W9-AVW-701

COMPLETE COOKERY

Pasta & Italian

This is a Dempsey Parr book
First printed in 2000

Dempsey Parr is an imprint of Parragon
Parragon
Queen Street House
4 Queen Street
Bath BA1 1HE, UK

ISBN: 1-84084-958-4

Printed in Italy

Note

Cup measurements in this book are for American cups.
Tablespoons are assumed to be 15 ml. Unless otherwise stated,
milk is assumed to be whole, eggs are large,
and pepper is freshly ground black pepper.

Contents

Italian Food Region by Region

There are two main culinary zones in Italy: the wine and olive zone, which lies around Umbria, Liguria, and the South; and the cattle country, where the olive tree will not flourish – Emilia-Romagna, Lombardy, and Veneto – but where milk and butter are widely produced. Tuscany, however, is the exception – it uses both butter and oil in its cooking because both cattle and olive trees thrive in the area.

Piedmont

The food here is substantial, peasant-type fare, although the expensive fragrant white truffle is found in this region. Truffles can be finely slivered or grated and added to many of the more sophisticated dishes. There is an abundance of wild mushrooms throughout the region. Garlic features strongly in the recipes and polenta, gnocchi, and rice are eaten in larger quantities than pasta, the former being offered as a first course when soup is not served. A large variety of game is also widely available.

Lombardy

Milan is home to the wonderful risotto named after the city and also the Milanese soufflé flavored strongly with lemon. Veal dishes, including *vitello tonnato* and *osso buco*, are specialties of the region and other excellent meat dishes, particularly pot roasts, feature widely. The lakes of the area produce a wealth of fresh fish. Rice and polenta are again popular but pasta also appears in many guises. The famous sweet yeasted cake *panettone* is a product of this region.

Trentino-Alto Adige

The foods are robust and basic here, where fish are plentiful. In the Trentino area particularly, pasta and simple meat dishes are popular, while in the Adige, soups, and pot roasts are favored, often with added dumplings and spiced sausages.

Veneto

Polenta is served with almost everything here. The land is intensively farmed, providing mostly cereals and wine. Pasta is less in evidence, with gnocchi and rice more favored. Fish, particularly shellfish, is in abundance and especially good seafood salads are widely available. There are also excellent robust soups and risottos flavored with the seafood and sausages of the area.

Liguria

All along the Italian Riviera can be found excellent trattorias which produce amazing fish dishes flavored with the local olive oil. Pesto sauce flavored with basil, cheese, and pine nuts comes from this area, along with other excellent sauces. Fresh herbs abound, widely used in many dishes, including the famous pizzas.

Emilia-Romagna

Tortellini and lasagne feature widely here, along with many other pasta dishes, as do *saltimbocca* and other veal dishes. Parma is famous for its ham, *prosciutto di Parma*, thought to be the best in the world. Balsamic vinegar is also produced here, from wine which is distilled until it is dark brown and extremely strongly flavored.

Tuscany

Tuscany has everything: an excellent coastal area providing splendid fish, hills covered in vineyards, and fertile plains where every conceivable vegetable and fruit grows. There is plenty of game in the region, providing many interesting recipes; tripe cooked in a thick tomato sauce is popular along with many liver recipes; beans in many guises appear frequently, as well as pot roasts, steaks, and full-bodied soups, all of which are well flavored. Florence has a wide variety of specialties, while Siena boasts the famous candied fruit cake called *Panforte di Siena*.

Umbria/Marches

Inland Umbria is famous for its pork, and the character of the cuisine is marked by the use of the local fresh ingredients, including lamb, game, and fish from the lakes. Spit-roasting and broiling is popular, and the excellent local olive oil is used both in cooking and to pour over dishes before serving. Black truffles, olives, fruit, and herbs are plentiful and feature in many recipes. First-class sausages and cured pork come from the Marches, particularly on the Umbrian border, and pasta features all over the region.

Lazio

Here, there are many pasta dishes with delicious sauces, gnocchi in various forms, and plenty of dishes featuring lamb and veal (*saltimbocca* being just one), and a variety of meats, all with plenty of herbs and seasonings giving really robust flavors and delicious sauces. Vegetables feature along with fantastic fruits; and beans appear both in soups and many other dishes.

Abruzzi and Molise

The cuisine here is deeply traditional, with local hams and cheeses from the mountain areas, interesting sausages with plenty of garlic and other seasonings, cured meats, and wonderful fish and seafood. Lamb features widely: tender, juicy, and well-flavored with herbs.

Campania

Naples is the home of pasta dishes, served with a splendid tomato sauce (with many variations). Pizza is said to have been created in Naples. Fish abounds, with *fritto misto* and *fritto pesce* being great favorites. Fish stews are robust and varied and shellfish in particular is often served with pasta. Cutlets and steaks are excellent, served with strong sauces flavored with garlic, tomatoes, and herbs: pizzaiola steak is one of the favorites. Mozzarella cheese is produced locally and used to create the crispy Mozzarella in Carozza, again served with a garlicky tomato sauce. Sweet dishes are popular too, often with flaky pastry and Ricotta cheese, and the seasonal fruit salads are laced with wine or liqueur.

Puglia (Apulia)

The ground in this region is stony but it produces good fruit, olive groves, vegetables, and herbs, and, of course, there is a large amount of seafood from the sea. Many of the excellent pasta dishes are exclusive to the region both in shape and ingredients. Mushrooms abound and are always added to the local pizzas. Oysters and mussels are plentiful, and so is octopus. Brindisi is famous for its shellfish – both the seafood salads and risottos are truly memorable. But it is not all fish or pasta: lamb is roasted and stewed to perfection and so is veal, always with plenty of herbs.

Basilicata

Here potent wines are produced to accompany a robust cuisine largely based on pasta, lamb, pork, game, and abundant dairy produce. The salamis and cured meats are excellent, as are the mountain hams. Lamb is flavored with the herbs and grasses on which it feeds. Wonderful thick soups – true minestrone – are produced in the mountains, and eels and fish are plentiful in the lakes. Chilli peppers are grown in this region and appear in many of the recipes. The cheeses are excellent, good fruit is grown, and interesting local bread is baked in huge loaves.

Calabria

This is the toe of Italy, where orange and lemon groves flourish along with olive trees and a profusion of vegetables, especially eggplants which are cooked in a variety of ways. Chicken, rabbit, and guinea fowl are often on the menu. Pizzas feature largely, often with a fishy topping. Mushrooms grow well in the Calabrian climate and feature in many dishes from sauces and stews to salads. Pasta comes with a great variety of sauces including baby artichokes, eggs, meat, cheese, mixed vegetables, the large sweet bell peppers of the region, and of course garlic. The fish is excellent too and fresh tuna and swordfish are available, along with many other varieties. Many desserts and cakes are flavored with aniseed, honey, and almonds and feature the plentiful figs of the region.

Sicily

This is the largest island in the Mediterranean and the cuisine is based mainly on fish and vegetables. Fish soups, stews, and salads appear in unlimited forms, including tuna, swordfish, mussels, and many more; citrus fruits are widely grown along with almonds and pistachio nuts, and the local wines, including the dark, sweet, dessert wine Marsala, are excellent. Meat is often given a long, slow cooking, or else is ground and shaped before cooking. Game is plentiful and is often cooked in sweet-sour sauces containing the local black olives. Pasta abounds again with more unusual sauces as well as the old favorites. All Sicilians have a love of desserts, cakes, and especially ice-cream. *Cassata* and other ice-creams from Sicily are famous all over the world.

Sardinia

The national dish of Sardinia is suckling pig or newborn lamb cooked on an open fire or spit, and rabbit, game, and a variety of meat dishes are also very popular. There is fresh fruit of almost every kind in abundance. Fish is also top quality, with excellent sea bass, lobsters, tuna, mullet, eels, and mussels in good supply. Myrtle (*mirto*), a local herb, is added to everything from chicken dishes to the local liqueur; and along with the cakes and breads of Sardinia, myrtle will long remain a fond memory of the island when you have returned home.

COOKING WITH PASTA

Pasta has existed in one form or another since the days of the Roman Empire and remains one of the most versatile ingredients in the kitchen. It can be combined with almost anything from meat to fish, vegetables to fruit, and is even delicious served with simple herb sauces. No store cupboard should be without a supply of dried pasta, which, combined with a few other stock ingredients, can be turned into a mouth-watering and nutritious meal within minutes.

Most pasta is made from durum wheat flour and contains protein and carbohydrates. It is a good source of slow-release energy and has the additional advantage of being value for money.

There is an enormous range of different types of pasta, some of which are listed on the opposite page. Many are available both dried and fresh. Unless you have access to a good Italian delicatessen, it is probably not worth buying fresh unfilled pasta, but even supermarkets sell high-quality tortellini, capelletti, ravioli, and agnolotti.

Best of all, make fresh pasta at home. It takes a little time, but is quite easy and well worth the effort. You can mix the dough by hand or prepare it in a food processor.

Pasta may be colored and flavored with extra ingredients that are usually added with the beaten egg:

Black: add 1 tsp squid or cuttlefish ink.
Green: add 4 oz well-drained, cooked spinach when kneading.
Purple: work 1 large, cooked beet in a food processor and add with an extra 2 oz ½ cup flour.
Red: add 2 tbsp tomato paste.

Always use a large saucepan for cooking pasta and bring lightly salted water to a boil. Add the pasta and 1 tbsp olive oil, but do not cover or the water will boil over. Quickly bring the water back to a rolling boil and avoid overcooking. When the pasta is tender, but still firm to the bite, drain, and toss with butter, olive oil, or your prepared sauce and serve as soon as possible.

The cooking times given here are guidelines only:

Fresh unfilled pasta: *2–3 minutes*
Fresh filled pasta: *8–10 minutes*
Dried unfilled pasta: *10–12 minutes*
Dried filled pasta: *15–20 minutes*

BASIC PASTA DOUGH

If you wish to make your own pasta for the dishes in this book, follow this simple recipe.

Serves 4

INGREDIENTS

4 cups durum wheat flour
4 eggs, lightly beaten
1 tbsp olive oil
salt

1 Lightly flour a work counter. Sift the flour with a pinch of salt into a mound. Make a well in the center and add the eggs and olive oil.

2 Using a fork or your fingertips, gradually work the mixture until the ingredients are combined. Knead vigorously for 10–15 minutes.

3 Set the dough aside to rest for 25 minutes, before rolling it out as thinly and evenly as possible.

TYPES OF PASTA

There are as many as 200 different pasta shapes and about three times as many names for them. New shapes are being designed – and named – all the time and the same shape may be called a different name in different regions of Italy.

anelli, anellini: *small rings for soup*

bucatini: *long, medium-thick tubes*

cannelloni: *large, thick, round pasta tubes*

capelli d'angelo: *thin strands of "angel hair"*

conchiglie: *ridged shells*

conchigliette: *little shells*

cresti di gallo: *curved-shaped*

ditali, ditalini: *short tubes*

eliche: *loose spirals*

farfalle: *bows*

fettuccine: *medium ribbons*

fusilli: *spirals*

gemelli: *two pieces wrapped together as "twins"*

lasagne: *flat, rectangular sheets*

linguini: *long, flat ribbons*

lumache: *snail-shaped shells*

lumaconi: *big shells*

macaroni: *long- or short-cut tubes*

orecchiette: *ear-shaped*

penne: *quill-shaped*

rigatoni: *thick, ridged tubes*

spaghetti: *fine or medium rods*

tagliarini: *thin ribbons*

tagliatelle: *broad ribbons*

vermicelli: *fine pasta, usually folded into skeins*

Cannelloni

Fusilli

Conchigliette

Orecchiette tricolori

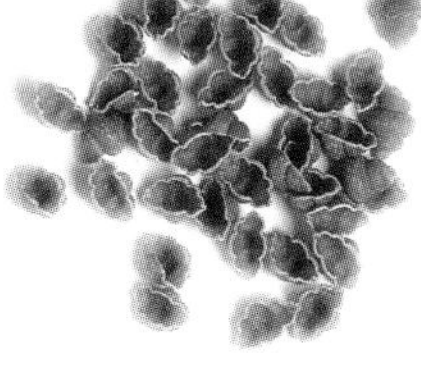

Conchiglie

Rigatoni

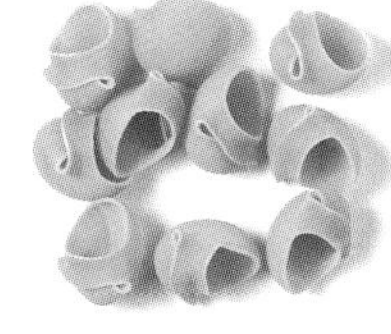

Lumaconi

Fettuccine

Spaghetti

Soups & Appetizers

Soups are an important part of Italian cuisine. They vary in consistency from light and delicate starters to hearty main meal soups. Although some may be puréed the ingredients never lose their delicious flavor.

Antipasto *means "before the main course" and what is served may be simple and inexpensive or highly elaborate. It usually comes in three categories: meat, fish, and vegetables. There are many varieties of cold meats, including ham, invariably sliced paper thin. All varieties of fish are enjoyed by the Italians, fresh sardines are particularly popular. Cook vegetables only until "al dente" and still slightly crisp so that they retain more nutrients and the colors remain bright.*

Use plenty of color – bell peppers, snow peas, and baby-corn-on-the-cobs are all readily available. Use Italian staples, such as extra-virgin olive oil and balsamic vinegar for a salad dressing, and sprinkle over Italian cheeses, such as Parmesan and Pecorino.

This chapter also contains a range of delicious side dishes which will complement your main meal. Whatever you are looking for to tempt those taste buds, you are sure to find it among these delicious delicacies.

Minestrone

Italian cooks have created some very heart-warming soups and this is the most famous of all.

Serves 8–10

INGREDIENTS

- 3 garlic cloves
- 3 large onions
- 2 celery stalks
- 2 large carrots
- 2 large potatoes
- 3 1/2 oz green beans
- 3 1/2 oz zucchini
- 4 tbsp butter
- 1/4 cup olive oil
- 2 oz rindless fatty bacon, finely diced
- 6 7/8 cups vegetable or chicken stock
- 1 bunch fresh basil, finely chopped
- 3 1/2 oz chopped tomatoes
- 2 tbsp tomato paste
- 3 1/2 oz Parmesan cheese peel
- 3 oz dried spaghetti, broken up
- salt and pepper
- freshly grated Parmesan cheese, to serve

1 Finely chop the garlic, onions, celery, carrots, potatoes, beans and zucchini.

2 Heat the butter and oil together in a large saucepan, add the bacon and cook for 2 minutes. Add the garlic and onion and fry for 2 minutes, then stir in the celery, carrots, and potatoes and fry for a further 2 minutes.

3 Add the beans to the pan and fry for 2 minutes. Stir in the zucchini and fry for a further 2 minutes. Cover the pan and cook all the vegetables, stirring frequently, for 15 minutes.

4 Add the stock, basil, tomatoes, tomato paste and cheese peel and season to taste. Bring to a boil, lower the heat and simmer for 1 hour. Remove and discard the cheese peel.

5 Add the spaghetti to the pan and cook for 20 minutes.

COOK'S TIP

There are almost as many recipes for minestrone as there are cooks in Italy! You can add almost any vegetables you like, including soaked dried beans.

Serve in large, warm soup bowls sprinkled with freshly grated Parmesan cheese.

Brown Lentil Soup with Pasta

In Italy, this soup is called Minestrade Lentiche. *A* minestra *is a soup cooked with pasta; in this case farfalline, a small bow-shaped variety, is used. Served with lentils, this hearty soup is a meal in itself.*

Serves 4

INGREDIENTS

- 4 rashers sliced bacon, cut into small squares
- 1 onion, chopped
- 2 garlic cloves, minced
- 2 celery stalks, chopped
- $^{1}/_{4}$ cup farfalline or spaghetti broken into small pieces
- 1 x 14$^{1}/_{2}$ oz can brown lentils, drained
- 5 cups hot ham or vegetable stock
- 2 tbsp chopped, fresh mint

1 Place the bacon in a large skillet together with the onions, garlic and celery. Dry fry for 4–5 minutes, stirring, until the onion is tender and the bacon is just beginning to brown.

2 Add the farfalline or spaghetti pieces to the skillet and cook, stirring, for about 1 minute to coat the pasta in the oil.

3 Add the lentils and the stock and bring to a boil. Reduce the heat and leave to simmer for 12–15 minutes or until the pasta is tender.

4 Remove the skillet from the heat and stir in the chopped fresh mint.

5 Transfer the soup to warm soup bowls and serve immediately.

COOK'S TIP

If you prefer to use dried lentils, add the stock before the pasta and cook for 1–1$^{1}/_{4}$ hours until the lentils are tender. Add the pasta and cook for a further 12–15 minutes.

VARIATION

Any type of pasta can be used in this recipe, try fusilli, conchiglie, or rigatoni, if you prefer.

1

Vegetable Soup with Cannelini Beans

This wonderful combination of beans, vegetables, and vermicelli is made even richer by the addition of pesto and dried mushrooms.

Serves 4

INGREDIENTS

- 1 small eggplant
- 2 large tomatoes
- 1 potato, peeled
- 1 carrot, peeled
- 1 leek
- 14½ oz can cannelini beans
- 3¾ cups hot vegetable or chicken stock
- 2 tsp dried basil
- ½ oz dried porcini mushrooms, soaked for 10 minutes in enough warm water to cover
- ¼ cup vermicelli
- 3 tbsp pesto
- freshly grated Parmesan cheese, to serve (optional)

1 Slice the eggplant into rings about ½ inch thick, then cut each ring into 4 pieces.

2 Cut the tomatoes and potato into small dice. Cut the carrot into sticks, about 1 inch long and cut the leek into rings.

3 Place the cannelini beans and their liquid in a large saucepan. Add the eggplant, tomatoes, potatoes, carrot, and leek, stirring to mix.

4 Add the stock to the pan and bring to a boil. Reduce the heat and leave to simmer for 15 minutes.

5 Add the basil, dried mushrooms, their soaking liquid and the vermicelli and simmer for 5 minutes or until all of the vegetables are tender.

6 Remove the pan from the heat and stir in the pesto.

7 Serve with freshly grated Parmesan cheese, if using.

COOK'S TIP

Porcini are a wild mushroom grown in southern Italy. When dried and rehydrated they have a very intense flavor, so although they are expensive to buy only a small amount are required to add flavor to soups or risottos.

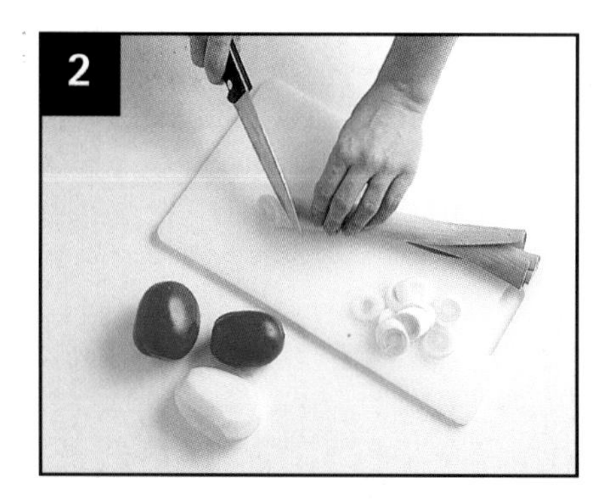

2

3

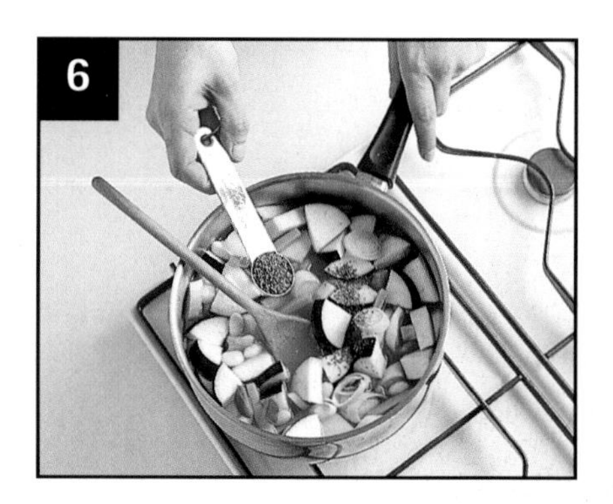

6

Italian Cream of Tomato Soup

Plum tomatoes are ideal for making soups and sauces, as they have denser, less watery flesh than round varieties.

Serves 4

INGREDIENTS

4 tbsp unsalted butter
1 large onion, chopped
2½ cups vegetable stock
2 lb Italian plum tomatoes, skinned and roughly chopped
pinch of baking soda
2 cups dried fusilli
1 tbsp superfine sugar
⅝ cup heavy cream
salt and pepper
fresh basil leaves, to garnish
deep-fried croutons, to serve

1 Melt the butter in a large pan, add the onion and fry for 3 minutes. Add 1¼ cups of vegetable stock to the pan, with the chopped tomatoes and baking soda. Bring the soup to a boil and simmer for 20 minutes.

2 Remove the pan from the heat and set aside to cool. Purée the soup in a blender or food processor and pour through a fine strainer back into the saucepan.

3 Add the remaining vegetable stock and the fusilli to the pan, and season to taste with salt and pepper.

4 Add the sugar to the pan, bring to a boil, then lower the heat and simmer for about 15 minutes.

5 Pour the soup into a warm tureen, swirl the heavy cream around the surface of the soup and garnish with fresh basil leaves. Serve immediately.

VARIATION

To make orange and tomato soup, simply use half the quantity of vegetable stock, topped up with the same amount of fresh orange juice and garnish the soup with orange peel. Or to make tomato and carrot soup, add half the quantity again of vegetable stock with the same amount of carrot juice and 1¼ cups grated carrot to the recipe, cooking the carrot with the onion.

Potato & Parsley Soup with Pesto

Fresh pesto is a treat to the taste buds and very different in flavor from the jars of pesto available from supermarkets.

Serves 4

INGREDIENTS

- 3 slices rindless, smoked, fatty bacon
- 2 tbsp butter
- 1 lb mealy potatoes
- 1 lb onions
- 2 1/2 cups chicken stock
- 2 1/2 cups milk
- 3/4 cup dried conchigliette
- 5/8 cup heavy cream
- chopped fresh parsley
- salt and black pepper
- freshly grated Parmesan cheese and garlic bread, to serve

PESTO SAUCE:

- 1 cup finely chopped fresh parsley
- 2 garlic cloves, minced
- 2/3 cup pine nuts, minced
- 2 tbsp chopped fresh basil leaves
- 2/3 cup freshly grated Parmesan cheese
- white pepper
- 5/8 cup olive oil

1 To make the pesto sauce, put all of the ingredients in a blender or food processor and process for 2 minutes, or blend together by hand (see Cook's Tip).

2 Finely chop the bacon, potatoes, and onions. Fry the bacon in a large pan over a medium heat for 4 minutes. Add the butter, potatoes, and onions and cook for 12 minutes, stirring constantly.

3 Add the stock and milk to the pan, bring to a boil and simmer for 10 minutes. Add the conchigliette and simmer for a further 12–14 minutes.

4 Blend in the cream and simmer for 5 minutes. Add the parsley and 2 tbsp pesto sauce. Transfer the soup to serving bowls and serve with Parmesan cheese and fresh garlic bread.

COOK'S TIP

If you are making pesto by hand, it is best to use a mortar and pestle. Thoroughly grind together the parsley, garlic, pine nuts and basil to make a paste, then mix in the cheese and pepper. Finally, gradually beat in the oil.

2

4

4

Pea & Egg Noodle Soup with Parmesan Cheese Croutons

This is a delicious and filling treat on cold winter evenings.

Serves 4

INGREDIENTS

3 slices smoked, rindless fatty bacon, diced
1 large onion, chopped
1 tbsp butter
$2^1/_2$ cups dried peas, soaked in cold water for 2 hours and drained
10 cups chicken stock
8 oz dried egg noodles
$^5/_8$ cup heavy cream
salt and pepper
chopped fresh parsley, to garnish
Parmesan cheese croutons (see Cook's Tip, below), to serve

1 Put the bacon, onion, and butter into a large saucepan and cook over a low heat for about 6 minutes.

2 Add the peas and the chicken stock to the pan and bring to a boil. Season lightly with salt and pepper, cover and simmer for $1\frac{1}{2}$ hours.

3 Add the egg noodles to the pan and simmer for a further 15 minutes.

4 Pour in the cream and blend thoroughly. Transfer to a warm tureen, garnish with parsley and top with Parmesan cheese croutons (see Cook's Tip, right). Serve immediately.

VARIATION

Other pulses, such as dried small navy beans, borlotti, or pinto beans, may be substituted for the peas in this recipe.

COOK'S TIP

To make Parmesan cheese croutons, cut a French stick into slices. Coat each slice lightly with olive oil and sprinkle with Parmesan cheese. broil for about 30 seconds.

1

2

3

Artichoke Soup

This refreshing chilled soup is ideal for al fresco dining.

Serves 4

INGREDIENTS

1 tbsp olive oil
1 onion, chopped
1 garlic clove, minced
2 x 14 oz can artichoke hearts, drained
$2^1/_2$ cups hot vegetable stock
$^2/_3$ cup light cream
2 tbsp fresh thyme, stalks removed
2 sun-dried tomatoes, cut into strips

1 Heat the oil in a large saucepan and fry the chopped onion and minced garlic until just softened.

2 Using a sharp knife, roughly chop the artichoke hearts. Add the artichoke pieces to the onion and garlic mixture in the pan. Pour in the hot vegetable stock, stirring.

3 Bring the mixture to a boil, then reduce the heat and leave to simmer, covered, for about 3 minutes.

4 Place the mixture into a food processor and blend until smooth. Alternatively, push the mixture through a strain to remove any lumps.

5 Return the soup to the saucepan. Stir the light cream and fresh thyme into the soup.

6 Transfer the soup to a large bowl, cover, and leave to chill in the refrigerator for about 3–4 hours.

7 Transfer the chilled soup to individual soup bowls and garnish with strips of sun-dried tomato. Serve with lots of fresh, crusty bread.

VARIATION

Try adding 2 tablespoons of dry vermouth, such as Martini, to the soup in step 5 if you wish.

1

2

5

Calabrian Mushroom Soup

The Calabrian mountains in southern Italy provide large amounts of wild mushrooms. They are rich in flavor and color and make a wonderful soup.

Serves 4

INGREDIENTS

- 2 tbsp olive oil
- 1 onion, chopped
- 1 lb mixed mushrooms, such as porcini, oyster, and button
- 1¼ cup milk
- 3¾ cups hot vegetable stock
- 8 slices of French stick
- 3 tbsp butter, melted
- 2 garlic cloves, minced
- 2¾ oz Gruyère cheese, finely grated
- salt and pepper

1 Heat the oil in a large skillet and cook the onion for 3–4 minutes or until soft and golden.

2 Wipe each mushroom with a damp cloth and cut any large mushrooms into smaller, bite-size pieces.

3 Add the mushrooms to the pan, stirring quickly to coat them in the oil.

4 Add the milk to the pan, bring to a boil, cover and leave to simmer for about 5 minutes. Gradually stir in the hot vegetable stock.

5 Under a preheated broil, toast the bread on both sides until golden.

6 Mix together the garlic and butter and spoon generously over the toast.

7 Place the toast in the bottom of a large tureen or divide it among 4 individual serving bowls and pour over the hot soup. Top with the grated Gruyère cheese and serve at once.

COOK'S TIP

Mushrooms absorb liquid, which can lessen the flavor and affect cooking properties. Wipe them with a damp cloth rather than rinsing them in water.

VARIATION

Supermarkets stock a wide variety of wild mushrooms. If you prefer, use a combination of cultivated and wild mushrooms.

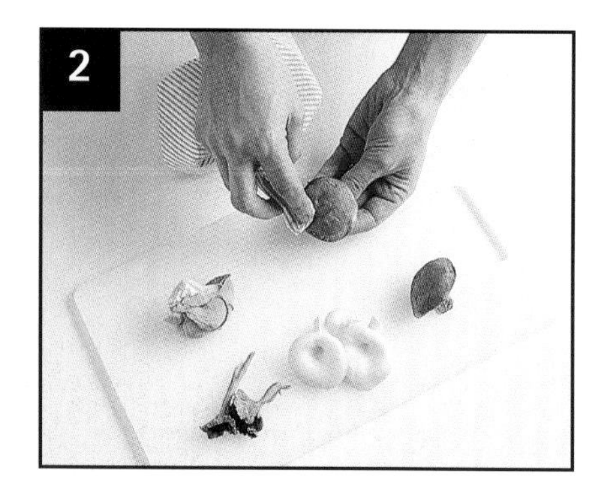

2

4

6

Tuscan Onion Soup

This soup is best made with white onions, which have a milder flavor than the more usual brown variety. If you cannot get hold of them, try using large Spanish onions instead.

Serves 4

INGREDIENTS

- $1^3/_4$ oz pancetta ham, diced
- 1 tbsp olive oil
- 4 large white onions, sliced thinly in rings
- 3 garlic cloves, chopped
- $3^3/_4$ cups hot chicken or ham stock
- 4 slices ciabatta or other Italian bread
- 3 tbsp butter
- $2^3/_4$ oz Gruyère or Cheddar
- salt and pepper

1. Dry fry the pancetta in a large saucepan for 3–4 minutes until it begins to brown. Remove the pancetta from the pan and set aside until required.

2. Add the oil to the pan and cook the onions and garlic over a high heat for 4 minutes. Reduce the heat, cover, and cook for 15 minutes until lightly caramelized.

3. Add the stock to the saucepan and bring to a boil. Reduce the heat and leave the mixture to simmer, covered, for about 10 minutes.

4. Toast the slices of ciabatta on both sides, under a preheated broil, for 2–3 minutes or until golden. Spread the ciabatta with butter and top with the Gruyère or Cheddar cheese. Cut the bread into bite-size pieces.

5. Add the reserved pancetta to the soup and season to taste with salt and pepper. Pour into 4 soup bowls and top with the toasted bread.

COOK'S TIP

Pancetta is similar to bacon, but it is air- and salt-cured for about 6 months. Pancetta is available from most delicatessens and some large supermarkets. If you cannot obtain pancetta use unsmoked bacon instead.

Chicken & Pasta Broth

This satisfying soup makes a good lunch or supper dish and you can use any vegetables that you have at hand. Children will love the tiny pasta shapes.

Serves 6

INGREDIENTS

12 oz boneless chicken breasts
2 tbsp sunflower oil
1 medium onion, diced
1 1/2 cups carrots, diced
9 oz cauliflower flowerets
3 3/4 cups chicken stock
2 tsp dried mixed herbs
4 1/2 oz small pasta shapes
salt and pepper
Parmesan cheese (optional) and crusty bread, to serve

1 Using a sharp knife, finely dice the chicken, discarding any skin.

2 Heat the oil in a large saucepan and quickly sauté the chicken and vegetables until they are lightly colored.

3 Stir in the stock and herbs. Bring to a boil and add the pasta shapes. Return to a boil, cover, and simmer for 10 minutes, stirring occasionally to prevent the pasta shapes sticking together.

4 Season with salt and pepper to taste and sprinkle with Parmesan cheese, if using. Serve with fresh crusty bread.

COOK'S TIP

You can use any small pasta shapes for this soup – try conchigliette or ditalini or even spaghetti broken up into small pieces. To make a fun soup for children you could add animal-shaped or alphabet pasta.

VARIATION

Broccoli flowerets can be used to replace the cauliflower flowerets. Substitute 2 tablespoons chopped fresh mixed herbs for the dried mixed herbs.

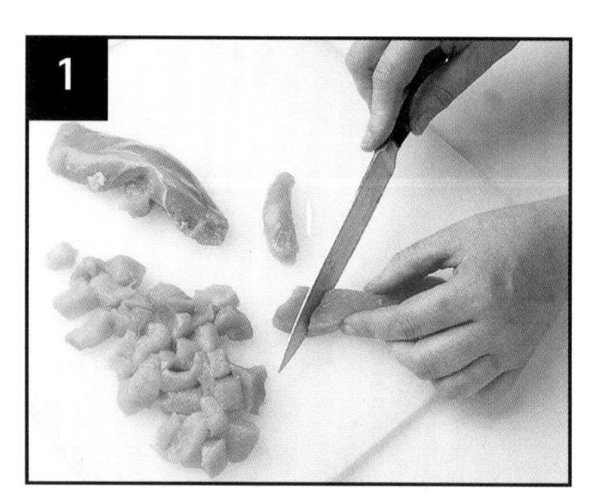

Cream of Lemon & Chicken Soup with Spaghetti

This delicately flavored summer soup is surprisingly easy to make.

Serves 4

INGREDIENTS

4 tbsp butter
8 shallots, thinly sliced
2 carrots, thinly sliced
2 celery stalks, thinly sliced
8 oz boned chicken breasts, finely chopped
3 lemons
5 cups chicken stock
8 oz dried spaghetti, broken into small pieces
5/8 cup heavy cream
salt and white pepper

TO GARNISH:
fresh parsley sprig
3 lemon slices, halved

1 Melt the butter in a large saucepan. Add the shallots, carrots, celery, and chicken and cook over a low heat, stirring occasionally, for 8 minutes.

2 Thinly pare the lemons and blanch the lemon peel in boiling water for 3 minutes. Squeeze the juice from the lemons.

3 Add the lemon peel and juice to the pan, together with the chicken stock. Bring slowly to a boil over a low heat and simmer for 40 minutes.

4 Add the spaghetti to the pan and cook for 15 minutes. Season to taste with salt and white pepper and add the cream. Heat through, but do not allow the soup to boil or it will curdle.

5 Pour the soup into a tureen or individual bowls, garnish with the parsley and half slices of lemon and serve immediately.

COOK'S TIP

You can prepare this soup up to the end of step 3 in advance, so that all you need do before serving is heat it through before adding the pasta and the finishing touches.

1

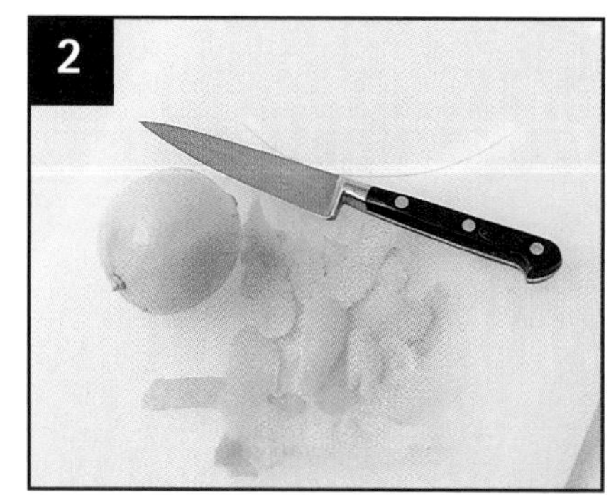
2

4

Mussel & Potato Soup

This quick and easy soup would make a delicious summer lunch served with fresh crusty bread.

Serves 4

INGREDIENTS

- 1 lb 10 oz mussels
- 2 tbsp olive oil
- 7 tbsp unsalted butter
- 2 slices rindless fatty bacon, chopped
- 1 onion, chopped
- 2 garlic cloves, minced
- 1/2 cup all-purpose flour
- 1 lb potatoes, thinly sliced
- 3/4 cup dried conchigliette
- 1 1/4 cups heavy cream
- 1 tbsp lemon juice
- 2 egg yolks
- salt and pepper

TO GARNISH:

- 2 tbsp finely chopped fresh parsley
- lemon wedges

1 Debeard the mussels and scrub them under cold water for 5 minutes. Discard any mussels that do not close immediately when sharply tapped.

2 Bring a large pan of water to a boil, add the mussels, oil, and a little pepper and cook until the mussels open.

3 Drain the mussels, reserving the cooking liquid. Discard any mussels that are closed. Remove the mussels from their shells.

4 Melt the butter in a large saucepan, add the bacon, onion, and garlic and cook for 4 minutes. Carefully stir in the flour. Measure 5 cups of the reserved cooking liquid and stir it into the pan.

5 Add the potatoes to the pan and simmer for 5 minutes. Add the conchigliette and simmer for a further 10 minutes.

6 Add the cream and lemon juice, season to taste with salt and pepper, then add the mussels to the pan.

7 Blend the egg yolks with 1–2 tbsp of the remaining cooking liquid, stir into the pan and cook for 4 minutes.

8 Ladle the soup into 4 warm individual soup bowls, garnish with the chopped fresh parsley and lemon wedges and serve immediately.

Italian Fish Soup

This colorful mixed seafood soup would be superbly complemented by a dry white wine.

Serves 4

INGREDIENTS

4 tbsp butter
1 lb assorted fish fillets, such as red mullet and snapper
1 lb prepared seafood, such as squid and shrimp
8 oz fresh crabmeat
1 large onion, sliced
1/4 cup all-purpose flour
5 cups fish stock
3/4 cup dried pasta shapes, such as ditalini or elbow macaroni
1 tbsp anchovy extract
grated peel and juice of 1 orange
1/4 cup dry sherry
1 1/4 cups heavy cream
salt and black pepper
crusty brown bread, to serve

1 Melt the butter in a large saucepan, add the fish fillets, seafood, crabmeat, and onion and cook gently over a low heat for 6 minutes.

2 Add the flour to the mixture, stirring thoroughly to avoid any lumps.

3 Gradually add the fish stock, stirring constantly, until the soup comes to a boil. Reduce the heat and simmer for 30 minutes.

4 Add the pasta to the pan and cook for a further 10 minutes.

5 Stir in the anchovy extract, orange peel, orange juice, sherry, and heavy cream. Season to taste with salt and pepper.

6 Heat the soup until completely warmed through. Transfer the soup to a tureen or to warm soup bowls and serve with crusty brown bread.

COOK'S TIP

The heads, tails, trimmings and bones of virtually any non-oily fish can be used to make fish stock. Simmer 2 lb fish pieces in a large saucepan with 5 fl oz white wine, 1 chopped onion, 1 sliced carrot, 1 sliced celery stalk, 4 black peppercorns, 1 bouquet garni and 7½ cups water for 30 minutes, then strain.

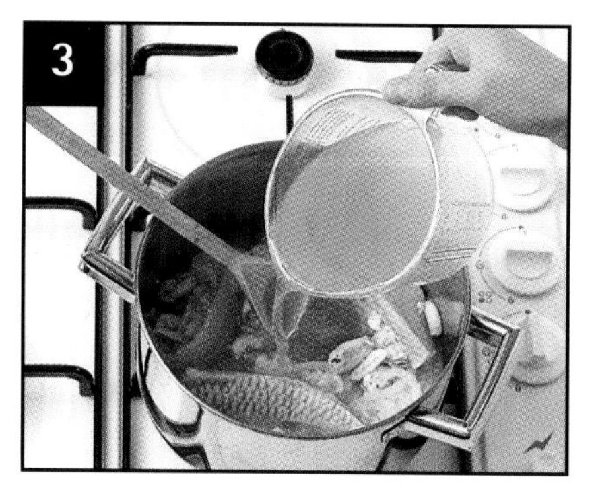

Tuscan Veal Broth

Veal plays an important role in Italian cuisine and there are dozens of recipes for all cuts of this meat.

Serves 4

INGREDIENTS

- 1/3 cup dried peas, soaked for 2 hours and drained
- 2 lb boned neck of veal, diced
- 5 cups beef or brown stock (see Cook's Tip)
- 2 1/2 cups water
- 1/3 cup barley, washed
- 1 large carrot, diced
- 1 small turnip (about 6 oz), diced
- 1 large leek, thinly sliced
- 1 red onion, finely chopped
- 3 1/2 oz chopped tomatoes
- 1 fresh basil sprig
- 3/4 cup dried vermicelli
- salt and white pepper

1 Put the peas, veal, stock, and water into a large saucepan and bring to a boil over a low heat. Using a slotted spoon, skim off any scum that rises to the surface of the liquid.

2 When all of the scum has been removed, add the barley and a pinch of salt to the mixture. Simmer gently over a low heat for 25 minutes.

3 Add the carrot, turnip, leek, onion, tomatoes, and basil to the pan, and season with salt and pepper to taste. Leave to simmer for about 2 hours, skimming the surface, using a draining spoon, from time to time. Remove the pan from the heat and set aside for 2 hours.

4 Set the pan over a medium heat and bring to a boil. Add the vermicelli and cook for 12 minutes. Season with salt and pepper to taste and remove and discard the basil. Ladle into soup bowls and serve immediately.

COOK'S TIP

The best brown stock is made with veal bones and shin of beef roasted with drippings in the oven for 40 minutes. Transfer the bones to a large pan and add sliced leeks, onion, celery, and carrots, a bouquet garni, white wine vinegar and a thyme sprig and cover with cold water. Simmer over a very low heat for about 3 hours. Strain and blot the fat from the surface with paper towels.

1

2

3

Baked Eggplant & Tomatoes

This dish is a bit like an eggplant lasagne with layers of eggplant, tomato sauce, and Mozzarella combining with Parmesan cheese to create a wonderfully tasty starter.

Serves 4

INGREDIENTS

3–4 tbsp olive oil
2 garlic cloves, minced
2 large eggplants
3½ oz Mozzarella cheese, sliced thinly
7 oz sieved tomatoes
1¾ oz Parmesan cheese, grated

1 Heat 2 tablespoons of the olive oil in a large skillet. Add the garlic to the skillet and sauté for 30 seconds.

2 Slice the eggplant lengthwise. Add the slices to the pan and cook in the oil for 3–4 minutes on each side or until tender. (You will probably have to cook them in batches, so add the remaining oil as necessary.)

3 Remove the eggplant with a draining spoon and drain on absorbent paper towels.

4 Place a layer of eggplant slices in a shallow ovenproof dish. Cover the eggplant with a layer of Mozzarella and then pour over a third of the sieved tomatoes. Continue layering in the same order, finishing with a layer of sieved tomatoes on top.

5 Generously sprinkle the grated Parmesan cheese over the top and bake in a preheated oven at 400°F for 25–30 minutes.

6 Transfer to serving plates and serve warm or chilled.

COOK'S TIP

A simple tomato sauce can be bought from most supermarkets. Alternatively, you can purée and sieve a can of tomatoes and season with salt and pepper.

2

2

4

Bruschetta with Tomatoes

Using ripe tomatoes and the best olive oil will make this Tuscan dish absolutely delicious.

Serves 4

INGREDIENTS

- $10^1/_2$ oz cherry tomatoes
- 4 sun-dried tomatoes
- 4 tbsp extra virgin olive oil
- 16 fresh basil leaves, shredded
- 8 slices ciabatta
- 2 garlic cloves, peeled
- salt and pepper

1 Using a sharp knife, cut the cherry tomatoes in half.

2 Using a sharp knife, slice the sun-dried tomatoes into strips.

3 Place the cherry tomatoes and sun-dried tomatoes in a bowl. Add the olive oil and the shredded basil leaves and toss to mix well. Season to taste with a little salt and pepper.

4 Using a sharp knife, cut the garlic cloves in half. Lightly toast the ciabatta bread.

5 Rub the garlic, cut-side down, over both sides of the toasted ciabatta bread.

6 Top the ciabatta bread with the tomato mixture and serve immediately.

COOK'S TIP

Ciabatta is an Italian rustic bread which is slightly holey and quite chewy. It is very good in this recipe as it absorbs the full flavor of the garlic and extra virgin olive oil.

VARIATION

Plum tomatoes are also good in this recipe. Halve them, then cut them into wedges. Mix them with the sun-dried tomatoes in step 3.

1

2

5

Casserole of Beans in Tomato Sauce

This quick and easy casserole can be eaten as a healthy supper dish or as a side dish to accompany sausages or grilled fish.

Serves 4

INGREDIENTS

1 x 14 oz can cannellini beans
1 x 14 oz can borlotti beans
2 tbsp olive oil
1 stick celery
2 garlic cloves, chopped
6 oz baby onions, halved
1 lb tomatoes
2 3/4 oz arugula

1 Drain both cans of beans and reserve 6 tbsp of the liquid.

2 Heat the oil in a large pan. Add the celery, garlic, and onions and sauté for 5 minutes or until the onions are golden.

3 Cut a cross in the base of each tomato and plunge them into a bowl of boiling water for 30 seconds until the skins split. Remove them with a draining spoon and leave until cool enough to handle. Peel off the skin and chop the flesh. Add the tomato flesh and the reserved bean liquid to the pan and cook for 5 minutes.

4 Add the beans to the pan and cook for a further 3–4 minutes or until the beans are hot.

5 Stir in the arugula and allow to wilt slightly before serving.

COOK'S TIP

Another way to peel tomatoes is once you have cut a cross in the base, push it on to a fork and hold it over a gas flame, turning it slowly so that the skin heats evenly all over. The skin will start to bubble and split, and should then slide off easily.

VARIATION

For a spicier tasting dish, add 1–2 teaspoons of hot pepper sauce with the beans in step 4.

1

2

3

Omelet Strips in Tomato Sauce

These omelet strips are delicious smothered in tomato sauce.

Serves 4

INGREDIENTS

2 tbsp butter
1 onion, finely chopped
2 garlic cloves, chopped
4 eggs, beaten
$\frac{2}{3}$ cup milk
$2\frac{3}{4}$ oz Gruyère cheese, diced
1 x 14 oz can tomatoes, chopped
1 tbsp rosemary, stalks removed
$\frac{2}{3}$ cup vegetable stock
freshly grated Parmesan cheese, for sprinkling
crusty bread, to serve

1 Melt the butter in a large skillet. Add the onion and garlic and cook for 4–5 minutes, until softened.

2 Beat together the eggs and milk and add the mixture to the skillet.

3 Using a spatula, gently raise the cooked edges of the omelet and tip any uncooked egg around the edge of the pan.

4 Scatter over the cheese. Cook for 5 minutes, turning once, until golden on both sides. Remove from the pan and roll up.

5 Add the tomatoes, rosemary, and vegetable stock to the skillet, stirring, and bring to a boil.

6 Leave the tomato sauce to simmer for about 10 minutes until reduced and thickened.

7 Slice the omelet into strips and add to the tomato sauce in the skillet. Cook for 3–4 minutes until very hot.

8 Sprinkle the freshly grated Parmesan cheese over the omelet strips in tomato sauce and serve with fresh crusty bread.

VARIATION

Try adding $3\frac{1}{2}$ oz diced pancetta or unsmoked bacon in step 1 and cooking the meat with the onions.

Black Olive Pâté

The flavor of olives is accentuated by the anchovies and the pâté is wonderful served as an appetizer on thin pieces of toast with a very dry white wine.

Serves 4

INGREDIENTS

6 oz black olives, pitted and chopped
finely grated peel and juice of 1 lemon
$1^1/_2$ oz unsalted butter
4 canned anchovy fillets, strained and rinsed
2 tbsp extra virgin olive oil
$^1/_2$ oz ground almonds

1 If you are making the pâté by hand, chop the olives very finely and then mash them along with the lemon peel, juice, and butter, using a fork or potato masher. Alternatively, place the roughly chopped olives, lemon peel, juice, and butter in a food processor and blend until all of the ingredients are finely chopped.

2 Using a sharp knife, chop the strained anchovies and add them to the olive and lemon mixture. Mash the pâté by hand or blend it in a food processor for about 20 seconds.

3 Gradually whisk in the olive oil and stir in the ground almonds. Place the black olive pâté in a serving bowl.

4 Leave the pâté to chill in the refrigerator for about 30 minutes. Serve accompanied by thin pieces of toast.

COOK'S TIP

Extra-virgin olive oil is the finest grade of olive oil. It is made from the first, cold pressing of hand-gathered olives.

COOK'S TIP

The pâté will keep for up to 5 days in a serving bowl in the refrigerator if you pour a thin layer of extra-virgin olive oil over the top of the pâté to seal it. Then use the oil to brush on the toast before spreading the pâté.

1

2

3

Deep-Fried Risotto Balls

The Italian name for this dish translates as "telephone wires" which refers to the strings of melted Mozzarella cheese; the surprise contained within the risotto balls.

Serves 4

INGREDIENTS

2 tbsp olive oil
1 medium onion, finely chopped
1 garlic clove, chopped
$^{1}/_{2}$ red bell pepper, diced
$^{3}/_{4}$ cup risotto rice, washed
1 tsp dried oregano
$1^{2}/_{3}$ cup hot vegetable or chicken stock
$^{1}/_{2}$ scant cup dry white wine
$2^{3}/_{4}$ oz Mozzarella cheese
oil, for deep-frying
fresh basil sprig, to garnish

1 Heat the oil in a skillet and cook the onion and garlic for 3–4 minutes or until just softened.

2 Add the bell pepper, rice, and oregano to the pan. Cook for 2–3 minutes, stirring to coat the rice in the oil.

3 Mix the stock together with the wine and add to the pan a ladleful at a time, waiting for the liquid to be absorbed by the rice before you add the next ladleful of liquid.

4 Once all of the liquid has been absorbed and the rice is tender (it should take about 15 minutes in total), remove the pan from the heat and leave until the mixture is cool enough to handle.

5 Cut the cheese into 12 pieces. Taking about a tablespoon of risotto, shape the mixture around the cheese pieces to make 12 balls.

6 Heat the oil until a piece of bread browns in 30 seconds. Cook the risotto balls in batches of 4 for 2 minutes until golden.

7 Remove the risotto balls with a draining spoon and drain thoroughly on absorbent paper towels. Garnish with a sprig of basil and serve hot.

VARIATION

Although Mozzarella is the traditional cheese for this recipe and creates the stringy "telephone wire" effect, other cheeses may be used if you prefer.

1

2

5

Roasted Bell Peppers

These bell peppers can be used as an antipasto, as a side dish, or as a relish to accompany meat and fish.

Serves 4

INGREDIENTS

2 each, red, yellow, and orange bell peppers
4 tomatoes, halved
1 tbsp olive oil
3 garlic cloves, chopped
1 onion, sliced in rings
2 tbsp fresh thyme
salt and pepper

1 Halve and seed the bell peppers. Place them, cut-side down, on a cookie sheet and cook under a preheated broiler for 10 minutes.

2 Add the tomatoes to the cookie sheet and broil for 5 minutes or until the skins of the bell peppers and tomatoes are charred.

3 Put the bell peppers into a plastic bag for 10 minutes to sweat, which will make the skin easier to peel. Remove the tomato skins and roughly chop the flesh.

4 Peel the skins from the bell peppers and slice the flesh into strips.

5 Heat the oil in a large skillet and fry the garlic and onion for 3–4 minutes or until softened.

6 Add the bell peppers and tomatoes to the skillet and cook for 5 minutes. Stir in the fresh thyme and season to taste with salt and pepper.

7 Transfer to serving bowls and serve warm or chilled.

COOK'S TIP

Preserve the bell peppers in the refrigerator by placing them in a sterilized jar and pouring olive oil over the top to seal. Alternatively, heat $1/4$ cup white wine vinegar with a bay leaf and 4 juniper berries and bring to a boiling point. Pour over the bell peppers and set aside until completely cold. Pack into sterilized jars – they will keep for up to 1 month.

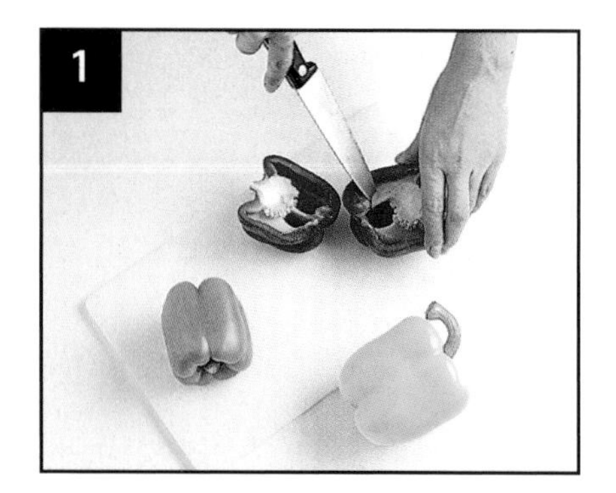

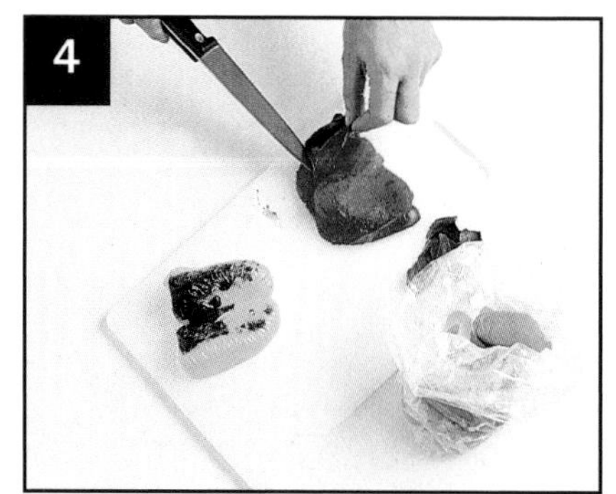

Spinach & Ricotta Patties

"Nudo" or naked is the word used to describe this mixture, which can also be made into thin pancakes or used as a filling for tortelloni.

Serves 4

INGREDIENTS

1 lb fresh spinach
9 oz ricotta cheese
1 egg, beaten
2 tsp fennel seeds, lightly minced
1 3/4 oz pecorino or Parmesan cheese, finely grated
1 oz all-purpose flour, mixed with 1 tsp dried thyme
5 tbsp butter
2 garlic cloves, minced
salt and pepper

1 Wash the spinach and trim off any long stalks. Place in a pan, cover, and cook for 4–5 minutes until wilted. This will probably have to be done in batches as the volume of spinach is quite large. Place in a colander and leave to drain and cool.

2 Mash the ricotta and beat in the egg and the fennel seeds. Season with plenty of salt and pepper, then stir in the pecorino or Parmesan cheese.

3 Squeeze as much excess water as possible from the spinach and finely chop the leaves. Stir into the cheese mixture.

4 Taking about 1 tablespoon of the spinach and cheese mixture, shape it into a ball, and flatten it slightly to form a patty. Gently roll in the seasoned flour. Continue this process until all of the mixture has been used up.

5 Half fill a large skillet with water and bring to a boil. Carefully add the patties and cook for 3–4 minutes or until they rise to the surface. Remove with a draining spoon.

6 Melt the butter in a pan. Add the garlic and cook for 2–3 minutes. Pour the garlic butter over the patties, season with freshly ground black pepper, and serve at once.

COOK'S TIP

Once it is washed, spinach holds enough water on the leaves to cook without adding any extra liquid. If you use frozen spinach instead of fresh, simply defrost it and squeeze out the excess water.

1

2

3

Sweet & Sour Baby Onions

This is a typical Sicilian dish, combining honey and vinegar to give a delicate sweet and sour flavor. Serve hot as an accompaniment or cold with cured meats.

Serves 4

INGREDIENTS

12 oz baby or pickling onions
2 tbsp olive oil
2 fresh bay leaves, torn into strips
thinly pared peel of 1 lemon
1 tbsp soft brown sugar
1 tbsp honey
4 tbsp red wine vinegar

1 Soak the onions in a bowl of boiling water – this will make them easier to peel. Using a sharp knife, peel and halve the onions.

2 Heat the oil in a large skillet. Add the bay leaves and onions to the pan and cook for 5–6 minutes over a medium-high heat or until browned all over.

3 Cut the lemon peel into thin matchsticks. Add to the skillet with the sugar and honey. Cook for 2–3 minutes, stirring occasionally, until the onions are lightly caramelized.

4 Add the red wine vinegar to the skillet, being careful because it will spit. Cook for about 5 minutes, stirring, or until the onions are tender and the liquid has all but disappeared.

5 Transfer the onions to a serving dish and serve at once.

COOK'S TIP

Adjust the piquancy of this dish to your liking by adding more sugar for a sweeter, more caramelized taste or extra red wine vinegar for a sharper, tarter flavor.

COOK'S TIP

To make the onions easier to peel, place them in a large saucepan, pour over boiling water, and leave for 10 minutes. Drain the onions thoroughly, and when they are cold enough to handle, peel them.

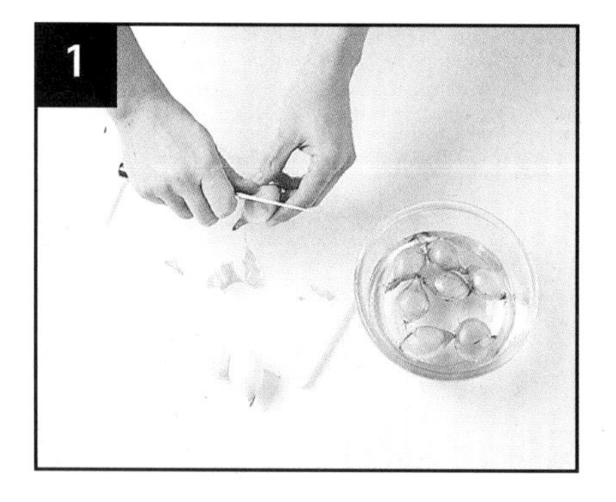

1

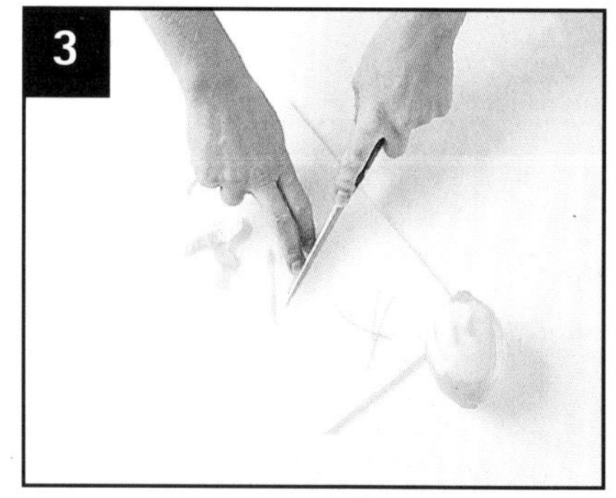

3

4

Tuscan Bean Salad with Tuna

The combination of beans and tuna is a favorite with the people of Tuscany. The hint of honey and lemon in the dressing makes this salad refreshing as well as hearty.

Serves 4

INGREDIENTS

1 small white onion or 2 scallions, finely chopped
2 x 14 oz cans lima beans, drained
2 medium tomatoes
$6^1/_2$ oz can tuna, drained
2 tbsp flat leaf parsley, chopped
2 tbsp olive oil
1 tbsp lemon juice
2 tsp honey
1 garlic clove, minced

1 Place the chopped onions or scallions and lima beans in a bowl and mix well to combine.

2 Using a sharp knife, cut the tomatoes into wedges. Add the tomatoes to the onion and bean mixture.

3 Flake the tuna with a fork and add it to the onion and bean mixture together with the parsley.

4 In a screw-top jar, mix together the olive oil, lemon juice, honey, and garlic. Shake the jar until the dressing emulsifies and thickens.

5 Pour the dressing over the bean salad. Toss the ingredients together using 2 spoons and serve.

COOK'S TIP

This salad will keep for several days in a covered container in the refrigerator. Make up the dressing just before serving and toss the ingredients together to mix well.

VARIATION

Substitute fresh salmon for the tuna if you wish to create a luxurious version of this recipe for a special occasion.

1

2

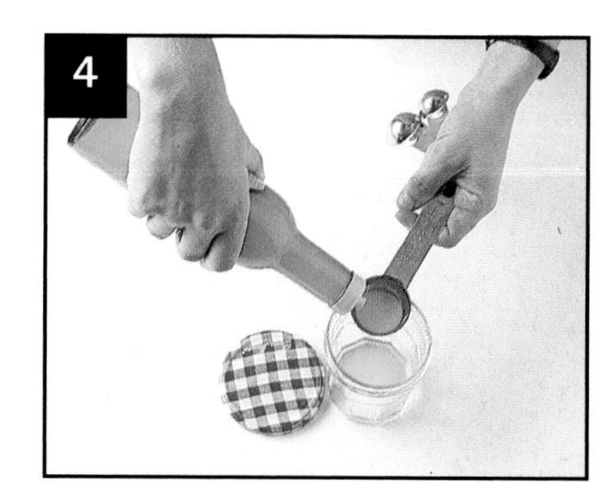
4

Stewed Artichokes

This is a traditional Roman dish. The artichokes are stewed in olive oil with fresh herbs.

Serves 4

INGREDIENTS

4 small globe artichokes
4 garlic cloves, peeled
2 bay leaves
finely grated peel and juice of 1 lemon
olive oil
2 tbsp fresh marjoram
lemon wedges, to serve

1 Using a sharp knife, carefully peel away the tough outer leaves surrounding the artichokes. Trim the stems to about 1 inch.

2 Using a knife, cut each artichoke in half and scoop out the heart.

3 Place the artichokes in a large heavy-bottomed pan. Pour over enough olive oil to half cover the artichokes in the pan.

4 Add the garlic cloves, bay leaves, and half of the grated lemon peel.

5 Start to heat the artichokes gently, cover the pan, and continue to cook over a low heat for about 40 minutes. The artichokes should be stewed in the oil, not fried.

6 Once the artichokes are tender, remove them with a draining spoon and drain thoroughly. Remove the bay leaves.

7 Transfer the artichokes to warm serving plates. Serve the artichokes sprinkled with the remaining grated lemon peel, fresh marjoram, and a little lemon juice.

COOK'S TIP

To prevent the artichokes from oxidizing and turning brown before cooking, brush them with a little lemon juice. In addition, use the oil used for cooking the artichokes for salad dressings – it will impart a lovely lemon and herb flavor.

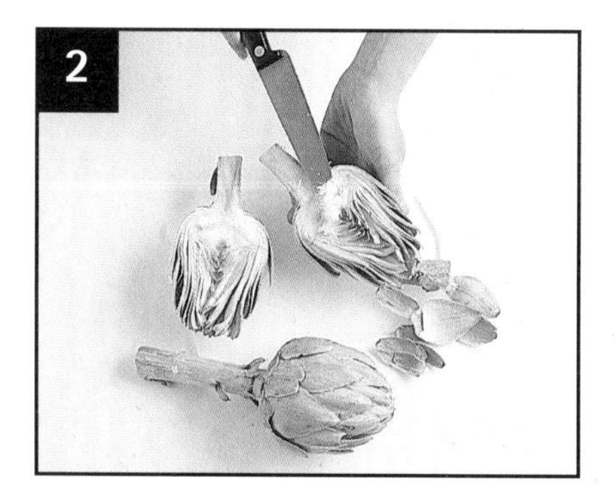
2

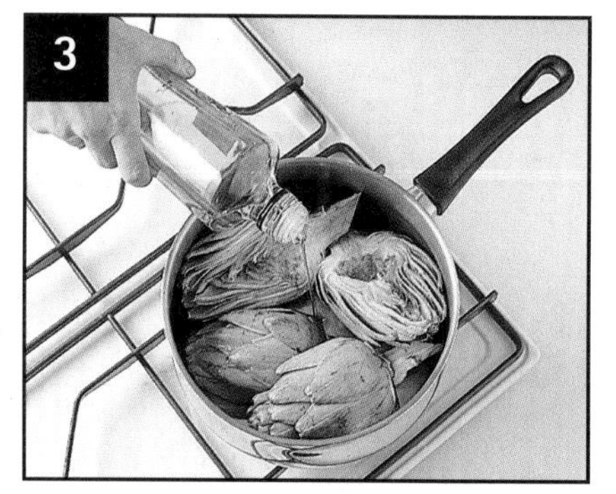
3

6

Italian Potato Salad

Potato salad is always a favorite, but it is even more delicious with the addition of sun-dried tomatoes and fresh parsley.

Serves 4

INGREDIENTS

1 lb baby potatoes, unpeeled, or larger potatoes, halved
4 tbsp unsweetened yogurt
4 tbsp mayonnaise
8 sun-dried tomatoes
2 tbsp flat leaf parsley, chopped
salt and pepper

1 Rinse and clean the potatoes and place them in a large pan of water. Bring to a boil and cook for 8–12 minutes or until just tender. (The cooking time will vary according to the size of your potatoes.)

2 Using a sharp knife, cut the sun-dried tomatoes into thin slices.

3 To make the dressing, mix together the yogurt and mayonnaise in a bowl and season to taste with a little salt and pepper. Stir in the sun-dried tomato slices and the chopped flat leaf parsley.

4 Remove the potatoes with a draining spoon, drain them thoroughly, and then set them aside to cool. If you are using larger potatoes, cut them into 2 inch chunks.

5 Pour the dressing over the potatoes and toss to mix.

6 Leave the potato salad to chill in the refrigerator for about 20 minutes, then serve as a starter or as an accompaniment.

COOK'S TIP

It is easier to cut the larger potatoes once they are cooked. Although smaller pieces of potato will cook more quickly, they tend to disintegrate and become mushy.

1

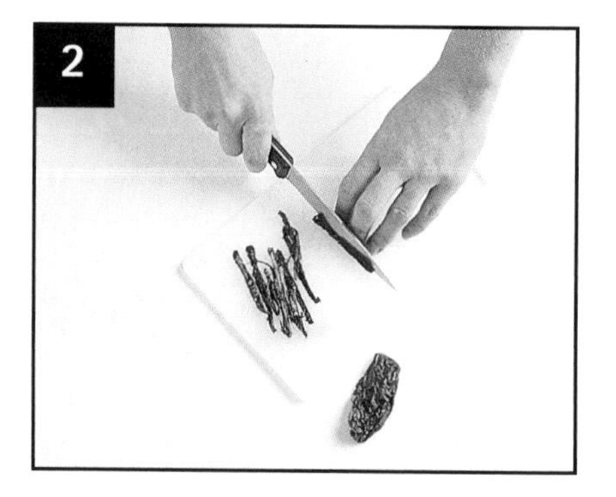

Yellow Bell Pepper Salad

A colorful combination of yellow bell peppers, red radishes, and celery combine to give a wonderfully crunchy texture and fresh taste.

Serves 4

INGREDIENTS

- 4 rashers streaky bacon, chopped
- 2 yellow bell peppers
- 8 radishes, washed and trimmed
- 1 celery stalk, finely chopped
- 3 plum tomatoes, cut into wedges
- 3 tbsp olive oil
- 1 tbsp fresh thyme

1 Dry fry the chopped bacon in a skillet for 4–5 minutes or until crispy. Remove the bacon from the skillet, set aside, and leave to cool until required.

2 Using a sharp knife, halve and seed the bell peppers. Slice the bell peppers into long strips.

3 Using a sharp knife, halve the radishes and cut them into wedges.

4 Mix together the bell peppers, radishes, celery, and tomatoes and toss the mixture in the olive oil and fresh thyme. Season to taste with a little salt and pepper.

5 Transfer the salad to serving plates and garnish with the reserved crispy bacon.

COOK'S TIP

Tomatoes are actually berries and are related to potatoes. There are many different shapes and sizes of this versatile fruit. The one most used in Italian cooking is the plum tomato, which is very flavorsome.

COOK'S TIP

Pre-packaged diced bacon can be purchased from most supermarkets, which helps to save on preparation time.

1

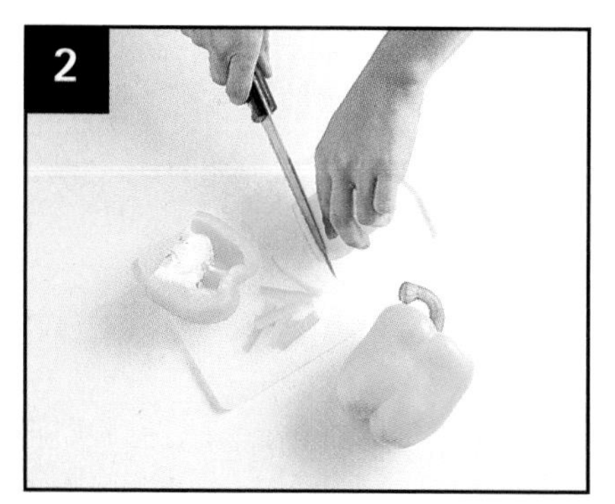

2

3

Sweet & Sour Eggplant Salad

This cooked salad from Sicily was first brought to Italy by the Moors.

Serves 4

INGREDIENTS

6 tbsp olive oil
1 onion, chopped
2 garlic cloves, chopped
2 celery stalks, chopped
1 lb eggplant
1 x 14 oz can tomatoes, chopped
1³/₄ oz green olives, stoned and chopped
1 oz granulated sugar
2¹/₃ cup red wine vinegar
1 oz capers, drained
salt and pepper
1 tbsp flat leaf parsley, roughly chopped, to garnish

1 Heat 2 tablespoons of the oil in a large skillet. Add the prepared onions, garlic, and celery to the skillet and cook, stirring, for 3–4 minutes.

2 Using a sharp knife, slice the eggplant into thick rounds, then cut each round into 4 pieces.

3 Add the eggplant pieces to the skillet with the remaining olive oil and fry for 5 minutes or until golden.

4 Add the tomatoes, olives, and sugar to the pan, stirring until the sugar has dissolved.

5 Add the red wine vinegar, reduce the heat, and leave to simmer for 10–15 minutes or until the sauce is thick and the eggplant are tender.

6 While the pan is still on the heat, stir in the capers. Season to taste with salt and pepper.

7 Transfer to serving plates and garnish with the chopped fresh parsley.

COOK'S TIP

This salad is best served cold the day after it is made, which allows the flavors to mingle and be fully absorbed.

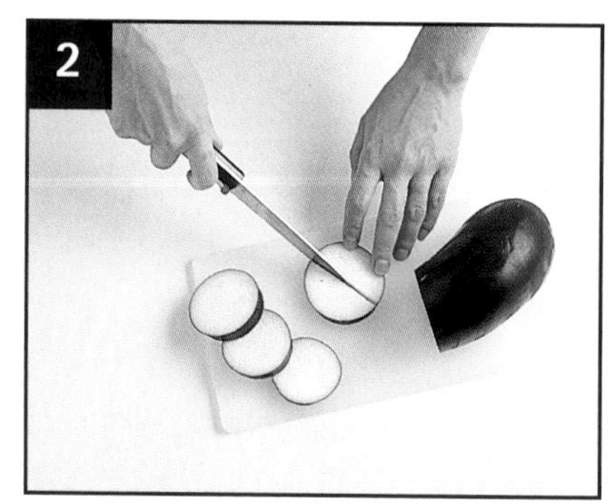

Lentil & Tuna Salad

In this recipe, lentils, combined with spices, lemon juice, and tuna, make a wonderfully tasty and filling salad.

Serves 4

INGREDIENTS

3 tbsp virgin olive oil
1 tbsp lemon juice
1 tsp wholegrain mustard
1 garlic clove, minced
$^1/_2$ tsp cumin powder
$^1/_2$ tsp ground coriander
1 small red onion
2 ripe tomatoes
1 x 14 oz can lentils, drained
1 x 6$^1/_2$ oz can tuna, drained
2 tbsp fresh cilantro, chopped
pepper

1 Using a sharp knife, seed the tomatoes and chop them into fine dice.

2 Using a sharp knife, finely chop the red onion.

3 To make the dressing, whisk together the virgin olive oil, lemon juice, mustard, garlic, cumin powder, and ground coriander in a small bowl. Set aside until required.

4 Mix together the chopped onion, diced tomatoes, and drained lentils in a large bowl.

5 Flake the tuna and stir it into the onion, tomato, and lentil mixture.

6 Stir in the chopped fresh cilantro.

7 Pour the dressing over the lentil and tuna salad and season with freshly ground black pepper. Serve at once.

VARIATION

Nuts would add extra flavor and texture to this salad.

COOK'S TIP

Lentils are a good source of protein and contain important vitamins and minerals. Buy them dried for soaking and cooking yourself, or buy canned varieties for speed and convenience.

1

3

4

Deep-Fried Seafood

Deep-fried seafood is popular all around the Mediterranean, where fish of all kinds is fresh and abundant. Serve with garlic mayonnaise and lemon wedges.

Serves 4

INGREDIENTS

7 oz prepared squid
7 oz raw jumbo shrimp, peeled
5½ oz whitebait
oil, for deep-frying
1½ oz all-purpose flour
1 tsp dried basil
salt and pepper

TO SERVE:
garlic mayonnaise (see Cook's Tip)
lemon wedges

1 Carefully rinse the squid, shrimp, and whitebait under cold running water, completely removing any dirt or grit.

2 Using a sharp knife, slice the squid into rings, leaving the tentacles whole.

3 Heat the oil in a large saucepan to 350°–375°F or until a cube of bread browns in 30 seconds.

4 Place the flour in a bowl and season with the salt, pepper, and basil.

5 Roll the squid, shrimp, and whitebait in the seasoned flour until coated all over. Carefully shake off any excess flour.

6 Cook the seafood in the heated oil in batches for 2–3 minutes or until crispy and golden all over. Remove all of the seafood with a draining spoon and leave to drain thoroughly on kitchen paper.

7 Transfer the deep-fried seafood to serving plates and serve with garlic mayonnaise (see Cook's Tip) and lemon wedges.

COOK'S TIP

To make garlic mayonnaise for serving with the deep-fried seafood, crush 2 garlic cloves, stir into 8 tablespoons of mayonnaise and season with salt and pepper and a little chopped parsley.

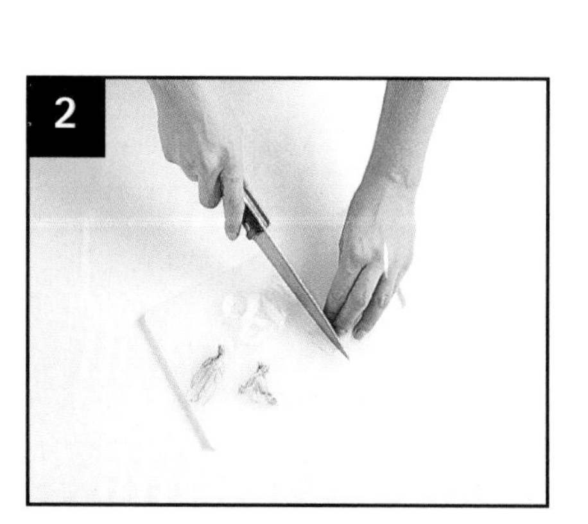
2

5

6

Ravioli alla Parmigiana

This soup is the traditional Minestra served at Easter and Christmas in the province of Parma.

Serves 4

INGREDIENTS

10 oz basic pasta dough (see page 6)
5 cups veal stock
freshly grated Parmesan cheese, to serve

FILLING:
1 cup freshly grated Parmesan cheese
$1^2/_3$ cup fine white bread crumbs
2 eggs
$^1/_2$ cup Espagnole Sauce (see Cook's Tip, below)
1 small onion, finely chopped
1 tsp freshly grated nutmeg

1 Make the basic pasta dough (see page 6). Carefully roll out 2 sheets of the pasta dough and cover with a damp dish cloth while you make the filling for the ravioli.

2 To make the filling, mix together the freshly grated Parmesan cheese, fine white bread crumbs, eggs, espagnole sauce (see Cook's Tip, right), finely chopped onion, and the freshly grated nutmeg in a large mixing bowl.

3 Place spoonfuls of the filling at regular intervals on 1 sheet of pasta dough. Cover with the second sheet of pasta dough, cut into squares, and seal the edges.

4 Bring the veal stock to a boil in a large saucepan. Add the ravioli to the pan and cook for about 15 minutes.

5 Transfer the soup and ravioli to warm serving bowls and serve at once, generously sprinkled with Parmesan cheese.

COOK'S TIP

For espagnole sauce, melt 2 tbsp butter and stir in ¼ cup all-purpose flour. Cook over a low heat, stirring, until lightly colored. Add 1 tsp tomato paste, then stir in 1⅛ cups hot veal stock, 1 tbsp Madeira wine, and 1½ tsp white wine vinegar. Dice 1 oz each bacon, carrot, and onion and ½ oz each celery, leek, and fennel. Fry with a thyme sprig and a bay leaf in oil until soft. Drain, add to the sauce, and simmer for 4 hours. Strain before using.

2

3

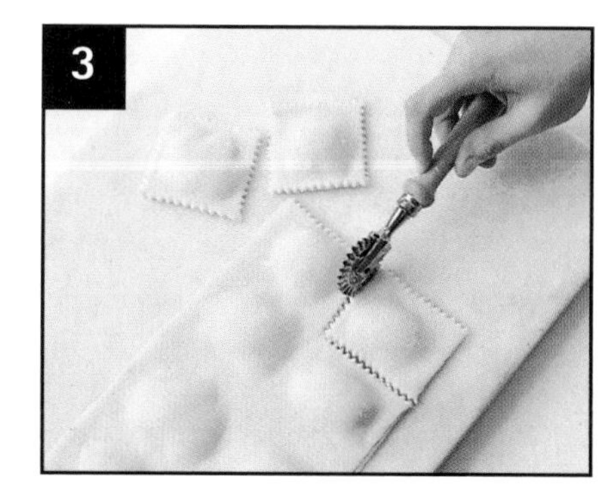

3

Spaghetti alla Carbonara

Ensure that all of the cooked ingredients are as hot as possible before adding the eggs, so they cook on contact.

Serves 4

INGREDIENTS

15 oz dried spaghetti
2 tbsp olive oil
1 large onion, thinly sliced
2 garlic cloves, chopped
6 oz rindless bacon, cut into thin strips
2 tbsp butter
6 oz mushrooms, thinly sliced
1¼ cups heavy cream
3 eggs, beaten
1 cup freshly grated Parmesan cheese, plus extra to serve (optional)
salt and pepper
fresh sage sprigs, to garnish

1 Warm a large serving dish or bowl. Bring a large pan of lightly salted water to a boil. Add the spaghetti and 1 tbsp of the oil and cook until tender but still firm to the bite. Drain, return to the pan, and keep warm.

2 Meanwhile, heat the remaining oil in a skillet over a medium heat. Add the onion and fry until it is transparent. Add the garlic and bacon and fry until the bacon is crisp. Transfer to the warm plate.

3 Melt the butter in the skillet. Add the mushrooms and fry, stirring occasionally, for 3–4 minutes. Return the bacon mixture to the pan. Cover and keep warm.

4 Mix together the cream, eggs, and cheese in a large bowl and then season to taste with salt and pepper.

5 Working very quickly, tip the spaghetti into the bacon and mushroom mixture and pour over the eggs. Toss the spaghetti quickly into the egg and cream mixture, using 2 forks, and serve at once. If you wish, serve with extra grated Parmesan cheese.

COOK'S TIP

The key to success with this recipe is not to overcook the egg. That is why it is important to keep all the ingredients hot enough just to cook the egg and to work rapidly to avoid scrambling it.

Smoked Ham Linguini

Served with freshly made Italian bread or tossed with pesto, this makes a mouth-watering light lunch.

Serves 4

INGREDIENTS

1 lb dried linguini
1 lb green broccoli flowerets
8 oz Italian smoked ham
$^5/_8$ cup Italian Cheese Sauce (see Cook's Tip, below right)
salt and pepper
Italian bread, to serve

1 Bring a large pan of lightly salted water to a boil. Add the linguini and broccoli flowerets and cook for 10 minutes, until the linguini is tender but still firm to the bite.

2 Drain the linguini and broccoli thoroughly, set aside, and keep warm.

3 Meanwhile, make the Italian Cheese Sauce (see Cook's Tip, right).

4 Cut the Italian smoked ham into thin strips. Toss the linguini, broccoli, and ham into the Italian Cheese Sauce and gently warm through over a very low heat.

5 Transfer the pasta mixture to a warm serving dish. Sprinkle with black pepper and serve with Italian bread.

COOK'S TIP

There are many types of Italian bread which would be suitable to serve with this dish. Ciabatta is made with olive oil and is available plain and with different ingredients, such as olives or sun-dried tomatoes.

COOK'S TIP

For Italian Cheese Sauce, melt 2 tbsp butter in a pan and stir in ¼ cup all-purpose flour. Cook, stirring, over a low heat until the roux is light in color and crumbly in texture. Stir in 1¼ cups hot milk. Cook, stirring, for 15 minutes until thick and smooth. Add a pinch of nutmeg, a pinch of dried thyme, 2 tbsp white wine vinegar, and season. Stir in 3 tbsp heavy cream and mix. Stir in ½ cup grated Mozzarella cheese, ⅔ cup grated Parmesan cheese, 1 tsp English mustard, and 2 tbsp sour cream.

1

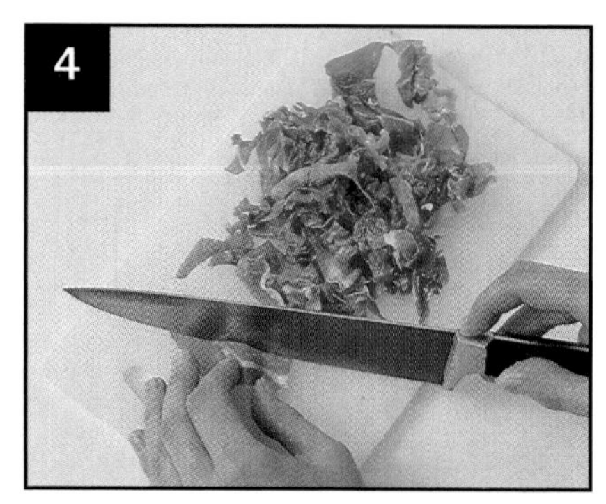
4

4

Rotelle with Spicy Italian Sauce

This filling vegetarian dish is perfect for an inexpensive and quick lunch.

Serves 4

INGREDIENTS

5 tbsp olive oil
3 garlic cloves, minced
2 fresh red chilies, chopped
1 green chili, chopped
$^7/_8$ cup Italian Red Wine Sauce (see Cook's Tip)
$3^1/_2$ cups dried rotelle
salt and pepper
warm Italian bread, to serve

1 Make the Italian Red Wine Sauce (see Cook's Tip, right).

2 Heat 4 tbsp of the oil in a saucepan. Add the garlic and chilies and fry for 3 minutes.

3 Stir in the Italian Red Wine Sauce (see Cook's Tip, right), season with salt and pepper to taste, and simmer gently over a low heat for 20 minutes.

4 Bring a large saucepan of lightly salted water to a boil. Add the rotelle and the remaining oil and cook for 8 minutes, until just tender but still firm to the bite. Drain the pasta.

5 Toss the rotelle in the spicy sauce, transfer to a warm serving dish, and serve with warm Italian bread.

COOK'S TIP

Take care when using fresh chilies as they can burn your skin. Handle them as little as possible – wear protective gloves. Always wash your hands thoroughly afterwards and don't touch your face or eyes before you have washed your hands. Remove chili seeds before chopping the chilies, as they are the hottest part and should not be allowed to slip into the food.

COOK'S TIP

To make Italian Red Wine Sauce, first make a demi-glace sauce by combining $^5/_8$ cup each Brown Stock (see page 36) and Espagnole Sauce (see page 70), cook for 10 minutes, and strain. Meanwhile, combine $^1/_2$ cup red wine, 2 tbsp red wine vinegar, 4 tbsp chopped shallots, 1 bay leaf, and 1 thyme sprig in a small saucepan. Bring to a boil and reduce by about three-quarters. Add the demi-glace sauce and simmer for 20 minutes. Season with pepper and strain.

Tagliarini with Gorgonzola

This simple, creamy pasta sauce is a classic Italian recipe.

Serves 4

INGREDIENTS

2 tbsp butter
8 oz Gorgonzola cheese, roughly crumbled
5/8 cup heavy cream
2 tbsp dry white wine
1 tsp cornstarch
4 fresh sage sprigs, finely chopped
14 oz dried tagliarini
2 tbsp olive oil
salt and white pepper

1 Melt the butter in a heavy-bottomed saucepan. Stir in 6 oz of the Gorgonzola cheese and melt, over a low heat, for about 2 minutes.

2 Add the cream, wine, and cornstarch and beat with a whisk until fully incorporated.

3 Stir in the sage and season to taste with salt and white pepper. Bring to a boil over a low heat, whisking constantly, until the sauce thickens. Remove from the heat and set aside while you cook the pasta.

4 Bring a large saucepan of lightly salted water to a boil. Add the tagliarini and 1 tbsp of the olive oil. Cook the pasta for 12–14 minutes or until just tender, drain thoroughly, and toss in the remaining olive oil. Transfer the pasta to a serving dish and keep warm.

5 Return the saucepan containing the sauce to a low heat to reheat the sauce, whisking constantly. Spoon the Gorgonzola sauce over the tagliarini, generously sprinkle over the remaining cheese, and serve immediately.

COOK'S TIP

Gorgonzola is one of the world's oldest veined cheeses and, arguably, its finest. When buying, always check that it is creamy yellow with delicate green veining. Avoid hard or discolored cheese. It should have a rich, piquant aroma, not a bitter smell. If you find Gorgonzola too strong or rich, you could substitute Danish blue.

Polenta Kabobs

Here, skewers of thyme-flavored polenta, wrapped in prosciutto, are grilled or barbecued.

Serves 4

INGREDIENTS

6 oz instant polenta
scant 3¾ cups water
2 tbsp fresh thyme, stalks removed
8 slices prosciutto (about 2¾ oz)
1 tbsp olive oil
salt and pepper
fresh green salad, to serve

1 Cook the polenta, using 3¼ cups of water to 6 oz polenta, stirring occasionally. Alternatively, follow the instructions on the package.

2 Add the fresh thyme to the polenta mixture and season to taste with salt and pepper.

3 Spread out the polenta, about 1 inch thick, on to a board. Set aside to cool.

4 Using a sharp knife, cut the cooled polenta into 1-inch cubes.

5 Cut the prosciutto slices into 2 pieces lengthways. Wrap the prosciutto around the polenta cubes.

6 Thread the prosciutto wrapped polenta cubes onto skewers.

7 Brush the kabobs with oil and cook under a preheated broiler, turning frequently, for 7–8 minutes. Alternatively, grill the kabobs until golden. Transfer to serving plates and serve with a green salad.

VARIATION

Try flavoring the polenta with chopped oregano, basil, or marjoram instead of the thyme, if you prefer. You should use 3 tablespoons of chopped herbs to every 12 oz instant polenta.

4

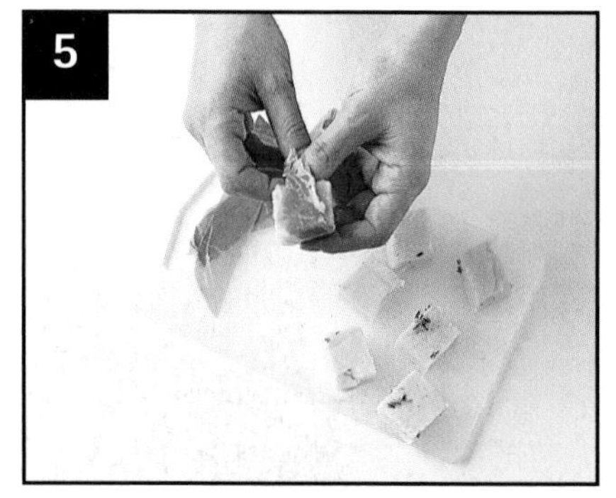

5

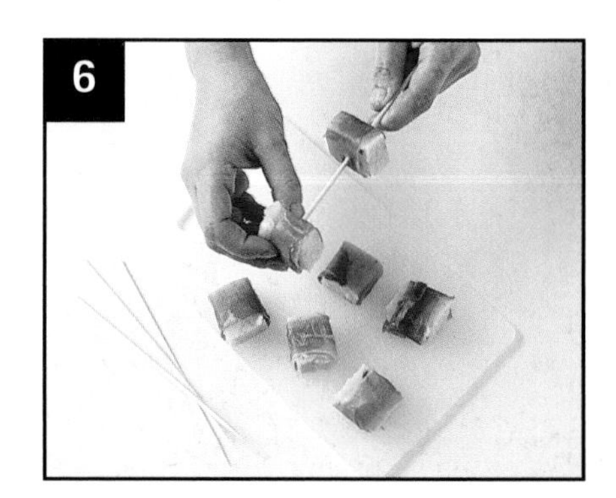

6

Potato Gnocchi with Tomato Sauce

Freshly made potato gnocchi are delicious, especially when they are topped with a fragrant tomato sauce.

Serves 4

INGREDIENTS

12 oz mealy potatoes (those suitable for baking or mashing), halved
2 3/4 oz self-rising flour, plus extra for rolling out
2 tsp dried oregano
2 tbsp oil
1 large onion, chopped
2 garlic cloves, chopped
1 x 14 oz can chopped tomatoes
1/2 vegetable stock cube dissolved in 1/3 cup boiling water
salt and pepper
2 tbsp basil, shredded, plus whole leaves to garnish
Parmesan cheese, grated, to serve

1 Bring a large pan of water to a boil. Add the potatoes and cook for 12–15 minutes or until tender. Drain and leave to cool.

2 Peel and then mash the potatoes with the salt and pepper, sifted flour, and oregano. Mix together with your hands to form a dough.

3 Heat the oil in a pan. Add the onions and garlic and cook for 3–4 minutes. Add the tomatoes and stock, and cook, uncovered, for 10 minutes. Season with salt and pepper to taste.

4 Roll the potato dough into a sausage about 1 inch in diameter. Cut the sausage into 1 inch lengths. Flour your hands, press a fork into each piece to create a series of ridges on one side, and the indent of your index finger on the other.

5 Bring a large pan of water to a boil and cook the gnocchi, in batches, for 2–3 minutes. They should rise to the surface when cooked. Drain and keep warm.

6 Stir the basil into the tomato sauce and pour over the gnocchi. Garnish with basil leaves and freshly ground black pepper. Sprinkle with Parmesan and serve.

VARIATION

Try serving the gnocchi with pesto sauce (see page 200) for a change.

2

3

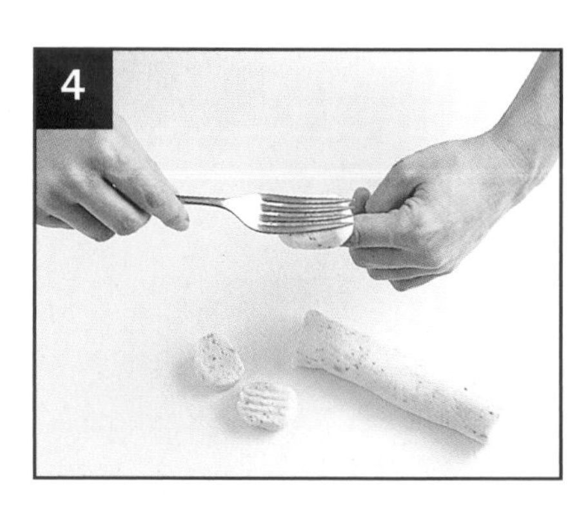

4

Meat & Poultry

Poultry and meat are popular ingredients in Italy. Dishes range from easy, economic mid-week suppers to sophisticated and elegant meals for special occasions. Most meat is sold ready-boned and cut across the grain. Veal is a great favorite and widely available. Pork is also popular, cooked with lots of fragrant herbs, with roast pork being the traditional dish of Umbria. Lamb is often served for special occasions, cooked on a spit, or roasted in the oven with wine, garlic and herbs. Poultry dishes also provide some of Italy's finest food; every part of the chicken is used up, and the leftovers are generally used for making nutritious soups. Turkey, goose, duck, partridge, and guinea fowl are also popular, as is wild game, especially in Sardinia. The recipes in this chapter include traditional family favorites and new combinations – you will be astonished at how easily these dishes are to prepare.

Sicilian Spaghetti

This delicious Sicilian dish originated as a handy way of using up leftover cooked pasta.

Serves 4

INGREDIENTS

- 5/8 cup olive oil, plus extra for brushing
- 2 eggplant
- 3 cups ground beef
- 1 onion, chopped
- 2 garlic cloves, minced
- 2 tbsp tomato paste
- 14 oz can chopped tomatoes
- 1 tsp Worcestershire sauce
- 1 tsp chopped fresh marjoram or oregano or 1/2 tsp dried marjoram or oregano
- 1/2 cup spitted black olives, sliced
- 1 green, red, or yellow bell pepper, cored, seeded, and chopped
- 6 oz dried spaghetti
- 1 cup freshly grated Parmesan cheese
- salt and pepper
- fresh oregano or parsley sprigs, to garnish

1 Brush a 8 inch loose-based round cake pan with oil, line the base with baking parchment, and brush with oil.

2 Slice the eggplant. Heat a little oil in a pan and fry the eggplant in batches until browned on both sides. Add more oil, as necessary. Drain on paper towels.

3 Put the beef, onion, and garlic in a saucepan and cook over a medium heat, stirring, until browned. Add the tomato paste, tomatoes, Worcestershire sauce, marjoram or oregano, and salt and pepper. Simmer, stirring, for 10 minutes. Add the olives and bell pepper and cook for 10 minutes.

4 Bring a pan of salted water to a boil. Add the spaghetti and 1 tbsp olive oil and cook until tender but still firm to the bite. Drain and turn the spaghetti into a bowl. Add the meat mixture and cheese and toss with 2 forks.

5 Arrange eggplant slices over the base and up the sides of the pan. Add the spaghetti and then cover with the rest of the eggplant slices. Bake in a preheated oven at 400°F for 40 minutes. Leave to stand for 5 minutes, then invert on to a serving dish. Discard the baking parchment. Garnish with the fresh herbs and serve.

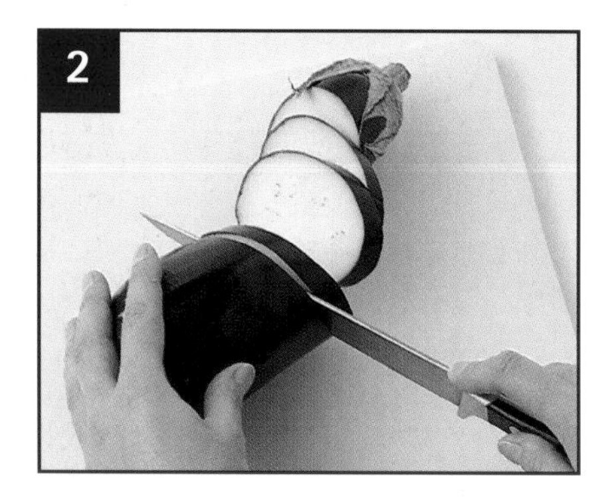

Beef & Pasta Bake

The combination of macaroni and beef korma gives this a really authentic flavor.

Serves 4

INGREDIENTS

2 lb steak, cut into cubes
5/8 cup beef stock
1 lb dried macaroni
1 1/4 cups heavy cream
1/2 tsp garam masala
salt
fresh cilantro, to garnish
naan bread, to serve

KORMA PASTE:
1/2 cup blanched almonds
6 garlic cloves
1 inch piece fresh gingerroot, coarsely chopped
6 tbsp beef stock
1 tsp ground cardamom
4 cloves, minced
1 tsp cinnamon
2 large onions, chopped
1 tsp coriander seeds
2 tsp ground cumin seeds
pinch of cayenne pepper
6 tbsp of sunflower oil

1 To make the korma paste, grind the almonds finely using a pestle and mortar. Put the ground almonds and the rest of the korma paste ingredients into a food processor or blender and process to make a very smooth paste.

2 Put the steak in a shallow dish and spoon over the korma paste, turning to coat the steak well. Leave in the refrigerator to marinate for 6 hours.

3 Transfer the steak to a large saucepan, and simmer over a low heat, adding a little beef stock if required, for 35 minutes.

4 Meanwhile, bring a large saucepan of lightly salted water to a boil. Add the macaroni and cook for 10 minutes, until tender, but still firm to the bite. Drain the pasta thoroughly and transfer to a deep casserole. Add the steak, heavy cream, and garam masala.

5 Bake in a preheated oven at 400°F for 30 minutes. Remove the casserole from the oven and allow to stand for about 10 minutes. Garnish the bake with fresh cilantro and serve with naan.

VARIATION

You could also make this dish using diced chicken and chicken stock, instead of steak and beef stock.

Spaghetti Bolognese

You can use this classic meat sauce for lasagne, cannelloni, or any other baked pasta dishes.

Serves 4

INGREDIENTS

3 tbsp olive oil
2 garlic cloves, minced
1 large onion, finely chopped
1 carrot, diced
2 cups lean ground beef, veal, or chicken
3 oz chicken livers, finely chopped
3 1/2 oz lean prosciutto, diced
5/8 cup Marsala wine
10 oz can chopped plum tomatoes
1 tbsp chopped fresh basil leaves
2 tbsp tomato paste
salt and pepper
1 lb dried spaghetti

1 Heat 2 tbsp of the olive oil in a large saucepan. Add the garlic, onion, and carrot and fry for 6 minutes.

2 Add the ground beef, veal, or chicken, chicken livers, and prosciutto to the pan and cook over a medium heat for 12 minutes, until well browned.

3 Stir in the Marsala, tomatoes, basil, and tomato paste and cook for 4 minutes. Season. Cover and simmer for 30 minutes.

4 Remove the lid from the pan, stir and simmer for a further 15 minutes.

5 Meanwhile, bring a large pan of lightly salted water to a boil. Add the spaghetti and the remaining oil and cook for about 12 minutes, until tender but still firm to the bite. Drain and transfer to a serving dish. Pour the sauce over the pasta, toss, and serve hot.

VARIATION

Chicken livers are an essential ingredient in a classic Bolognese sauce to which they add richness. However, if you prefer not to use them, you can substitute the same quantity of ground beef.

Fresh Spaghetti with Italian Meatballs in Tomato Sauce

This well-loved Italian dish is famous across the world. Make the most of it by using high-quality steak for the meatballs.

Serves 4

INGREDIENTS

- 2½ cups brown bread crumbs
- ⅝ cup milk
- 2 tbsp butter
- ¼ cup whole-wheat flour
- ⅞ cup beef stock
- 14 oz can chopped tomatoes
- 2 tbsp tomato paste
- 1 tsp sugar
- 1 tbsp finely chopped fresh tarragon
- 1 large onion, chopped
- 4 cups ground steak
- 1 tsp paprika
- 4 tbsp olive oil
- 1 lb fresh spaghetti
- salt and pepper
- fresh tarragon sprigs, to garnish

1 Place the bread crumbs in a bowl, add the milk, and set aside to soak for 30 minutes.

2 Melt half the butter in a pan. Add the flour and cook, stirring constantly, for 2 minutes. Gradually stir in the beef stock and cook, stirring constantly, for a further 5 minutes. Add the tomatoes, tomato paste, sugar, and tarragon. Season well and simmer for 25 minutes.

3 Mix the onion, steak, and paprika into the bread crumbs and season to taste. Shape the mixture into 14 meatballs.

4 Heat the oil and remaining butter in a skillet and fry the meatballs, turning frequently, until brown all over. Place them in a deep casserole, pour over the tomato sauce, cover, and bake in a preheated oven at 350°F for 25 minutes.

5 Bring a large saucepan of lightly salted water to a boil. Add the fresh spaghetti, bring back to a boil, and cook for about 2–3 minutes, until tender, but still firm to the bite.

6 Meanwhile, remove the meatballs from the oven and allow them to cool for 3 minutes. Serve the meatballs and their sauce with the spaghetti, garnished with tarragon sprigs.

2

2

4

Lasagne Verde

Today you can buy pre-cooked lasagne sheets from most supermarkets; otherwise prepare the lasagne sheets according to the instructions on the package.

Serves 4–6

INGREDIENTS

butter, for oiling
14 sheets pre-cooked lasagne
3 3/4 cups Béchamel Sauce
3/4 cup grated mozzarella cheese
fresh basil (optional), to garnish

MEAT SAUCE:
1/8 cup olive oil
4 cups ground beef
1 large onion, chopped
1 celery stalk, diced
4 cloves garlic, minced
1/4 cup all purpose flour
1 1/4 cups beef stock
5/8 cup red wine
1 tbsp chopped fresh parsley
1 tsp chopped fresh marjoram
1 tsp chopped fresh basil
2 tbsp tomato paste
salt and pepper

1 To make the meat sauce, heat the olive oil in a large skillet. Add the ground beef and fry, stirring frequently, until browned all over. Add the onion, celery, and garlic and cook for 3 minutes.

2 Sprinkle over the flour and cook, stirring constantly, for 1 minute. Gradually stir in the stock and red wine, season well with salt and pepper and add the parsley, marjoram, and basil. Bring to a boil, lower the heat and simmer for 35 minutes. Add the tomato paste and simmer for a further 10 minutes.

3 Lightly grease an ovenproof dish with butter. Arrange sheets of lasagne over the base of the dish, spoon over a layer of meat sauce, then Béchamel Sauce. Place another layer of lasagne on top and repeat the process twice, finishing with a layer of Béchamel Sauce. Sprinkle over the grated mozzarella cheese.

4 Bake the lasagne in a preheated oven at 375°F for 35 minutes, until the top is golden brown and bubbling. Garnish with fresh basil, if liked, and serve immediately.

Tagliarini with Meatballs in Red Wine & Oyster Mushroom Sauce

A different twist is given to this traditional pasta dish with a rich, but subtle, sauce.

Serves 4

INGREDIENTS

2 cups white bread crumbs
5/8 cup milk
2 tbsp butter
9 tbsp olive oil
3 cups sliced oyster mushrooms
1/4 cup whole-wheat flour
7/8 cup beef stock
5/8 cup red wine

4 tomatoes, skinned and chopped
1 tbsp tomato paste
1 tsp brown sugar
1 tbsp finely chopped fresh basil
12 shallots, chopped

4 cups ground steak
1 tsp paprika

1 lb dried egg tagliarini
salt and pepper
fresh basil sprigs, to garnish

1 Soak the bread crumbs in the milk for 30 minutes.

2 Heat half the butter and 4 tbsp of the oil in a pan. Fry the mushrooms for 4 minutes, then stir in the flour and cook for 2 minutes. Add the stock and wine and simmer for 15 minutes. Add the tomatoes, tomato paste, sugar, and basil. Season well and simmer for 30 minutes.

3 Mix the shallots, steak, and paprika with the bread crumbs and season. Shape the mixture into 14 meatballs.

4 Heat 4 tbsp of the remaining oil and the remaining butter in a large skillet. Fry the meatballs, turning frequently, until brown all over. Transfer to a deep casserole, pour over the red wine and the mushroom sauce, cover, and bake in a preheated oven at 350°F for 30 minutes.

5 Bring a pan of salted water to a boil. Add the pasta and the remaining oil and cook until tender. Drain and transfer to a serving dish. Remove the casserole from the oven and cool for 3 minutes. Pour the meatballs and sauce on to the pasta, garnish with the basil sprigs, and serve.

3

3

4

Neapolitan Veal Cutlets with Mascarpone Cheese & Marille

The delicious combination of apple, onion, and mushroom perfectly complements the delicate flavor of veal.

Serves 4

INGREDIENTS

7/8 cup butter
4 x 9 oz veal cutlets, trimmed
1 large onion, sliced
2 apples, peeled, cored, and sliced
6 oz button mushrooms
1 tbsp chopped fresh tarragon
8 black peppercorns
1 tbsp sesame seeds
14 oz dried marille
scant 1/2 cup extra virgin olive oil
3/4 cup mascarpone cheese, broken into small pieces
salt and pepper
2 large beef tomatoes, cut in half
leaves of 1 fresh basil sprig
fresh basil leaves, to garnish

1 Melt 4 tbsp of the butter in a skillet. Fry the veal over a low heat for 5 minutes on each side. Transfer to a dish and keep warm.

2 Fry the onion and apples in the pan until lightly browned. Transfer to a dish, place the veal on top, and keep warm.

3 Melt the remaining butter in the skillet. Gently fry the mushrooms, tarragon, and peppercorns over a low heat for 3 minutes. Sprinkle over the sesame seeds.

4 Bring a pan of salted water to a boil. Add the pasta and 1 tbsp of the oil. Cook until tender, but still firm to the bite. Drain and transfer to a serving plate.

5 Top the pasta with the mascarpone and sprinkle over the remaining olive oil. Place the onions, apples, and veal cutlets on top of the pasta. Spoon the mushrooms, and peppercorns on to the cutlets, place the tomatoes and basil leaves around the edge, and place in a preheated oven at 300°F for 5 minutes.

6 Season to taste with salt and pepper, garnish with fresh basil leaves, and serve immediately.

1

2

3

Orecchioni with Pork in Cream Sauce, Garnished with Quail Eggs

This unusual and attractive dish is surprisingly quick and easy to make.

Serves 4

INGREDIENTS

1 lb pork tenderloin, thinly sliced
4 tbsp olive oil
8 oz button mushrooms, sliced
7/8 cup Italian Red Wine Sauce (see page 76)
1 tbsp lemon juice
pinch of saffron
3 cups dried orecchioni
4 tbsp heavy cream
12 quail eggs (see Cook's Tip, below)
salt

1 Pound the slices of pork between 2 sheets of plastic wrap until they are wafer thin, then cut into strips.

2 Heat the olive oil in a large skillet, add the pork and stir-fry for 5 minutes. Add the mushrooms to the pan and stir-fry for a further 2 minutes.

3 Pour over the Italian Red Wine Sauce, lower the heat and simmer gently for 20 minutes.

4 Meanwhile, bring a large saucepan of lightly salted water to a boil. Add the lemon juice, saffron, and orecchioni and cook for 12 minutes, until tender but still firm to the bite. Drain the pasta and keep warm.

5 Stir the cream into the pan with the pork and heat gently for a few minutes.

6 Boil the quail eggs for 3 minutes, cool them in cold water and remove the shells.

7 Transfer the pasta to a large, warm serving plate, top with the pork and the sauce, and garnish with the eggs.

COOK'S TIP

In this recipe, the quail eggs are soft-cooked. As they are extremely difficult to shell when warm, it is important that they are thoroughly cooled first. Otherwise, they will break up unattractively.

Chicken & Wild Mushroom Lasagne

You can use your favorite mushrooms, such as chanterelles or oyster mushrooms, for this delicately flavored dish.

Serves 4

INGREDIENTS

butter, for greasing
14 sheets pre-cooked lasagne
3 3/4 cups Béchamel Sauce
1 cup grated Parmesan cheese

CHICKEN & WILD MUSHROOM SAUCE:
2 tbsp olive oil
2 garlic cloves, minced
1 large onion, finely chopped
8 oz wild mushrooms, sliced
2 1/2 cups ground chicken
3 oz chicken livers, finely chopped
4 oz prosciutto, diced
5/8 cup Marsala wine
10 oz can chopped tomatoes
1 tbsp chopped fresh basil leaves
2 tbsp tomato paste
salt and pepper

1 To make the chicken and wild mushroom sauce, heat the olive oil in a large saucepan. Add the garlic, onion, and mushrooms and cook, stirring frequently, for 6 minutes.

2 Add the ground chicken, chicken livers, and prosciutto and cook over a low heat for 12 minutes, until the meat has browned.

3 Stir the Marsala wine, tomatoes, basil, and tomato paste into the mixture in the pan and cook for 4 minutes. Season to taste with salt and pepper, cover and simmer for 30 minutes. Uncover the pan, stir, and simmer for a further 15 minutes.

4 Lightly grease an ovenproof dish with butter. Arrange sheets of lasagne over the base of the dish, spoon over a layer of chicken and wild mushroom sauce, then spoon over a layer of Béchamel Sauce. Place another layer of lasagne on top and repeat the process twice, finishing with a layer of Béchamel Sauce. Sprinkle over the grated cheese and bake in a preheated oven at 375°F for 35 minutes until golden brown and bubbling. Serve immediately.

2

3

4

Mustard Baked Chicken with Pasta Shells

Chicken pieces are cooked in a succulent, mild mustard sauce, then coated in poppy seeds and served on a bed of fresh pasta shells.

Serves 4

INGREDIENTS

8 chicken pieces
(about 4 oz each)
4 tbsp butter, melted
4 tbsp mild mustard (see Cook's Tip)
2 tbsp lemon juice
1 tbsp brown sugar
1 tsp paprika
3 tbsp poppy seeds
14 oz fresh pasta shells
1 tbsp olive oil
salt and pepper

1 Arrange the chicken pieces, smooth side down, in a single layer in a large ovenproof dish.

2 Mix together the butter, mustard, lemon juice, sugar, and paprika in a bowl and season to taste with salt and pepper. Brush the mixture over the upper surfaces of the chicken pieces and bake in a preheated oven at 400°F for 15 minutes.

3 Remove the dish from the oven and carefully turn over the chicken pieces. Coat the upper surfaces of the chicken with the remaining mustard mixture, sprinkle the chicken pieces with poppy seeds and return to the oven for a further 15 minutes.

4 Meanwhile, bring a large pan of lightly salted water to a boil. Add the pasta shells and olive oil and cook until tender, but still firm to the bite.

5 Drain the pasta and arrange on a warmed serving dish. Top with the chicken, pour over the sauce and serve immediately.

COOK'S TIP

Dijon is the type of mustard most often used in cooking, as it has a clean and only mildly spicy flavor. German mustard has a sweet-sour taste, with Bavarian mustard being slightly sweeter. American mustard is mild and sweet.

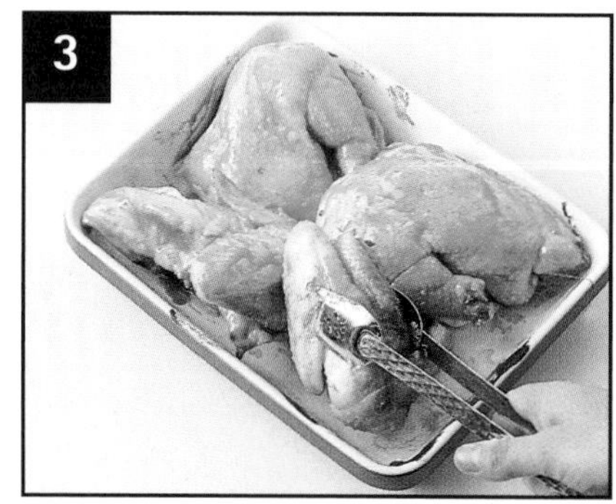

Chicken Suprêmes Filled with Jumbo Shrimp on a Bed of Pasta

These mouth-watering mini-packets of chicken and shrimp will delight your guests.

Serves 4

INGREDIENTS

4 tbsp butter, plus extra for greasing
4 x 7 oz chicken suprêmes, trimmed
4 oz large spinach leaves, trimmed and blanched in hot salted water
4 slices of prosciutto
12–16 raw jumbo shrimp, shelled and deveined
1 lb dried tagliatelle
1 tbsp olive oil
3 leeks, shredded
1 large carrot, grated
5/8 cup thick mayonnaise
2 large cooked beet
salt

1 Grease 4 large pieces of foil and set aside. Place each suprême between 2 pieces of baking parchment and pound with a rolling pin to flatten.

2 Divide half of the spinach between the suprêmes, add a slice of ham to each and top with more spinach. Place 3–4 shrimp on top of the spinach. Fold the pointed end of the suprême over the shrimp, then fold over again to form a parcel. Wrap in foil, place on a baking sheet and bake in a preheated oven at 400°F for 20 minutes.

3 Bring a pan of salted water to a boil. Add the pasta and oil and cook until tender. Drain and transfer to a serving dish.

4 Melt the butter in a skillet. Fry the leeks and carrots for 3 minutes. Transfer the vegetables to the center of the pasta.

5 Work the mayonnaise and 1 beet in a food processor or blender until smooth. Rub through a strainer and pour around the pasta and vegetables.

6 Cut the remaining beet into diamond shapes and place them neatly around the mayonnaise. Remove the foil from the chicken and, using a sharp knife, cut the suprêmes into thin slices. Arrange the slices on top of the vegetables and pasta, and serve.

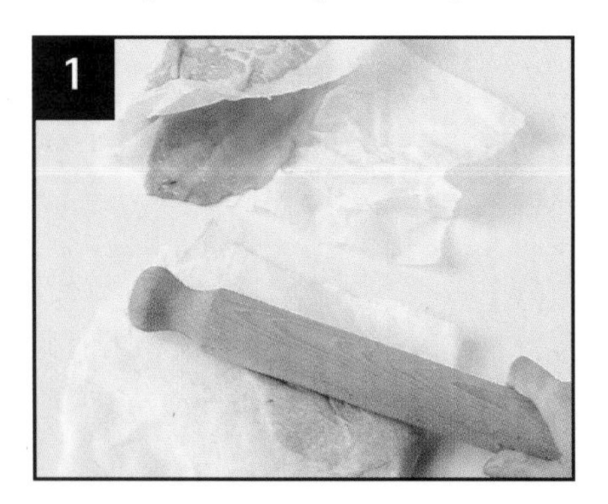
1

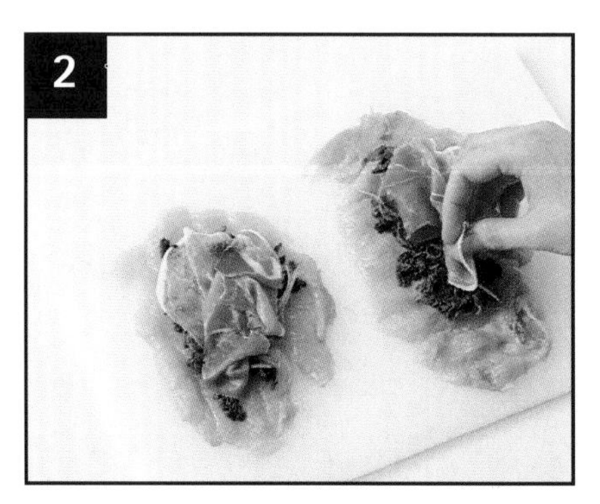
2

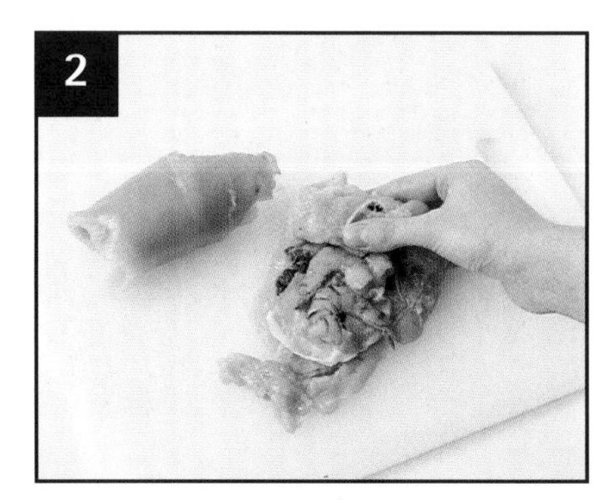
2

Chicken with Green Olives & Pasta

Olives are a popular flavoring for poultry and game in the Apulia region of Italy, where this recipe originates.

Serves 4

INGREDIENTS

- 3 tbsp olive oil
- 2 tbsp butter
- 4 chicken breasts, part boned
- 1 large onion, finely chopped
- 2 garlic cloves, minced
- 2 red, yellow or green bell peppers, cored, seeded, and cut into large pieces
- 9 oz button mushrooms, sliced or quartered
- 6 oz tomatoes, skinned and halved
- $^5/_8$ cup dry white wine
- $1^1/_2$ cups pitted green olives
- 4–6 tbsp heavy cream
- 14 oz dried pasta
- salt and pepper
- chopped flat leaf parsley, to garnish

1 Heat 2 tbsp of the oil and the butter in a skillet. Add the chicken breasts and fry until golden brown all over. Remove the chicken from the pan.

2 Add the onion and garlic to the pan and fry over a medium heat until beginning to soften. Add the bell peppers and mushrooms and cook for 2–3 minutes. Add the tomatoes and season to taste with salt and pepper. Transfer the vegetables to a casserole and arrange the chicken on top.

3 Add the wine to the pan and bring to a boil. Pour the wine over the chicken. Cover and cook in a preheated oven at 350°F for 50 minutes.

4 Add the olives to the casserole and mix in. Pour in the cream, cover and return to the oven for 10–20 minutes.

5 Meanwhile, bring a large pan of lightly salted water to a boil. Add the pasta and the remaining oil and cook until tender, but still firm to the bite. Drain the pasta well and transfer to a serving dish.

6 Arrange the chicken on top of the pasta, spoon over the sauce, garnish with the parsley and serve immediately. Alternatively, place the pasta in a large serving bowl and serve separately.

1

2

3

Parma-Wrapped Chicken

There is a delicious surprise inside these chicken breast packets!

Serves 4

INGREDIENTS

- 4 chicken breasts, skin removed
- $3\frac{1}{2}$ oz full fat soft cheese, flavored with herbs and garlic
- 8 slices prosciutto
- $\frac{2}{3}$ cup red wine
- $\frac{2}{3}$ cup chicken stock
- 1 tbsp brown sugar

1 Using a sharp knife, make a horizontal slit along the length of each chicken breast to form a pocket.

2 Beat the cheese with a wooden spoon to soften it. Spoon the cheese into the pocket of the chicken breasts.

3 Wrap 2 slices of prosciutto around each chicken breast and secure in place with string.

4 Pour the wine and chicken stock into a large skillet and bring to a boil. When the mixture is just starting to boil, add the sugar and stir to dissolve.

5 Add the chicken breasts to the mixture in the skillet. Leave to simmer for 12–15 minutes or the chicken is tender and the juices run clear when a skewer is inserted into the thickest part of the meat.

6 Remove the chicken from the pan, set aside and keep warm.

7 Reheat the sauce and boil until reduced and thickened. Remove the string from the chicken and cut into slices. Pour the sauce over the chicken to serve.

VARIATION

Try adding 2 finely chopped sun-dried tomatoes to the soft cheese in step 2, if you prefer.

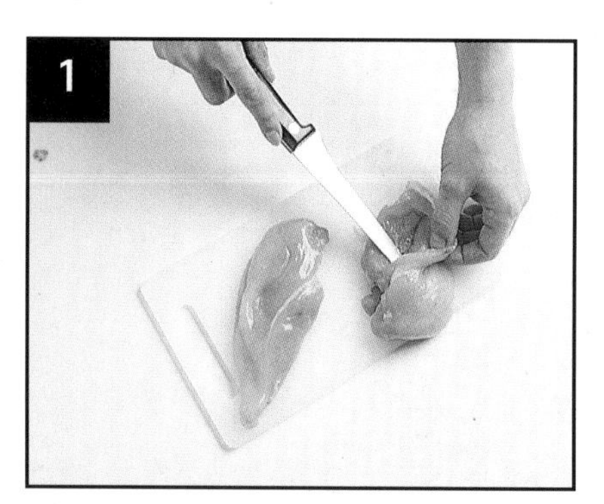

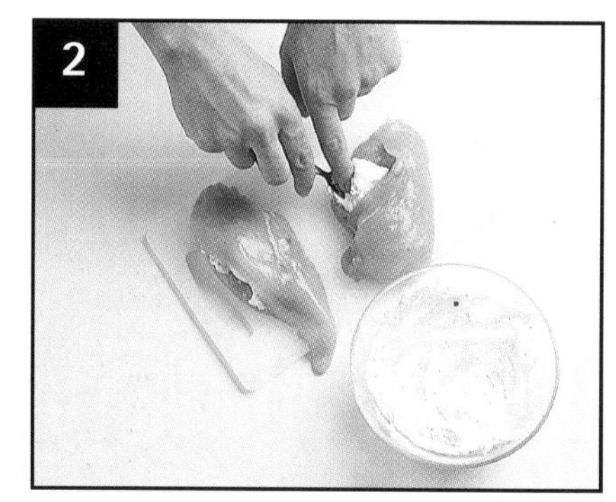

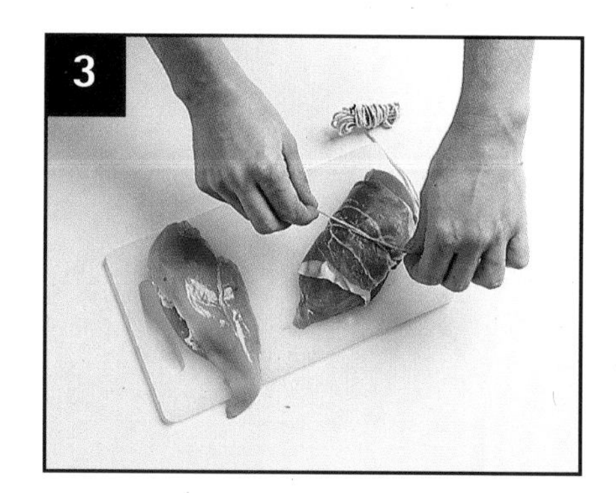

Chicken with Balsamic Vinegar

A rich caramelized sauce, flavored with balsamic vinegar and wine, gives this chicken dish a piquant flavor.

Serves 4

INGREDIENTS

4 chicken thighs, boned
2 garlic cloves, minced
3/4 cup red wine
3 tbsp white wine vinegar
1 tbsp oil
1 tbsp butter
4 shallots
3 tbsp balsamic vinegar
2 tbsp fresh thyme
salt and pepper
cooked polenta or rice, to serve

1 Using a sharp knife, make a few slashes in the skin of the chicken. Brush the chicken with the minced garlic and place in a non-metallic dish.

2 Pour the wine and white wine vinegar over the chicken and season to taste with salt and pepper. Cover and leave to marinate in the refrigerator overnight.

3 Remove the chicken pieces with a perforated spoon, draining well, and reserve the marinade.

4 Heat the oil and butter in a skillet. Add the shallots and cook for 2–3 minutes or until they begin to soften.

5 Add the chicken pieces to the pan and cook for 3–4 minutes, turning, until browned all over. Reduce the heat and add half of the reserved marinade. Cover and cook for 15–20 minutes, adding more marinade when necessary.

6 Once the chicken is tender, add the balsamic vinegar and thyme and cook for a further 4 minutes.

7 Transfer the chicken and marinade to serving plates and serve with polenta or rice.

COOK'S TIP

To make the chicken pieces look a little neater, use wooden skewers to hold them together or secure them with a length of string.

Broiled Chicken with Pesto Toasts

This Italian-style dish is richly flavored with pesto, which is a mixture of basil, olive oil, pine nuts, and Parmesan cheese. Either red or green pesto can be used for this recipe.

Serves 4

INGREDIENTS

8 part-boned chicken thighs
olive oil, for brushing
1 2/3 cups sieved tomatoes
1/2 cup green or red pesto sauce
12 slices French bread
1 cup freshly grated Parmesan cheese
1/2 cup pine nuts or slivered almonds
basil sprig, to garnish

1 Arrange the chicken in a single layer in a wide flameproof dish and brush lightly with oil. Place under a preheated broiler for about 15 minutes, turning occasionally until golden brown.

2 Pierce with a skewer to ensure that the there is no trace of pink in the juices.

3 Pour off any excess fat. Warm the sieved tomatoes and half the pesto sauce in a small pan and pour over the chicken. broil for a few more minutes, turning until coated.

4 Meanwhile, spread the remaining pesto on to the slices of bread. Arrange the bread over the chicken and sprinkle with the Parmesan cheese. Scatter the pine nuts over the cheese. Broil for 2–3 minutes, until browned and bubbling. Serve hot garnished with a basil sprig.

COOK'S TIP

Leaving the skin on means the chicken will have a higher fat content but many people like the rich taste and crispy skin especially when it is blackened by the grill. The skin also keeps in the cooking juices.

Chicken Pepperonata

All the sunshine colors and flavors of the Mediterranean are combined in this easy dish.

Serves 4

INGREDIENTS

8 skinless chicken thighs
2 tbsp whole-wheat flour
2 tbsp olive oil
1 small onion, sliced thinly
1 garlic clove, minced
1 each large red, yellow, and green bell peppers, sliced thinly
14 oz can chopped tomatoes
1 tbsp chopped oregano
salt and pepper
fresh oregano, to garnish
crusty whole-wheat bread, to serve

1 Remove the skin from the chicken thighs and toss in the flour.

2 Heat the oil in a wide pan and fry the chicken quickly until sealed and lightly browned, then remove from the pan. Add the onion to the pan and gently fry until soft. Add the garlic, bell peppers, tomatoes, and oregano, then bring to a boil, stirring.

3 Arrange the chicken over the vegetables, season well with salt and pepper, then cover the pan tightly and simmer for 20–25 minutes or until the chicken is completely cooked and tender.

4 Season to taste, garnish with oregano and serve with crusty whole-wheat bread.

COOK'S TIP

If you do not have fresh oregano, use canned tomatoes with herbs already added.

COOK'S TIP

For extra flavor, halve the peppers and broil under a preheated broiler until the skins are charred. Leave to cool then remove the skins and seeds. Slice the bell peppers thinly and use in the recipe.

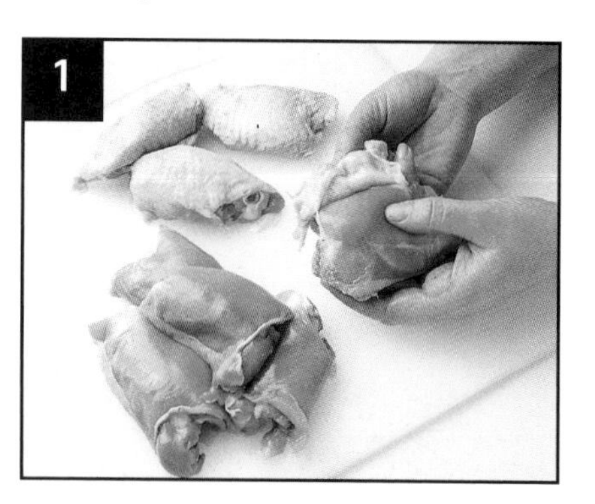

Italian Chicken Spirals

Steaming allows you to cook without fat, and these little foil packets retain all the natural juices of the chicken while cooking conveniently over the pasta while it boils.

Serves 4

INGREDIENTS

4 skinless, boneless, chicken breasts
1 cup fresh basil leaves
2 tbsp hazelnuts
1 garlic clove, minced
2 cups whole-wheat pasta spirals
2 sun-dried tomatoes
or fresh tomatoes
1 tbsp lemon juice
1 tbsp olive oil
1 tbsp capers
1/2 cup black olives
salt and pepper

1 Beat the chicken breasts with a rolling pin to flatten evenly.

2 Place the basil and hazelnuts in a food processor and process until finely chopped. Mix with the garlic, salt, and pepper.

3 Spread the basil mixture over the chicken breasts and roll up from one short end to enclose the filling. Wrap the chicken roll tightly in foil so that they hold their shape, then seal the ends well.

4 Bring a large pan of lightly salted water to a boil and cook the pasta until tender, but still firm to the bite.

5 Place the chicken parcels in a steamer basket or colander set over the pan, cover tightly, and steam for 10 minutes. Meanwhile, dice the tomatoes.

6 Drain the pasta and return to the pan with the lemon juice, olive oil, tomatoes, capers, and olives. Heat through.

7 Pierce the chicken with a skewer to make sure that the juices run clear and not pink, then slice the chicken, arrange over the pasta and serve.

VARIATION

Sun-dried tomatoes have a wonderful, rich flavor, but if you can't find them use fresh tomatoes.

2

3

6

Parma-Wrapped Chicken Cushions

Stuffed with creamy ricotta, nutmeg, and spinach, then wrapped with wafer thin slices of prosciutto and gently cooked in white wine.

Serves 4

INGREDIENTS

1/2 cup frozen spinach, defrosted
1/2 cup ricotta cheese
pinch grated nutmeg
4 skinless, boneless chicken breasts, each weighing 6 oz
4 prosciutto slices
2 tbsp butter
1 tbsp olive oil
12 small onions or shallots
1 1/2 cups button mushrooms, sliced
1 tbsp all-purpose flour
2/3 cup dry white or red wine
1 1/4 cups chicken stock
salt and pepper

1 Put the spinach into a strainer and press out the water with a spoon. Mix with the ricotta and nutmeg and season with salt and pepper to taste.

2 Using a sharp knife, slit each chicken breast through the side and enlarge each cut to form a pocket. Fill with the spinach mixture, reshape the chicken breasts, wrap each breast tightly in a slice of ham and secure with toothpicks. Cover and chill in the refrigerator.

3 Heat the butter and oil in a skillet and brown the chicken breasts for 2 minutes on each side. Transfer the chicken to a large, shallow ovenproof dish and keep warm until required.

4 Fry the onions and mushrooms for 2–3 minutes until lightly browned. Stir in the all-purpose flour then gradually add the wine and stock. Bring to a boil, stirring constantly. Season and spoon the mixture around the chicken.

5 Cook the chicken uncovered in a preheated oven, 400°F, for 20 minutes. Turn the breasts over and cook for a further 10 minutes. Remove the toothpick and serve with the sauce, together with carrot purée and green beans, if wished.

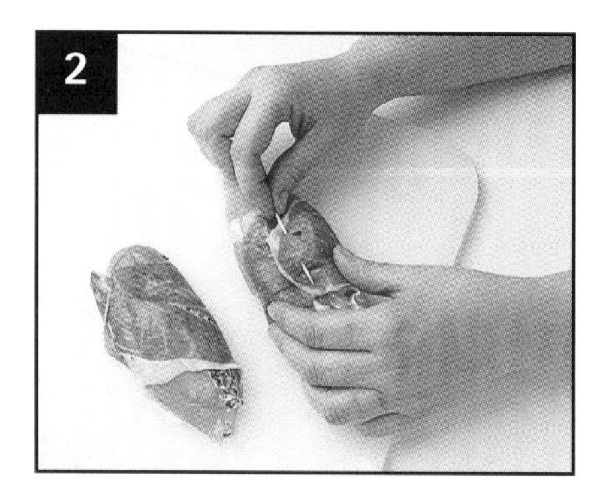
2

3

4

Boned Chicken with Parmesan

It's really very easy to bone a whole chicken, but if you prefer, you can ask a friendly butcher to do this for you.

Serves 6

INGREDIENTS

- 1 chicken, weighing about 5 lb
- 8 slices Mortadella or salami
- 2 cups fresh white or brown bread crumbs
- 1 cup freshly grated Parmesan cheese
- 2 garlic cloves, minced
- 6 tbsp chopped fresh basil or parsley
- 1 egg, beaten
- pepper
- fresh spring vegetables, to serve

1 Bone the chicken, keeping the skin intact. Dislocate each leg by breaking it at the thigh joint. Cut down each side of the backbone, taking care not to pierce the breast skin.

2 Pull the backbone clear of the flesh and discard. Remove the ribs, severing any attached flesh with a sharp knife.

3 Scrape the flesh from each leg and cut away the bone at the joint with a knife or shears.

4 Use the bones for stock. Lay out the boned chicken on a board, skin side down. Arrange the Mortadella slices over the chicken, overlapping slightly.

5 Put the bread crumbs, Parmesan, garlic, and basil or parsley in a bowl. Season well with pepper and mix. Stir in the beaten egg to bind the mixture together. Pile the mixture down the middle of the boned chicken, roll the meat around it and tie securely with fine cotton string.

6 Place in a roasting dish and brush lightly with olive oil. Roast in a preheated oven, 400°F, for 1½ hours or until the juices run clear when pierced.

7 Serve hot or cold, in slices, with fresh spring vegetables.

VARIATION

Replace the Mortadella with rashers of streaky bacon, if preferred.

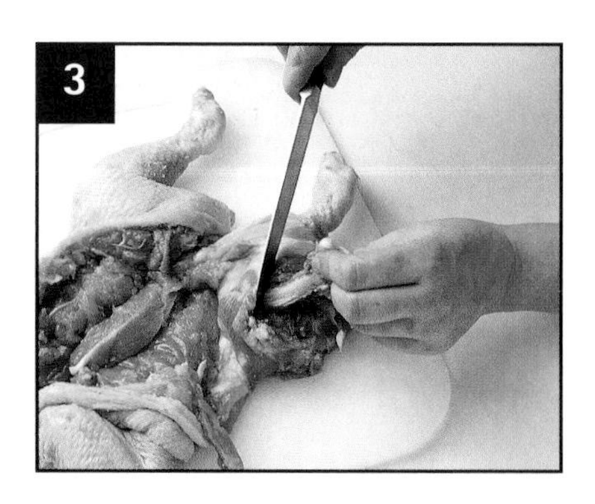

Saltimbocca

The Italian name for this dish, Saltimbocca, *means 'jump into the mouth'. The stuffed rolls are quick and easy to make and taste delicious.*

Serves 4

INGREDIENTS

4 turkey fillets or 4 veal escalopes, about 1 lb in total
$3^3/_4$ oz prosciutto
8 sage leaves
1 tbsp olive oil
1 onion, finely chopped
$^3/_4$ cup white wine
$^3/_4$ cup chicken stock

1 Place the turkey or veal between sheets of waxed paper. Pound the meat with a meat mallet or the end of a rolling pin to flatten it slightly. Cut each escalope in half.

2 Trim the prosciutto to fit each piece of turkey or veal and place over the meat. Lay a sage leaf on top. Roll up the escalopes and secure with a toothpick.

3 Heat the oil in a skillet and cook the onion for 3–4 minutes. Add the turkey or veal rolls to the pan and cook for 5 minutes until brown all over.

4 Pour the wine and stock into the pan and leave to simmer for 15 minutes if using turkey, and 20 minutes for veal, or until tender. Serve immediately.

VARIATION

Try a similar recipe called Bocconcini, *meaning 'little mouthfuls'. Follow the same method as here, but replace the sage leaf with a piece of Gruyère cheese.*

COOK'S TIP

If using turkey rather than veal, watch it carefully as turkey tends to turn dry very quickly if overcooked.

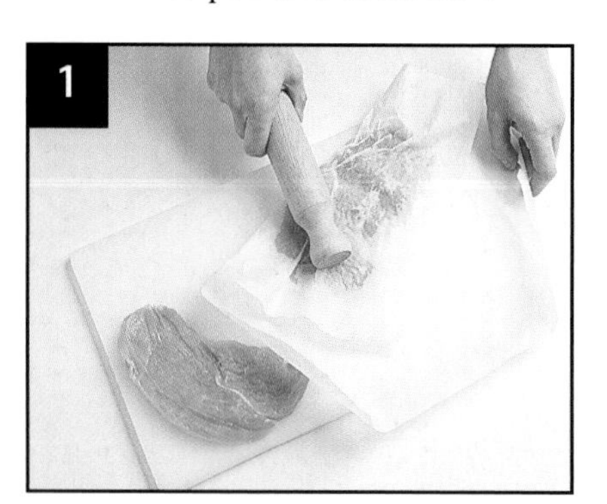
1

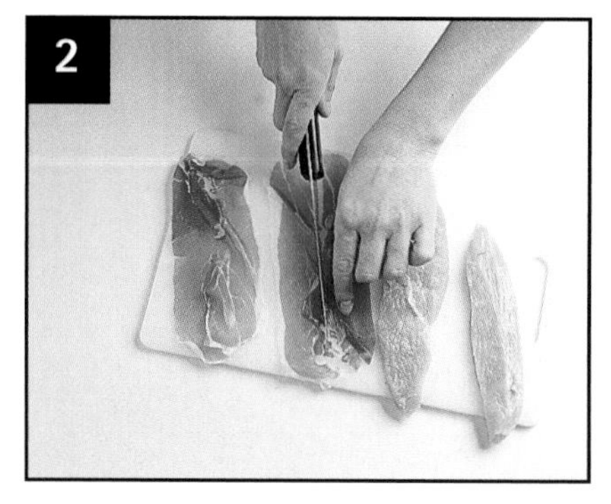
2

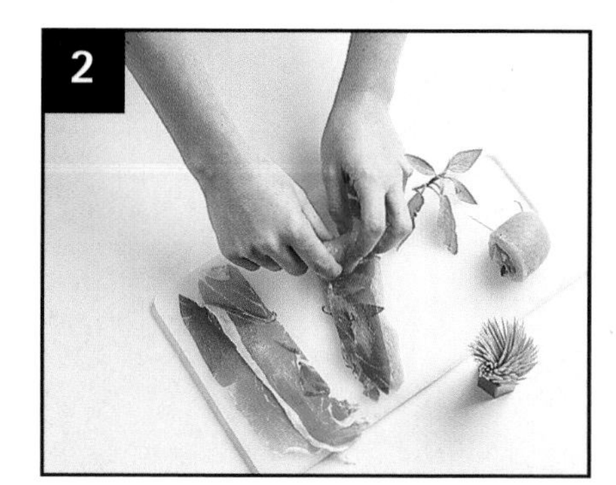
2

Sliced Breast of Duck with Linguine

A raspberry and honey sauce superbly counterbalances the richness of the duck.

Serves 4

INGREDIENTS

- 4 x $10\frac{1}{2}$ oz boned breasts of duck
- 2 tbsp butter
- $\frac{3}{8}$ cup finely chopped carrots
- 4 tbsp finely chopped shallots
- 1 tbsp lemon juice
- $\frac{5}{8}$ cup meat stock
- 4 tbsp clear honey
- $\frac{3}{4}$ cup fresh or thawed frozen raspberries
- $\frac{1}{4}$ cup all-purpose flour
- 1 tbsp Worcestershire sauce
- 14 oz fresh linguine
- 1 tbsp olive oil
- salt and pepper

TO GARNISH:

- fresh raspberries
- fresh sprig of flat-leaf parsley

1 Trim and score the duck breasts with a sharp knife and season well all over. Melt the butter in a skillet, add the duck breasts and fry all over until lightly colored.

2 Add the carrots, shallots, lemon juice, and half the meat stock and simmer over a low heat for 1 minute. Stir in half the honey and half the raspberries. Sprinkle over half the flour and cook, stirring constantly for 3 minutes. Season with pepper and add the Worcestershire sauce.

3 Stir in the remaining stock and cook for 1 minute. Stir in the remaining honey and remaining raspberries and sprinkle over the remaining flour. Cook for a further 3 minutes.

4 Remove the duck breasts from the pan, but leave the sauce to continue simmering over a very low heat.

5 Meanwhile, bring a large saucepan of lightly salted water to a boil. Add the linguine and olive oil and cook until tender, but still firm to the bite. Drain and divide between 4 individual plates.

6 Slice the duck breast lengthways into $\frac{1}{4}$ inch thick pieces. Pour a little sauce over the pasta and arrange the sliced duck in a fan shape on top of it. Garnish with raspberries and flat-leaf parsley and serve.

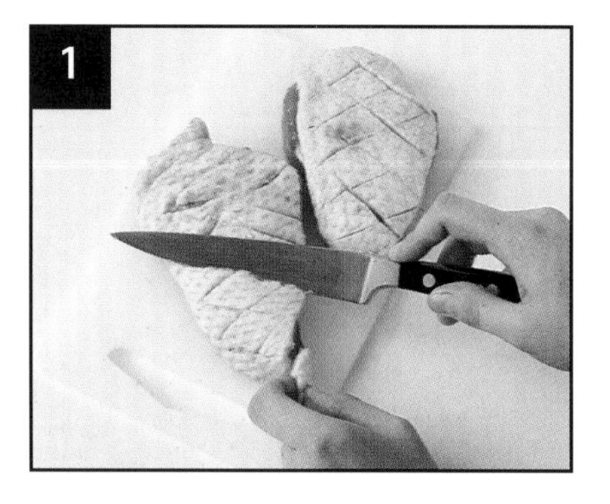

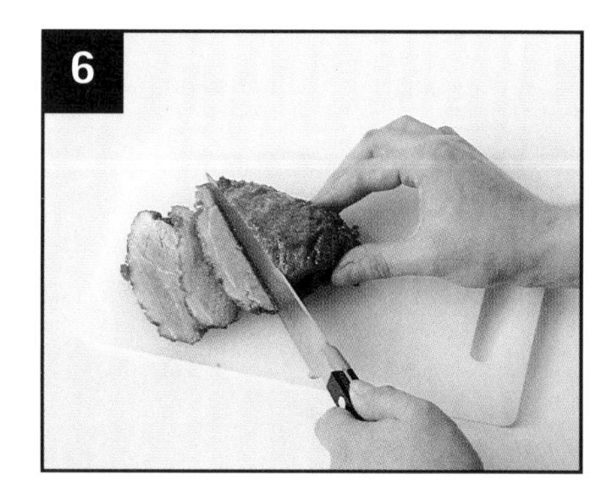

Breast of Pheasant Lasagne with Baby Onions & Green Peas

This scrumptious and unusual baked lasagne is virtually a meal in itself.

Serves 4

INGREDIENTS

butter, for greasing
14 sheets pre-cooked lasagne
3 3/4 cups Béchamel Sauce
3/4 cup grated mozzarella cheese

FILLING:
8 oz pork fat, diced
2 tbsp butter
16 small onions
8 large pheasant breasts, thinly sliced
1/4 cup all purpose flour
2 1/2 cups chicken stock
bouquet garni
1 lb fresh English peas, shelled
salt and pepper

1. To make the filling, put the pork fat into a pan of boiling, salted water and simmer for 3 minutes, then drain and pat dry.

2. Melt the butter in a large skillet. Add the pork fat and onions and cook for 3 minutes, until lightly browned.

3. Remove the pork fat and onions from the pan and set aside. Add the slices of pheasant and cook over a low heat for 12 minutes, until browned all over. Transfer to an ovenproof dish.

4. Stir the flour into the pan and cook until just brown, then blend in the stock. Pour over the pheasant, add the bouquet garni and cook in a preheated oven at 400°F for 5 minutes.

5. Remove the bouquet garni. Add the onions, pork fat, and peas and return to the oven for 10 minutes.

6. Put the pheasant breasts and pork in a food processor and grind finely.

7. Lower the oven temperature to 375°F. Lightly grease an ovenproof dish with butter. Make layers of lasagne, pheasant sauce, and Béchamel Sauce in the dish, ending with Béchamel sauce. Sprinkle over the cheese and bake in the oven for 30 minutes. Serve surrounded by the peas and onions.

2

3

6

Rigatoni & Pesto-Baked Partridge

Partridge has a more delicate flavor than many game birds and this subtle sauce perfectly complements it.

Serves 4

INGREDIENTS

- 8 partridge pieces (about 4 oz each)
- 4 tbsp butter, melted
- 4 tbsp Dijon mustard
- 2 tbsp lime juice
- 1 tbsp brown sugar
- 6 tbsp Pesto Sauce
- 1 lb dried rigatoni
- 1 tbsp olive oil
- 1 1/3 cups freshly grated Parmesan cheese
- salt and pepper

1 Arrange the partridge pieces, smooth side down, in a single layer in a large, ovenproof dish.

2 Mix together the butter, Dijon mustard, lime juice, and brown sugar in a bowl. Season to taste with salt and pepper.Brush this mixture over the uppermost surfaces of the partridge pieces and bake in a preheated oven at 400°F for 15 minutes.

3 Remove the dish from the oven and coat the partridge pieces with 3 tbsp of the Pesto Sauce. Return to the oven and bake for a further 12 minutes.

4 Remove the dish from the oven and carefully turn over the partridge pieces. Coat the top of the partridges with the remaining mustard mixture and return to the oven for a further 10 minutes.

5 Meanwhile, bring a large saucepan of lightly salted water to a boil. Add the rigatoni and olive oil and cook for about 10 minutes, until tender, but still firm to the bite. Drain and transfer to a large serving dish. Toss the pasta with the remaining Pesto Sauce and the Parmesan cheese.

6 Arrange the pieces of partridge on the serving dish with the rigatoni, pour over the cooking juices and serve immediately.

VARIATION

You could also prepare young pheasant in the same way.

2

2

3

Pork with Lemon & Garlic

This is a simplified version of a traditional dish from the Marche region, on the east coast of Italy. Pork fillet pockets are stuffed with prosciutto and herbs.

Serves 4

INGREDIENTS

1 lb pork fillet
1$^3/_4$ oz chopped almonds
2 tbsp olive oil
3$^1/_2$ oz prosciutto, finely chopped
2 garlic cloves, chopped
1 tbsp fresh oregano, chopped
finely grated peel of 2 lemons
4 shallots, finely chopped
$^3/_4$ cup ham or chicken stock
1 tsp sugar

1 Using a sharp knife, cut the pork fillet into 4 equal pieces. Place the pork between sheets of oiled paper and pound each piece with a meat mallet or the end of a rolling pin to flatten it.

2 Cut a horizontal slit in each piece of pork to make a pocket.

3 Place the almonds on a baking sheet. Lightly toast the almonds under a medium-hot broiler for 2–3 minutes or until golden.

4 Mix the almonds with 1 tablespoon of the olive oil, chopped prosciutto, garlic, oregano, and the finely grated peel from 1 lemon. Spoon the mixture into the pockets of the pork.

5 Heat the remaining oil in a large skillet. Add the shallots and cook for 2 minutes.

6 Add the pork to the skillet and cook for 2 minutes on each side or until browned all over.

7 Add the stock to the pan, bring to a boil, cover and leave to simmer for 45 minutes or until the pork is tender. Remove the meat from the pan, set aside and keep warm.

8 Using a zester, pare the remaining lemon. Add the peel and sugar to the pan, boil for 3–4 minutes or until reduced and syrupy. Pour over the pork fillets and serve immediately.

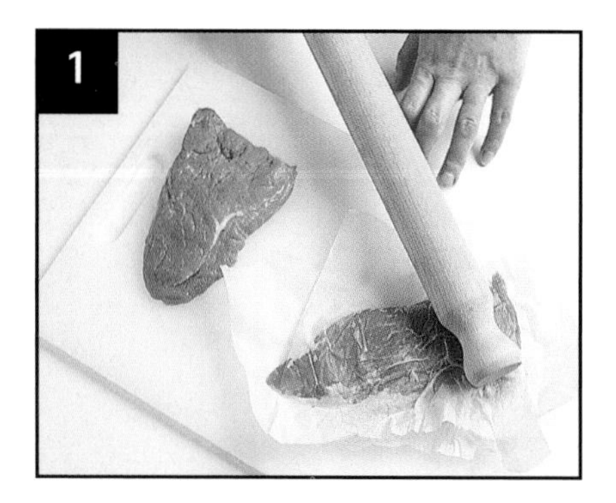
1

4

4

Neapolitan Pork Steaks

An Italian version of broiled pork steaks, this dish is easy to make and delicious to eat.

Serves 4

INGREDIENTS

2 tbsp olive oil
1 garlic clove, chopped
1 large onion, sliced
1 x 14 oz can tomatoes
2 tsp yeast extract
4 pork loin steaks, each about 4½ oz
2 ¾ oz black olives, pitted
2 tbsp fresh basil, shredded
freshly grated Parmesan cheese, to serve

1 Heat the oil in a large skillet. Add the onions and garlic and cook, stirring, for 3–4 minutes or until they just begin to soften.

2 Add the tomatoes and yeast extract to the skillet and leave to simmer for about 5 minutes or until the sauce starts to thicken.

3 Cook the pork steaks, under a preheated broiler, for 5 minutes on both sides, until the the meat is golden and cooked through. Set the pork steaks aside and keep warm.

4 Add the olives and fresh shredded basil to the sauce in the skillet and stir quickly to combine.

5 Transfer the steaks to warm serving plates. Top the steaks with the sauce, sprinkle with freshly grated Parmesan cheese, and serve immediately.

COOK'S TIP

Parmesan is a mature and exceptionally hard cheese produced in Italy. You only need to add a little as it has a very strong flavor.

COOK'S TIP

There are many types of canned tomato available – for example plum tomatoes, or tomatoes chopped in water, or chopped sieved tomatoes. The chopped variety are often canned with added flavors such as garlic, basil, onion, chili, and mixed herbs, and are a good storecupboard standby.

Pork Chops with Fennel & Juniper

The addition of juniper and fennel to the pork chops gives an unusual and delicate flavor to this dish.

Serves 4

INGREDIENTS

$^{1}/_{2}$ fennel bulb
1 tbsp juniper berries, lightly minced
about 2 tbsp olive oil
finely grated peel and juice of 1 orange
4 pork chops, each about $5^{1}/_{2}$ oz
fresh bread and a crisp salad, to serve

1 Using a sharp knife, finely chop the fennel bulb, discarding the green parts.

2 Grind the juniper berries in a mortar and pestle. Mix the minced juniper berries with the fennel flesh, olive oil, and orange peel.

3 Using a sharp knife, score a few cuts all over each chop.

4 Place the pork chops in a roasting pan or an ovenproof dish. Spoon the fennel and juniper mixture over the pork chops.

5 Carefully pour the orange juice over the top of each pork chop, cover, and leave to marinate in the refrigerator for about 2 hours.

6 Cook the pork chops, under a preheated broiler, for 10–15 minutes, depending on the thickness of the meat, until the meat is tender and cooked through, turning occasionally.

7 Transfer the pork chops to serving plates and serve with a crisp, fresh salad and plenty of fresh bread to mop up the cooking juices.

COOK'S TIP

Juniper berries are most commonly associated with gin, but they are often added to meat dishes in Italy for a delicate citrus flavor. They can be bought dried from most health food shops and some larger supermarkets.

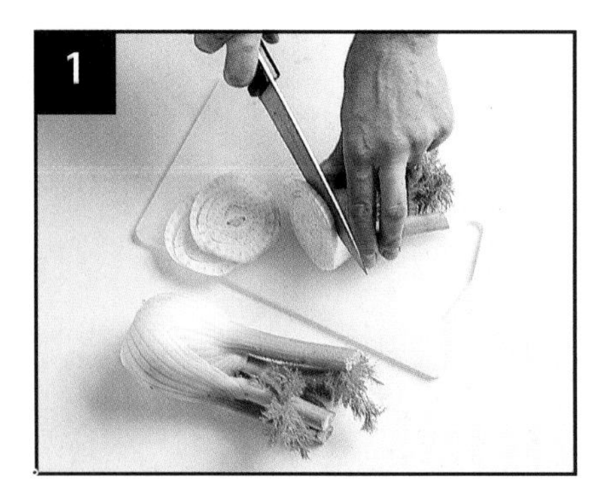

1

2

5

Cannelloni

It is easier to use dried pasta in this recipe – you can buy it ready made in tubes. If you are using fresh pasta, you must cut out squares and roll them yourself.

Serves 4

INGREDIENTS

20 tubes dried cannelloni (about 7 oz) or 20 square sheets of fresh pasta (12 oz)
9 oz ricotta cheese
5½ oz frozen spinach, defrosted
½ small red bell pepper, diced
2 scallions, chopped
⅔ cup hot vegetable or chicken stock
1 portion of Basil and Tomato Puréed Sauce (see page 90)
1 oz Parmesan or pecorino cheese, grated
salt and pepper

1 If you are using dried cannelloni, check the package directions; many varieties do not need pre-cooking. If necessary, pre-cook your pasta. Bring a large saucepan of water to a boil, add 1 tablespoon of oil, and cook the pasta for 3–4 minutes – it is easier to do this in batches.

2 In a bowl, mix together the ricotta, spinach, bell pepper, and scallions, and season to taste with salt and pepper.

3 Lightly butter an ovenproof dish, large enough to contain all of the pasta tubes in a single layer. Spoon the ricotta mixture into the pasta tubes and place them into the prepared dish. If you are using fresh sheets of pasta, spread the ricotta mixture along one side of each fresh pasta square and roll up to form a tube.

4 Mix together the stock and basil and tomato purée and pour it all over the pasta tubes.

5 Sprinkle the cheese over the cannelloni and bake in a preheated oven, 375°F for 20–25 minutes or until the pasta is cooked through.

VARIATION

If you would prefer a creamier version, omit the stock and the basil and tomato puréed sauce and replace with Béchamel Sauce.

1

3

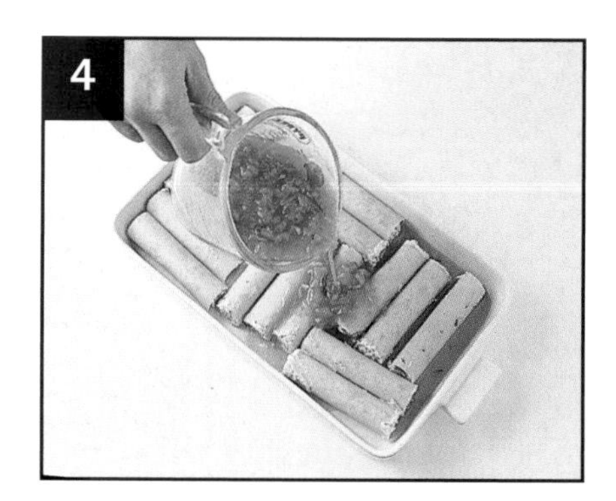
4

Italian Sausage & Bean Casserole

In this traditional Tuscan dish, Italian sausages are cooked with cannellini beans and tomatoes.

Serves 4

INGREDIENTS

8 Italian sausages
1 tbsp olive oil
1 large onion, chopped
2 garlic cloves, chopped
1 green bell pepper
8oz fresh tomatoes, skinned and chopped or 1 x 14 oz can tomatoes, chopped
2 tbsp sun-dried tomato paste
14 oz can cannellini beans
mashed potato or rice, to serve

1 Seed the bell pepper and cut it into thin strips.

2 Prick the Italian sausages all over with a fork. Cook them, under a preheated broiler, for 10–12 minutes, turning occasionally, until brown all over. Set aside and keep warm.

3 Heat the oil in a large skillet. Add the onion, garlic, and bell pepper to the skillet and cook for 5 minutes, stirring occasionally, or until softened.

4 Add the tomatoes to the skillet and leave the mixture to simmer for about 5 minutes, stirring occasionally, or until slightly reduced and thickened.

5 Stir the sun-dried tomato paste, cannellini beans, and Italian sausages into the mixture in the skillet. Cook for 4–5 minutes or until the mixture is piping hot. Add 4–5 tablespoons of water, if the mixture becomes too dry during cooking.

COOK'S TIP

Italian sausages are coarse in texture and have a strong flavor. They can be found in specialist sausage shops, Italian delicatessens, and some larger supermarkets. They are replaceable in this recipe only by game sausages.

6 Transfer the Italian sausage and bean casserole to serving plates and serve with mashed potato or cooked rice.

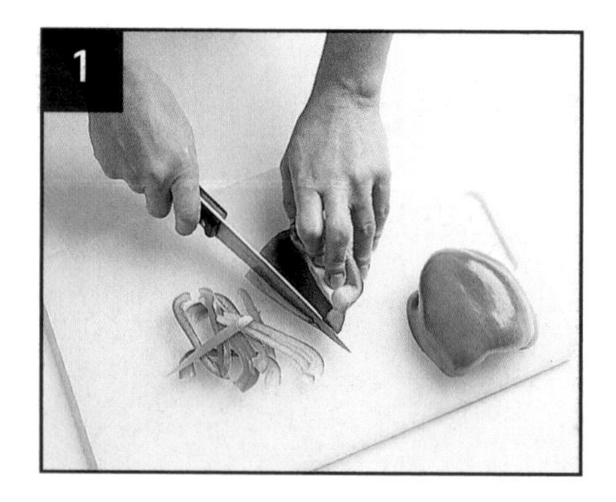
1

3

4

Rich Beef Stew

This slow-cooked beef stew is flavored with oranges, red wine, and porcini mushrooms.

Serves 4

INGREDIENTS

- 1 tbsp oil
- 1 tbsp butter
- 8 oz baby onions, peeled and halved
- 1 lb 5 oz stewing steak, diced into 1 1/2 inch chunks
- 1 1/4 cup beef stock
- 2/3 cup red wine
- 4 tbsp chopped oregano
- 1 tbsp sugar
- 1 orange
- 1 oz porcini or other dried mushrooms
- 8 oz fresh plum tomatoes
- cooked rice or potatoes, to serve

1 Heat the oil and butter in a large skillet. Add the onions and sauté for 5 minutes or until golden. Remove with a draining spoon, set aside and keep warm.

2 Add the beef to the pan and cook, stirring, for 5 minutes or until browned all over.

3 Return the onions to the skillet and add the stock, wine, oregano, and sugar, stirring to mix well. Transfer the mixture to an ovenproof casserole dish.

4 Pare the peel from the orange and cut it into strips. Slice the orange flesh into rings. Add the orange rings and the peel to the casserole. Cook in a preheated oven, at 350°F, for 1 1/4 hours.

5 Soak the porcini mushrooms for 30 minutes in a small bowl containing 4 tablespoons of warm water.

6 Peel and halve the tomatoes. Add the tomatoes, porcini mushrooms, and their soaking liquid to the casserole. Cook for a further 20 minutes until the beef is tender and the juices thickened. Serve with cooked rice or potatoes.

VARIATION

Instead of fresh tomatoes, try using 8 sun-dried tomatoes, cut into wide strips, if you prefer.

2

3

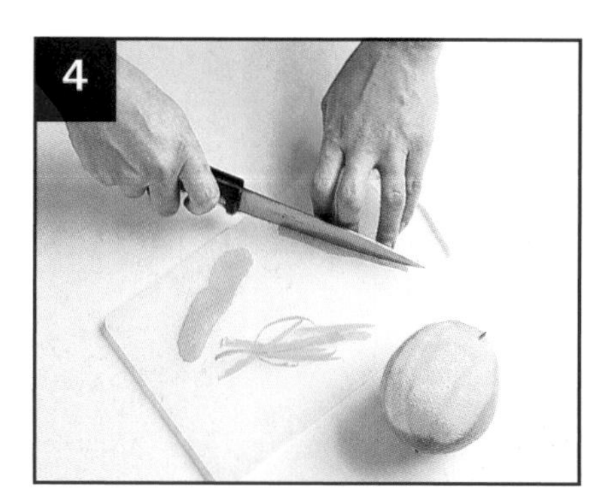
4

Roman Pan-Fried Lamb

Chunks of tender lamb, pan-fried with garlic and stewed in red wine, are a real Roman dish.

Serves 4

INGREDIENTS

1 tbsp oil
1 tbsp butter
1 lb 5 oz lamb (shoulder or leg), cut in 1 inch chunks
4 garlic cloves, peeled
3 sprigs thyme, stalks removed
6 canned anchovy fillets
2/3 cup red wine
2/3 cup lamb or vegetable stock
1 tsp sugar
1 3/4 oz black olives, pitted and halved
2 tbsp chopped parsley, to garnish
mashed potato, to serve

1 Heat the oil and butter in a large skillet. Add the lamb and cook for 4–5 minutes, stirring, until the meat is browned all over.

2 Using a pestle and mortar, grind together the garlic, thyme, and anchovies to make a smooth paste.

3 Add the wine and lamb or vegetable stock to the skillet. Stir in the garlic and anchovy paste together with the sugar.

4 Bring the mixture to a boil, reduce the heat, cover, and leave to simmer for 30–40 minutes or until the lamb is tender. For the last 10 minutes of the cooking time, remove the lid in order to allow the sauce to reduce slightly.

5 Stir the olives into the sauce and mix to combine.

6 Transfer the lamb and the sauce to a serving bowl and garnish with freshly chopped parsley. Serve with creamy mashed potatoes.

COOK'S TIP

Rome is the capital of both the region of Lazio and Italy and thus has become a focal point for specialities from all over Italy. Food from this region tends to be simple and quick to prepare, all with plenty of herbs and seasonings, giving really robust flavors.

1

2

3

Lamb Noisettes with Bay & Lemon

These lamb chops quickly become more elegant when the bone is removed to make noisettes.

Serves 4

INGREDIENTS

4 lamb chops
1 tbsp oil
1 tbsp butter
2/3 cup white wine
2/3 cup lamb or vegetable stock
2 bay leaves
pared peel of 1 lemon
salt and pepper

1 Using a sharp knife, carefully remove the bone from each lamb chop, keeping the meat intact. Alternatively, ask the butcher to prepare the lamb noisettes for you.

2 Shape the meat into rounds and secure with a piece of string.

3 In a large skillet, heat together the oil and butter until the mixture starts to froth. Add the lamb noisettes to the skillet and cook for 2–3 minutes on each side or until browned all over.

4 Remove the skillet from the heat, drain off all of the fat, and discard.

5 Return the skillet to the heat. Add the wine, stock, bay leaves, and lemon peel to the skillet and cook for 20–25 minutes or until the lamb is tender.

6 Season the lamb noisettes and sauce to taste with a little salt and pepper.

7 Transfer to serving plates. Remove the string from each noisette and serve with the sauce.

COOK'S TIP

Your local butcher will offer you good advice on how to prepare the lamb noisettes if you are wary of preparing them yourself.

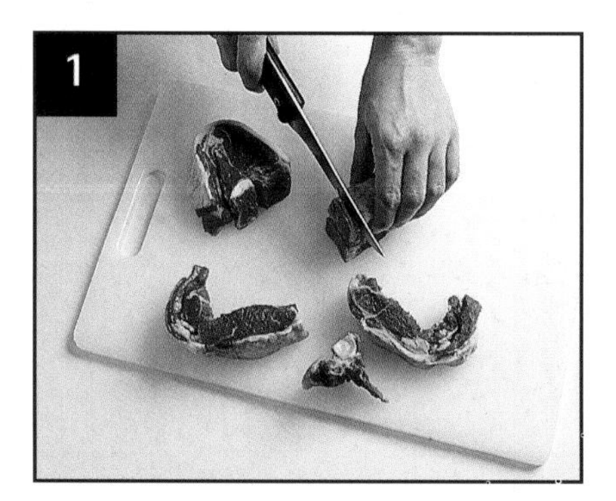
1

2

3

Pasticcio

A recipe with both Italian and Greek origins, this dish may be served hot or cold, cut into thick satisfying squares.

Serves 6

INGREDIENTS

2 cups dried fusilli
1 tbsp olive oil, plus extra for brushing
4 tbsp heavy cream
salt
fresh rosemary sprigs, to garnish
mixed salad, to serve

SAUCE:
2 tbsp olive oil
1 onion, thinly sliced
1 red bell pepper, cored, seeded, and chopped
2 garlic cloves, chopped
5 1/4 cups ground beef
14 oz can chopped tomatoes
1/2 cup dry white wine
2 tbsp chopped fresh parsley
2 oz can anchovies, drained and chopped
salt and pepper

TOPPING:
1 1/4 cups unsweetened yogurt
3 eggs
pinch of freshly grated nutmeg
1/2 cup freshly grated Parmesan cheese

1 To make the sauce, heat the oil in a skillet and fry the onion and red bell pepper for 3 minutes. Add the garlic and cook for 1 minute. Add the beef and cook until browned.

2 Add the tomatoes and wine to the pan and bring to a boil. Lower the heat and simmer for 20 minutes, until thickened. Stir in the parsley and anchovies and season to taste.

3 Bring a pan of salted water to a boil. Add the pasta and oil and cook for 10 minutes, until almost tender. Drain and transfer to a bowl. Stir in the cream.

4 For the topping, beat the yogurt, eggs, and nutmeg.

5 Brush an ovenproof dish with oil. Spoon in half the pasta and cover with half the meat sauce. Repeat, then spread over the topping and sprinkle with cheese.

6 Bake in a preheated oven at 375°F for 25 minutes until golden. Garnish with rosemary and serve with a mixed salad.

1

2

5

Tortellini

Tortellini were said to have been created in the image of the goddess Venus's navel. Whatever the story, these delicate filled pasta swirls offer a delicious blend of Italian flavors.

Serves 4

INGREDIENTS

4 oz boned chicken breast, skinned
2 oz prosciutto
1½ oz cooked spinach, well drained
1 tbsp finely chopped onion
2 tbsp freshly grated Parmesan cheese
pinch of ground allspice
1 egg, beaten
1 lb pasta dough (see page 6)
salt and pepper
2 tbsp chopped fresh parsley, to garnish

SAUCE:
1¼ cups light cream
2 garlic cloves, minced
4 oz button mushrooms, thinly sliced
4 tbsp freshly grated Parmesan cheese

1 Bring a pan of seasoned water to a boil. Add the chicken and poach for about 10 minutes. Cool slightly, then put in a food processor, with the prosciutto, spinach, and onion, and process until finely chopped. Stir in the Parmesan cheese, allspice, and egg and season to taste.

2 Thinly roll out the pasta dough and cut into 1½–2 inch rounds.

3 Place ½ tsp of the filling in the center of each round. Fold the pieces in half and press the edges to seal. Then wrap each piece around your index finger, cross over the ends, and curl the rest of the dough backward to make a navel shape. Re-roll the trimmings and repeat until all the dough is used up.

4 Bring a pan of salted water to a boil. Add the tortellini, in batches, bring back to a boil, and cook for 5 minutes. Drain and transfer to a serving dish.

5 To make the sauce, bring the cream and garlic to a boil in a small pan, then simmer for 3 minutes. Add the mushrooms and half the cheese, season, and simmer for 2–3 minutes. Pour the sauce over the tortellini. Sprinkle over the remaining Parmesan cheese, garnish with the parsley and serve.

1

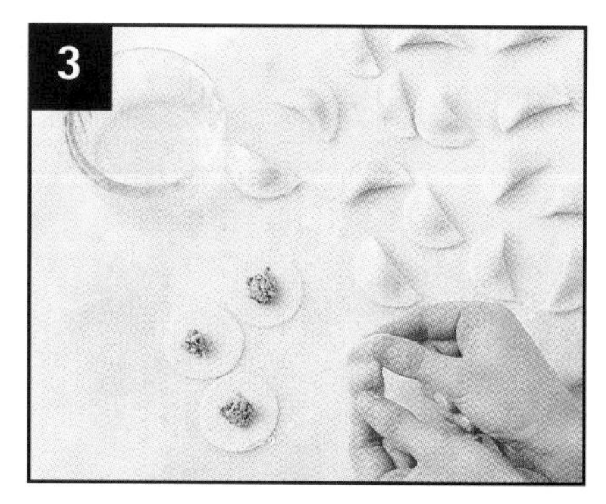
3

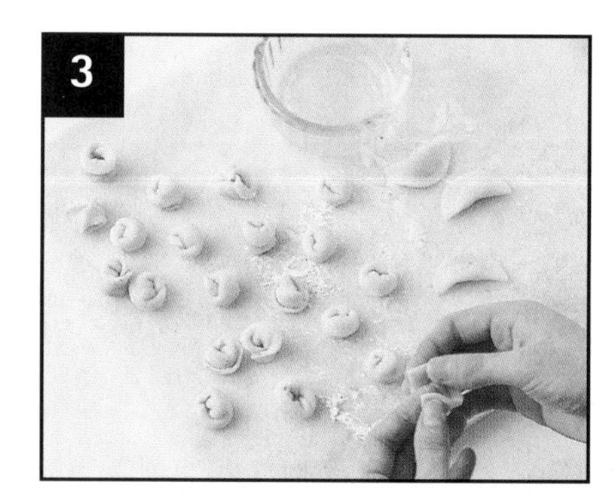
3

Fish & Seafood

Pasta is a natural partner for fish and seafood. Both are cooked quickly to preserve their flavor and texture, they are packed full of nutritional goodness, and the varieties available are almost infinite. These recipes feature exciting and tempting ways of cooking fish and meat to make a range of satisfying meals that are typically Italian. Fish is one of the most important food sources in Italy. The fish markets there are fascinating, with a huge variety of local fish on display. Fresh or frozen imported fish of all kinds from the Mediterranean are appearing increasingly in fishmongers and supermarkets, giving us access to dishes that were once only the preserve of the Italians. This chapter contains a wealth of fish and seafood recipes to suit all occasions.

Spaghetti alla Bucaniera

Brill was once known as poor man's turbot, an unfair description as it is a delicately flavored and delicious fish in its own right.

Serves 4

INGREDIENTS

- 3/4 cup all purpose flour
- 1 lb brill or sole fillets, skinned and chopped
- 1 lb hake fillets, skinned and chopped
- 6 tbsp butter
- 4 shallots, finely chopped
- 2 garlic cloves, minced
- 1 carrot, diced
- 1 leek, finely chopped
- 1 1/4 cups hard cider
- 1/4 cups medium sweet cider
- 2 tsp anchovy extract
- 1 tbsp tarragon vinegar
- 1 lb dried spaghetti
- 1 tbsp olive oil
- salt and pepper
- chopped fresh parsley, to garnish
- crusty brown bread, to serve

1 Season the flour with salt and pepper. Sprinkle 1/4 cup of the seasoned flour on to a shallow plate. Press the fish pieces into the seasoned flour to coat thoroughly.

2 Melt the butter in a flameproof casserole. Add the fish fillets, shallots, garlic, carrot, and leek and cook over a low heat, stirring frequently, for about 10 minutes.

3 Sprinkle over the remaining seasoned flour and cook, stirring constantly, for 2 minutes. Gradually stir in the cider, anchovy extract, and tarragon vinegar. Bring to a boil and simmer over a low heat for 35 minutes. Alternatively, bake in a preheated oven at 350°F for 30 minutes.

4 About 15 minutes before the end of the cooking time, bring a large pan of lightly salted water to a boil. Add the spaghetti and olive oil and cook for about 12 minutes, until tender but still firm to the bite. Drain the pasta thoroughly and transfer to a large serving dish.

5 Arrange the fish on top of the spaghetti and pour over the sauce. Garnish with chopped parsley and serve immediately with warm, crusty brown bread.

2

3

3

Vermicelli with Fillets of Red Mullet

This simple recipe perfectly complements the sweet flavor and delicate texture of the fish.

Serves 4

INGREDIENTS

$2\frac{1}{4}$ lb red mullet fillets
$1\frac{1}{4}$ cups dry white wine
4 shallots, finely chopped
1 garlic clove, minced
3 tbsp finely chopped mixed fresh herbs
finely grated peel and juice of 1 lemon
pinch of freshly grated nutmeg
3 anchovy fillets, roughly chopped
2 tbsp heavy cream
1 tsp cornstarch
1 lb dried vermicelli
1 tbsp olive oil
salt and pepper

TO GARNISH:
1 fresh mint sprig
lemon slices
lemon peel

1 Put the red mullet fillets in a large casserole. Pour over the wine and add the shallots, garlic, chopped herbs, lemon peel and juice, nutmeg, and anchovies. Season to taste with salt and pepper. Cover and bake in a preheated oven at 350°F for 35 minutes.

2 Carefully transfer the mullet to a warm dish. Set aside and keep warm while you prepare the sauce and pasta.

3 Pour the cooking liquid into a pan and bring to a boil. Simmer for 25 minutes, until reduced by half. Mix together the cream and cornstarch and stir into the sauce to thicken.

4 Meanwhile, bring a large pan of lightly salted water to a boil. Add the vermicelli and olive oil and cook for 8–10 minutes, until tender, but still firm to the bite. Drain the pasta and transfer to a warm serving dish.

5 Arrange the red mullet fillets on top of the vermicelli and pour over the sauce. Garnish with a fresh mint sprig, slices of lemon, and strips of lemon peel and serve immediately.

COOK'S TIP

The best red mullet is sometimes called golden mullet, although it is bright red in color.

Spaghetti al Tonno

The classic Italian combination of pasta and tuna is enhanced in this recipe with a delicious parsley sauce.

Serves 4

INGREDIENTS

7 oz can tuna, drained
2 oz can anchovies, drained
1 1/8 cups olive oil
1 cup roughly chopped flat leaf parsley
5/8 cup crème fraîche
1 lb dried spaghetti
2 tbsp butter
salt and pepper
black olives, to garnish
crusty bread, to serve

1 Remove any bones from the tuna. Put the tuna into a food processor or blender, together with the anchovies, 1 cup of the olive oil, and the flat leaf parsley. Process until the sauce is smooth.

2 Spoon the crème fraîche into the food processor or blender and process again for a few seconds to blend thoroughly. Season to taste with salt and black pepper.

3 Bring a large pan of lightly salted water to a boil. Add the spaghetti and the remaining olive oil and cook until tender but still firm to the bite.

4 Drain the spaghetti, return to the pan, and place over a medium heat. Add the butter and toss well to coat. Spoon in the sauce and quickly toss into the spaghetti, using 2 forks.

5 Remove the pan from the heat and divide the spaghetti between 4 warm individual serving plates. Garnish with the olives and serve immediately with warm, crusty bread.

VARIATION

For a change, add 1–2 garlic cloves to the sauce, substitute ½ cup chopped fresh basil for half the parsley, and garnish with capers instead of black olives.

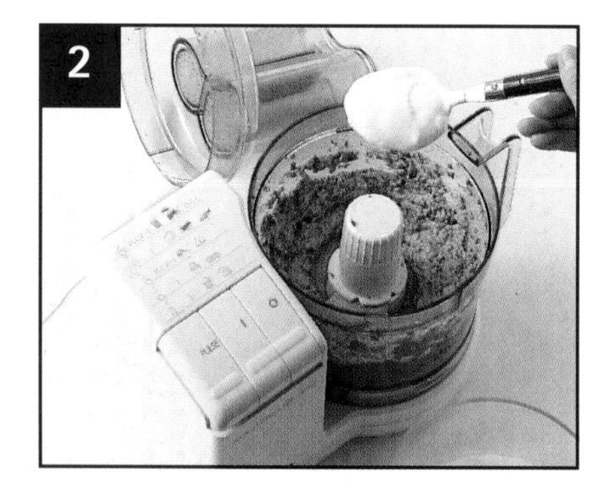

Cannelloni Filetti di Sogliola

This is a lighter dish than the better-known cannelloni stuffed with ground beef.

Serves 6

INGREDIENTS

12 small fillets of sole (about 4 oz each)
$^5/_8$ cup red wine
6 tbsp butter
$3^7/_8$ cups sliced button mushrooms
4 shallots, finely chopped
4 oz tomatoes, chopped
2 tbsp tomato paste
$^1/_2$ cup all purpose flour, sifted
$^5/_8$ cup of warm milk
2 tbsp heavy cream
6 dried cannelloni tubes
6 oz cooked, peeled shrimp, preferably freshwater
salt and pepper
1 fresh fennel sprig, to garnish

1 Brush the fillets with a little wine, season with salt, and pepper and roll them up, skin side inward. Secure with a skewer or toothpick.

2 Arrange the fish rolls in a single layer in a large skillet, add the remaining red wine and poach for about 4 minutes. Remove from the pan and reserve the cooking liquid.

3 Melt the butter in another pan. Fry the mushrooms and shallots for 2 minutes, then add the tomatoes and tomato paste. Season the flour and stir it into the pan. Stir in the reserved cooking liquid and half the milk. Cook over a low heat, stirring, for 4 minutes. Remove from the heat and stir in the cream.

4 Bring a large saucepan of lightly salted water to a boil. Add the cannelloni and cook for about 8 minutes until tender but still firm to the bite. Drain and set aside to cool.

5 Remove the skewers or toothpicks from the fish rolls. Put 2 sole fillets into each cannelloni tube with 2–3 shrimp and a little red wine sauce. Arrange the cannelloni in an ovenproof dish, pour over the sauce and bake in a preheated oven at 400°F for 20 minutes.

6 Serve the cannelloni with the red wine sauce, garnished with the remaining shrimp and a sprig of fennel.

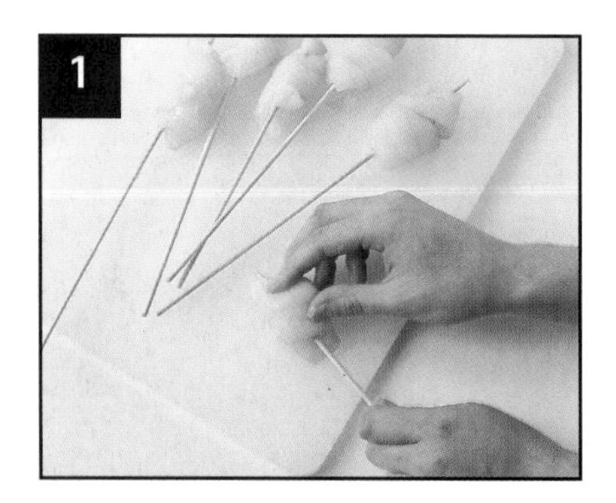
1

2

3

Spaghetti with Seafood Sauce

Peeled shrimp from the freezer can become the star ingredient in this colorful and tasty dish.

Serves 4

INGREDIENTS

- 8 oz dried spaghetti, broken into 6 inch pieces
- 2 tbsp olive oil
- 1 1/4 cups chicken stock
- 1 tsp lemon juice
- 1 small cauliflower, cut into flowerets
- 2 carrots, thinly sliced
- 4 oz snow peas
- 4 tbsp butter
- 1 onion, sliced
- 8 oz zucchini, sliced
- 1 garlic clove, chopped
- 12 oz frozen, cooked, peeled shrimp, defrosted
- 2 tbsp chopped fresh parsley
- 1/3 cup freshly grated Parmesan cheese
- 1/2 tsp paprika
- salt and pepper
- 4 unpeeled, cooked shrimp, to garnish

1 Bring a pan of lightly salted water to a boil. Add the spaghetti and 1 tbsp of the olive oil and cook until tender, but still firm to the bite. Drain the spaghetti and return to the pan. Toss with the remaining olive oil, cover and keep warm.

2 Bring the chicken stock and lemon juice to a boil. Add the cauliflower and carrots and cook for 3–4 minutes. Remove from the pan and set aside. Add the snow peas to the pan and cook for 1–2 minutes. Set aside with the other vegetables.

3 Melt half the butter in a skillet over a medium heat. Add the onion and zucchini and fry for about 3 minutes. Add the garlic and shrimp and cook for a further 2–3 minutes, until thoroughly heated through.

4 Stir in the reserved vegetables and heat through. Season to taste with salt and pepper and stir in the remaining butter.

5 Transfer the spaghetti to a warm serving dish. Pour over the sauce and add the chopped parsley. Toss well with 2 forks until coated. Sprinkle over the Parmesan cheese and paprika, garnish with the unpeeled shrimp, and serve immediately.

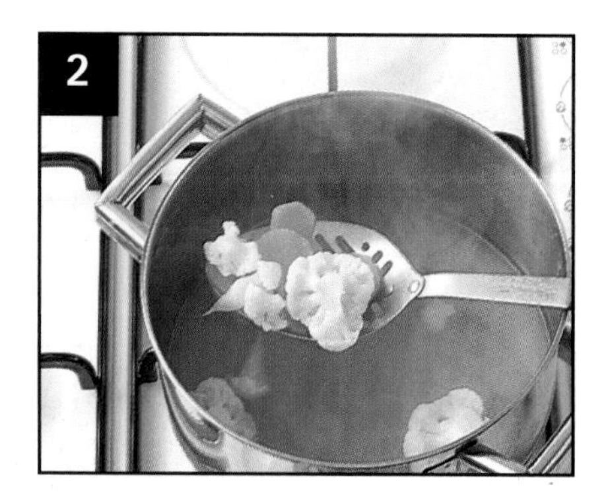

Spaghetti with Smoked Salmon

Made in moments, this is a luxurious dish to astonish and delight unexpected guests.

Serves 4

INGREDIENTS

1 lb dried buckwheat spaghetti
2 tbsp olive oil
$\frac{1}{2}$ cup crumbled feta cheese
salt
fresh cilantro or parsley leaves, to garnish

SAUCE:
$1\frac{1}{4}$ cups heavy cream
$\frac{5}{8}$ cup whiskey or brandy
$4\frac{1}{2}$ oz smoked salmon
pinch of cayenne pepper
black pepper
2 tbsp chopped fresh cilantro or parsley

1 Bring a large pan of lightly salted water to a boil. Add the spaghetti and 1 tbsp of the olive oil and cook until tender but still firm to the bite. Drain the spaghetti, return to the pan, and sprinkle over the remaining olive oil. Cover, shake the pan, set aside, and keep warm.

2 Pour the cream into a small saucepan and bring to simmering point, but do not let it boil. Pour the whiskey or brandy into another small saucepan and bring to simmering point, but do not allow it to boil. Remove both pans from the heat and mix together the cream and whiskey or brandy.

3 Cut the smoked salmon into thin strips and add to the cream mixture. Season to taste with cayenne and black pepper. Just before serving, stir in the chopped fresh cilantro or parsley.

4 Transfer the spaghetti to a warm serving dish, pour over the sauce, and toss thoroughly with 2 large forks. Scatter over the crumbled feta cheese, garnish with the cilantro or parsley leaves, and serve immediately.

COOK'S TIP

Serve this rich and luxurious dish with a green salad tossed in a lemony dressing.

Farfalle with a Medley of Seafood

You can use almost any kind of sea fish in this recipe. Red sea bream is an especially good choice.

Serves 4

INGREDIENTS

- 1 lb fillet of sea bream
- 4 tbsp butter
- 12 scallops, shelled
- 12 raw tiger shrimp
- 12 raw shrimp
- $4^{1}/_{2}$ oz freshwater shrimp
- juice and finely grated peel of 1 lemon
- pinch of saffron powder or threads
- 4 cups vegetable stock
- $^{5}/_{8}$ cup rose petal-infused white wine vinegar
- 1 lb dried farfalle
- 1 tbsp olive oil
- $^{5}/_{8}$ cup white wine
- 1 tbsp pink peppercorns
- 4 oz baby carrots
- $^{5}/_{8}$ cup heavy cream or fromage blanc
- salt and pepper

1 Peel and devein the shrimp. Thinly slice the sea bream. Melt the butter in a pan, add the sea bream, scallops, shrimp, and shrimp and cook for 1–2 minutes.

2 Season with black pepper. Add the lemon juice and grated peel. Very carefully add a pinch of saffron powder or a few strands of saffron to the cooking juices (not to the seafood).

3 Remove the seafood from the pan, set aside, and keep warm.

4 Return the pan to the heat and add the vegetable stock. Bring to a boil and reduce by one third. Add the rose petal vinegar and cook for 4 minutes, until reduced.

5 Bring a pan of salted water to a boil. Add the farfalle and olive oil and cook until tender, but still firm to the bite. Drain the pasta, transfer to a serving plate, and top with the seafood.

6 Add the wine, peppercorns, and carrots to the pan and reduce the sauce for 6 minutes. Add the cream or fromage blanc and simmer for 2 minutes.

7 Pour the sauce over the seafood and pasta and serve immediately.

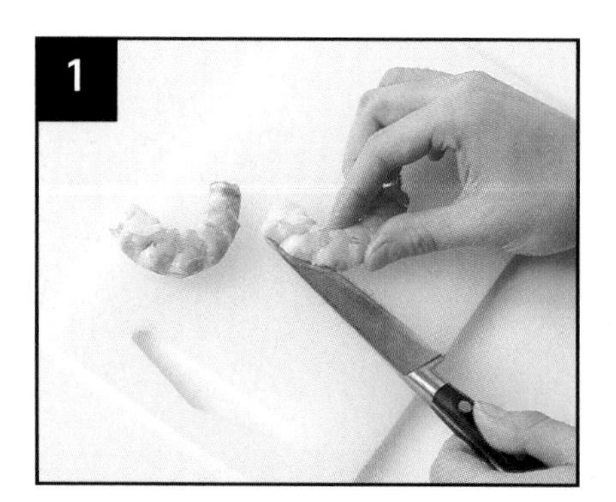

Ravioli of Lemon Sole & Haddock

This delicate-tasting dish is surprisingly satisfying for even the hungriest appetites.

Serves 4

INGREDIENTS

1 lb lemon sole fillets, skinned
1 lb haddock fillets, skinned
3 eggs beaten
1 lb cooked potato gnocchi
3 cups fresh bread crumbs
1/4 cup heavy cream
1 lb pasta dough (see page 6)
1 1/4 cups Italian Red Wine Sauce (see page 76)
2/3 cup freshly grated Parmesan cheese
salt and pepper

1 Flake the lemon sole and haddock fillets with a fork and transfer the flesh to a large mixing bowl.

2 Mix the eggs, cooked potato gnocchi, bread crumbs, and cream in a bowl until thoroughly combined. Add the fish to the bowl containing the gnocchi and season the mixture to taste with salt and black pepper.

3 Roll out the pasta dough on to a lightly floured surface and cut out 3 inch rounds using a plain cutter.

4 Place a spoonful of the fish stuffing on each round. Dampen the edges slightly and fold the pasta rounds over, pressing together to seal.

5 Bring a large saucepan of lightly salted water to a boil. Add the ravioli and cook for 15 minutes.

6 Drain the ravioli, using a draining spoon, and transfer to a large serving dish. Pour over the Italian Red Wine Sauce, sprinkle over the Parmesan cheese, and serve immediately.

COOK'S TIP

When making square ravioli, divide the dough into two. Wrap half in plastic wrap and thinly roll out the other half. Cover with a clean, damp dish cloth while you roll out the remaining dough. Spoon or pipe the filling at regular intervals and brush the spaces inbetween with water or beaten egg. Lift the second sheet of dough into position with a rolling pin and press firmly between the filling to seal and expel any air. Cut out the shapes with a ravioli cutter or a knife.

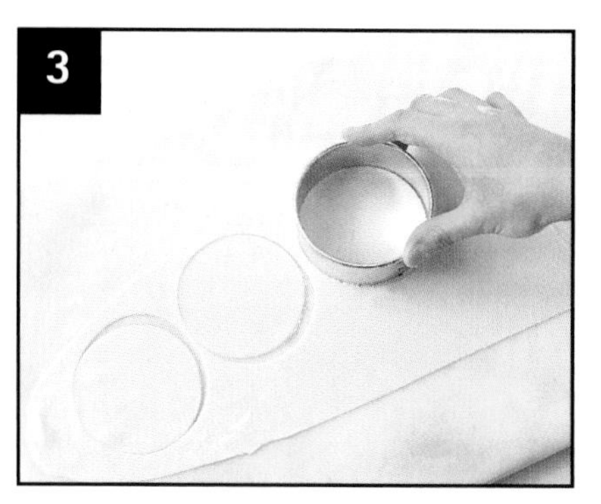

Pasta Packages

This is the ideal dish when you have guests because the packages can be prepared in advance and simply put in the oven when you are ready to eat.

Serves 4

INGREDIENTS

- 1 lb dried fettuccine
- 5/8 cup Pesto Sauce
- 4 tsp extra virgin olive oil
- 1 lb 10 oz large raw shrimp, peeled and deveined
- 2 garlic cloves, minced
- 1/2 cup dry white wine
- salt and pepper

1 Cut out 4 x 3 1/2 inch squares of baking paper.

2 Bring a large saucepan of lightly salted water to a boil. Add the fettuccine and cook for 2–3 minutes, until just softened. Drain and set aside.

3 Mix together the fettuccine and half of the Pesto Sauce. Spread out the paper squares and put 1 tsp olive oil in the middle of each. Divide the fettuccine between the the squares, divide the shrimp, and place on top of the fettuccine.

4 Mix together the remaining Pesto Sauce and the garlic and spoon it over the shrimp. Season each parcel with salt and black pepper and sprinkle with the white wine.

5 Dampen the edges of the baking paper and wrap the packages loosely, twisting the edges to seal.

6 Place the packages on a cookie sheet and bake in a preheated oven at 400°F for 10–15 minutes. Transfer the parcels to 4 individual serving plates and serve at once.

COOK'S TIP

Traditionally, these packages are designed to look like money bags. The resemblance is more effective with baking paper than with foil.

3

3

4

Macaroni & Shrimp Bake

This adaptation of an eighteenth-century Italian dish is baked until it is golden brown and sizzling, then cut into wedges like a cake.

Serves 4

INGREDIENTS

3 cups dried short-cut macaroni
1 tbsp olive oil, plus extra for brushing
6 tbsp butter, plus extra for greasing
2 small fennel bulbs, thinly sliced and fronds reserved
6 oz mushrooms, thinly sliced
6 oz peeled, cooked shrimp
pinch of cayenne pepper
1 1/4 cups Béchamel Sauce (see Cook's Tip, below)
2/3 cup freshly grated Parmesan cheese
2 large tomatoes, sliced
1 tsp dried oregano
salt and pepper

1 Bring a saucepan of salted water to a boil. Add the pasta and oil and cook until tender, but still firm to the bite. Drain and return to the pan. Add 2 tbsp of butter, cover, shake the pan, and keep warm.

2 Melt the remaining butter in a saucepan. Fry the fennel for 3–4 minutes. Stir in the mushrooms and fry for a further 2 minutes. Stir in the shrimp, then remove the pan from the heat.

3 Stir the cayenne pepper and shrimp mixture into the Béchamel sauce. Pour into a greased ovenproof dish and spread evenly. Sprinkle over the Parmesan cheese and arrange the tomato slices in a ring around the edge. Brush the tomatoes with olive oil and sprinkle over the oregano.

4 Bake in a preheated oven at 350°F for 25 minutes, until golden brown. Serve immediately.

COOK'S TIP

For Béchamel sauce, melt 2 tbsp butter. Stir in 1/4 cup flour. Cook, stirring, for 2 minutes. Gradually, stir in 1 1/4 cups warm milk. Add 2 tbsp finely chopped onion, 5 white peppercorns, and 2 parsley sprigs and season with salt, dried thyme, and grated nutmeg. Simmer, stirring, for 15 minutes. Strain before using.

2

3

3

Pasta Vongole

Fresh clams are available from most good fishmongers. If you prefer, used canned clams, which are less messy to eat but not so pretty to serve.

Serves 4

INGREDIENTS

$1^1/_2$ lb fresh clams or 1 x 10 oz can clams, drained
14 oz mixed seafood, such as shrimps, squid, and mussels, defrosted if frozen
2 tbsp olive oil
2 cloves garlic, finely chopped
$^2/_3$ cup white wine
$^2/_3$ cup fish stock
2 tbsp chopped tarragon
salt and pepper
$1^1/_2$ lb fresh pasta or 12 oz dried pasta

1 If you are using fresh clams, scrub them clean and discard any that are already open.

2 Heat the oil in a large skillet. Add the garlic and the clams to the pan and cook for 2 minutes, shaking the pan to ensure that all of the clams are coated in the oil.

3 Add the remaining seafood mixture to the pan and cook for a further 2 minutes.

4 Pour the wine and stock over the mixed seafood and garlic and bring to a boil. Cover the pan, reduce the heat, and leave to simmer for 8–10 minutes or until the shells open. Discard any clams or mussels that do not open.

5 Meanwhile, cook the pasta in a saucepan of boiling water according to the instructions on the packet or until it is cooked through, but still has bite. Drain.

6 Stir the tarragon into the sauce and season to taste.

7 Transfer the pasta to a serving plate and pour over the sauce.

VARIATION

Red clam sauce can be made by adding 8 tablespoons of tomato paste to the sauce along with the stock in step 4. Follow the same cooking method.

Baked Scallops with Pasta in Shells

This is another tempting seafood dish where the eye is delighted as much as the taste buds.

Serves 4

INGREDIENTS

12 scallops
3 tbsp olive oil
3 cups small, dried whole-wheat pasta shells
5/8 cup fish stock
1 onion, chopped
juice and finely grated peel of 2 lemons
5/8 cup heavy cream
2 cups grated hard cheese
salt and pepper
crusty brown bread, to serve

1 Remove the scallops from their shells. Scrape off the skirt and the black intestinal thread. Reserve the white part (the flesh) and the orange part (the coral or roe). Very carefully ease the flesh and coral from the shell with a short, but very strong knife.

2 Wash the shells thoroughly and dry them well. Put the shells on a cookie sheet, sprinkle lightly with about two thirds of the olive oil, and set aside.

3 Meanwhile, bring a large saucepan of lightly salted water to a boil. Add the pasta shells and remaining olive oil and cook for about 12 minutes, until tender, but still firm to the bite. Drain and spoon about 1 oz of pasta into each scallop shell.

4 Put the scallops, fish stock and onion in an ovenproof dish and season to taste with pepper. Cover with foil and bake in a preheated oven at 350°F for 8 minutes.

5 Remove the dish from the oven. Remove the foil and, using a draining spoon, transfer the scallops to the shells. Add 1 tbsp of the cooking liquid to each shell, together with a drizzle of lemon juice and a little cream, and top with the grated cheese.

6 Increase the oven temperature to 450°F and return the scallops to the oven for a further 4 minutes.

7 Serve the scallops in their shells with crusty brown bread and butter.

4

5

5

Saffron Mussel Tagliatelle

Saffron is the most expensive spice in the world, but you only ever need a small quantity. Saffron threads or powdered saffron may be used in this recipe.

Serves 4

INGREDIENTS

2 1/4 lb mussels
5/8 cup white wine
1 medium onion, finely chopped
2 tbsp butter
2 garlic cloves, minced
2 tsp cornstarch
1 1/4 cups heavy cream
pinch of saffron threads or saffron powder
juice of 1/2 lemon
1 egg yolk
1 lb dried tagliatelle
1 tbsp olive oil
salt and pepper
3 tbsp chopped fresh parsley, to garnish

1 Scrub and debeard the mussels under cold running water. Discard any that do not close when sharply tapped. Put the mussels in a pan with the wine and onion. Cover and cook over a high heat, shaking the pan, for 5–8 minutes, until the shells open.

2 Drain and reserve the cooking liquid. Discard any mussels that are still closed. Reserve a few mussels for the garnish and remove the remainder from their shells.

3 Strain the cooking liquid into a saucepan. Bring to a boil and reduce by about half. Remove the pan from the heat.

4 Melt the butter in a saucepan. Add the garlic and cook, stirring frequently, for 2 minutes, until golden brown. Stir in the cornstarch and cook, stirring, for minute. Gradually stir in the cooking liquid and the cream. Crush the saffron threads and add to the pan. Season with salt and pepper to taste and simmer over a low heat for 2–3 minutes, until thickened.

5 Stir in the egg yolk, lemon juice, and shelled mussels. Do not allow the mixture to boil.

6 Meanwhile, bring a pan of salted water to a boil. Add the pasta and oil and cook until tender, but still firm to the bite. Drain and transfer to a serving dish. Add the mussel sauce and toss. Garnish with the parsley and reserved mussels and serve.

4

4

5

Squid & Macaroni Stew

This scrumptious seafood dish is quick and easy to make, yet deliciously satisfying to eat.

Serves 4–6

INGREDIENTS

- 2 cups dried short-cut macaroni or other small pasta shapes
- 7 tbsp olive oil
- 2 onions, sliced
- 12 oz prepared squid, cut into 1½ inch strips
- 1 cup fish stock
- ⅝ cup red wine
- 12 oz tomatoes, skinned and thinly sliced
- 2 tbsp tomato paste
- 1 tsp dried oregano
- 2 bay leaves
- 2 tbsp chopped fresh parsley
- salt and pepper
- crusty bread, to serve

1 Bring a large saucepan of lightly salted water to a boil. Add the pasta and 1 tbsp of the olive oil and cook for 3 minutes. Drain, return to the pan, cover and keep warm.

2 Heat the remaining oil in a pan over a medium heat. Add the onions and fry until they are translucent. Add the squid and stock and simmer for 5 minutes. Pour in the wine and add the tomatoes, tomato paste, oregano, and bay leaves. Bring the sauce to a boil, season to taste and cook for 5 minutes.

3 Stir the pasta into the pan, cover and simmer for about 10 minutes, or until the squid and macaroni are tender and the sauce has thickened. If the sauce remains too liquid, uncover the pan and continue cooking for a few minutes.

4 Remove and discard the bay leaves. Reserve a little parsley and stir the remainder into the pan. Transfer to a warm serving dish and sprinkle over the remaining parsley. Serve with crusty bread to soak up the sauce.

COOK'S TIP

To prepare squid, peel off the outer skin, then cut off the head and tentacles. Extract the transparent flat oval bone from the body and discard. Remove the sac of black ink, then turn the body sac inside out. Wash in cold water. Cut off the tentacles and discard the rest; wash thoroughly.

2

3

4

Farfallini Buttered Lobster

This is one of those dishes that looks almost too lovely to eat – but you must!

Serves 4

INGREDIENTS

2 x 1 lb 9 oz lobsters, split into halves
juice and grated peel of 1 lemon
$^1/_2$ cup butter
4 tbsp fresh white bread crumbs
2 tbsp brandy
5 tbsp heavy cream or crème fraîche
1 lb dried farfallini
1 tbsp olive oil
$^2/_3$ cup freshly grated Parmesan cheese
salt and pepper

TO GARNISH:
1 kiwi fruit, sliced
4 unpeeled, cooked king shrimp
fresh dill sprigs

1 Carefully discard the stomach sac, vein, and gills from each lobster. Remove all the meat from the tail and chop. Crack the claws and legs, remove the meat, and chop. Transfer the meat to a bowl and add the lemon juice and grated lemon peel.

2 Clean the shells thoroughly and place in a warm oven at 325°F to dry out.

3 Melt 2 tbsp of the butter in a skillet. Add the bread crumbs and fry for about 3 minutes, until crisp and golden brown.

4 Melt the remaining butter in a saucepan. Add the lobster meat and heat through gently. Add the brandy and cook for a further 3 minutes, add the cream or crème fraîche, and season to taste with salt and black pepper.

5 Meanwhile, bring a large pan of lightly salted water to a boil. Add the farfallini and olive oil and cook for about 12 minutes, until tender but still firm to the bite. Drain and spoon the pasta into the clean lobster shells. Top with the buttered lobster and sprinkle with a little grated Parmesan cheese and the bread crumbs. Broil for 2–3 minutes, until golden brown.

6 Transfer the lobster shells to a warm serving dish, garnish with the lemon slices, kiwi fruit, king shrimp, and dill sprigs and serve immediately.

1

3

5

Steamed Pasta Pudding

A tasty mixture of creamy fish and pasta cooked in a bowl, unmolded and drizzled with tomato sauce presents macaroni in a new guise.

Serves 4

INGREDIENTS

- cup dried short-cut macaroni or other short pasta
- 1 tbsp olive oil
- 1 tbsp butter, plus extra for oiling
- 1 lb white fish fillets, such as cod or haddock
- 2–3 fresh parsley sprigs
- 6 black peppercorns
- $^1/_2$ cup heavy cream
- 2 eggs, separated
- 2 tbsp chopped fresh dill or parsley
- pinch of freshly grated nutmeg
- $^2/_3$ cup freshly grated Parmesan cheese
- salt and pepper
- fresh dill or parsley sprigs, to garnish
- tomato sauce to serve

1 Bring a pan of salted water to a boil. Add the pasta and olive oil and cook until tender, but still firm to the bite. Drain the pasta, return to the pan, add the butter, cover, and keep warm.

2 Place the fish in a skillet. Add the parsley sprigs, peppercorns, and enough water to cover. Bring to a boil, cover, and simmer for 10 minutes. Lift out the fish and set aside to cool. Reserve the cooking liquid.

3 Skin the fish and cut into bite-size pieces. Put the pasta in a bowl. Mix the cream, egg yolks, chopped dill or parsley, nutmeg, and cheese, pour into the pasta and mix. Spoon in the fish without breaking it. Add enough of the reserved cooking liquid to make a moist, but firm mixture. Whisk the egg whites until stiff, then fold them into the mixture.

4 Grease a heatproof bowl and spoon in the fish mixture to within 1½ inches of the rim. Cover with greased baking paper and foil and tie with string.

5 Stand the bowl on a trivet in a saucepan. Add boiling water to reach halfway up the sides. Cover and steam for 1½ hours.

6 Invert the pudding on to a serving plate. Pour over a little tomato sauce. Garnish and serve with the remaining tomato sauce.

2

3

3

Stuffed Squid

Whole squid are stuffed with a mixture of fresh herbs and sun-dried tomatoes and then cooked in a wine sauce.

Serves 4

INGREDIENTS

- 8 squid, cleaned and gutted but left whole (ask your fishmonger to do this)
- 6 canned anchovies, chopped
- 2 garlic cloves, chopped
- 2 tbsp rosemary, stalks removed and leaves chopped
- 2 sun-dried tomatoes, chopped
- $5^1/_2$ oz bread crumbs
- 1 tbsp olive oil
- 1 onion, finely chopped
- $^3/_4$ cup white wine
- $^3/_4$ cup fish stock
- cooked rice, to serve

1 Remove the tentacles from the body of the squid and chop the flesh finely.

2 Grind the anchovies, garlic, rosemary, and tomatoes to a paste in a mortar and pestle.

3 Add the bread crumbs and the chopped squid tentacles and mix. If the mixture is too dry to form a thick paste at this point, add 1 teaspoon of water.

4 Spoon the paste into the body sacs of the squid then tie a piece of cotton around the end of each sac to fasten them. Do not overfill the sacs because they will expand during cooking.

5 Heat the oil in a skillet. Add the onion and cook, stirring, for 3–4 minutes or until golden.

6 Add the stuffed squid to the pan and cook for 3–4 minutes or until brown all over.

7 Add the wine and stock and bring to a boil. Reduce the heat, cover, and simmer.

8 Remove the lid and cook for a further 5 minutes until the squid is tender and the juices reduced. Serve with cooked rice.

COOK'S TIP

If you cannot buy whole squid, use squid pieces and stir the paste into the sauce with the wine and stock.

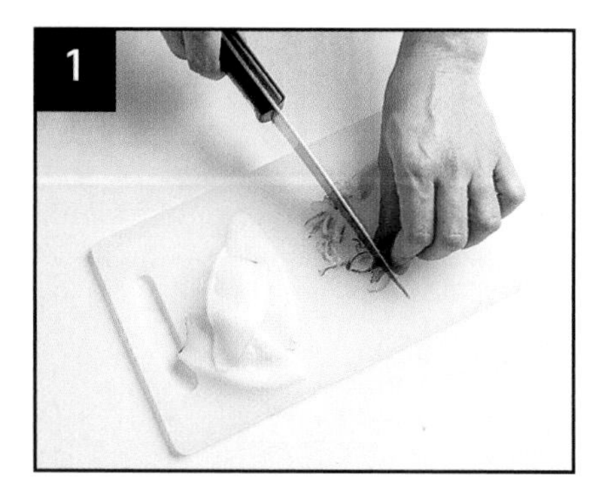
1

3

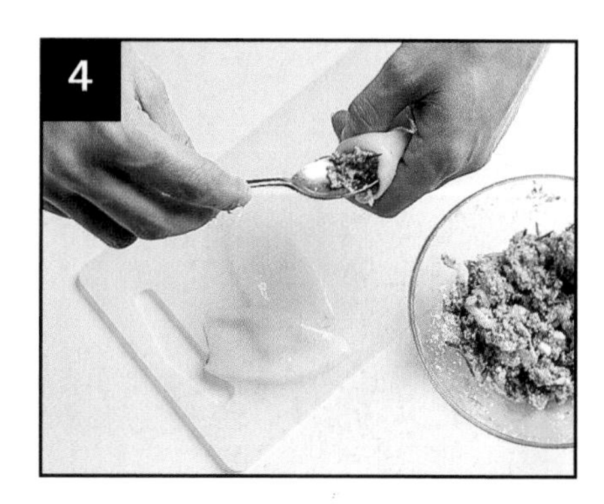
4

Sea Bass with Olive Sauce on a Bed of Macaroni

A favorite fish for chefs, the delicious sea bass is now becoming increasingly common in supermarkets and fish stores for family meals.

Serves 4

INGREDIENTS

1 lb dried macaroni
1 tbsp olive oil
8 x 4 oz sea bass medallions

TO GARNISH:
lemon slices
shredded leek
shredded carrot

SAUCE:
2 tbsp butter
4 shallots, chopped
2 tbsp capers
$1^1/_2$ cups pitted green olives, chopped
4 tbsp balsamic vinegar
$1^1/_4$ cups fish stock
$1^1/_4$ cups heavy cream
juice of 1 lemon
salt and pepper

1 To make the sauce, melt the butter in a skillet. Add the shallots and cook over a low heat for 4 minutes. Add the capers and olives and cook for a further 3 minutes.

2 Stir in the balsamic vinegar and fish stock, bring to a boil, and reduce by half. Add the cream, stirring, and reduce again by half. Season to taste with salt and pepper and stir in the lemon juice. Remove the pan from the heat, set aside, and keep warm.

3 Bring a large saucepan of lightly salted water to a boil. Add the pasta and olive oil and cook for about 12 minutes, until tender but still firm to the bite.

4 Meanwhile, lightly broil the sea bass medallions for 3–4 minutes on each side, until cooked through, but still moist.

5 Drain the pasta thoroughly and transfer to large individual serving dishes. Top the pasta with the fish medallions and pour over the olive sauce. Garnish with lemon slices, shredded leek, and shredded carrot, and serve immediately.

1

2

2

Genoese Seafood Risotto

The Genoese risotto is cooked in a different way from any of the other risottos. First, you cook the rice, then you prepare a sauce, then you mix the two together. The results are just as delicious though!

Serves 4

INGREDIENTS

- 5 cups hot fish or chicken stock
- 12 oz risotto rice, washed
- 3 tbsp butter
- 2 garlic cloves, chopped
- 9 oz mixed seafood, preferably raw, such as shrimp, squid, mussels, clams, and small shrimp
- 2 tbsp chopped oregano, plus extra for garnishing
- $1^3/_4$ oz pecorino or Parmesan cheese, grated

1 In a large saucepan, bring the stock to a boil. Add the rice and cook for about 12 minutes, stirring, until the rice is tender or according to the instructions on the packet. Drain thoroughly, reserving any excess liquid.

2 Heat the butter in a large skillet and add the garlic, stirring.

3 Add the raw mixed seafood to the skillet and cook for 5 minutes. If the seafood is already cooked, fry for 2–3 minutes.

4 Stir the oregano into the seafood mixture in the skillet.

5 Add the cooked rice to the pan and cook for 2–3 minutes, stirring, or until hot. Add the reserved stock if the mixture gets too sticky.

6 Add the pecorino or Parmesan cheese and mix well.

7 Transfer the risotto to warm serving dishes and serve immediately.

COOK'S TIP

The Genoese are excellent cooks, and they make particularly delicious fish dishes flavored with the local olive oil.

1

3

5

Smoked Cod Polenta

Using polenta as a crust for a gratin dish gives a lovely crispy outer texture and a smooth inside. It works well with smoked fish and chicken.

Serves 4

INGREDIENTS

12 oz instant polenta
$6\frac{1}{2}$ cups water
7 oz chopped frozen spinach, defrosted
3 tbsp butter
$1\frac{3}{4}$ oz pecorino cheese, grated
$\frac{3}{4}$ cup milk
1 lb smoked cod fillet, skinned and boned
4 eggs, beaten
salt and pepper

1 Cook the polenta, using $6\frac{1}{2}$ cups of water to 12 oz polenta, stirring occasionally. Alternatively, follow the directions on the package.

2 Stir the spinach, butter, and half of the pecorino cheese into the polenta. Season to taste with salt and pepper.

3 Divide the polenta among 4 individual ovenproof dishes, spreading the polenta evenly across the bottom and up the sides of the dishes.

4 In a large skillet, bring the milk to a boil. Add the fish and cook for 8–10 minutes, turning once, or until tender. Remove the fish with a draining spoon.

5 Remove the pan from the heat. Pour the eggs into the milk in the pan and mix together.

6 Using a fork, flake the fish into smaller pieces and place it in the center of the dishes.

7 Pour the milk and egg mixture over the fish.

8 Sprinkle with the remaining cheese and bake in a preheated oven at 375°F for 25–30 minutes or until set and golden. Serve hot.

VARIATION

Try using 12 oz cooked chicken breast with 2 tablespoons of chopped tarragon, instead of the fish, if you prefer.

Sardinian Red Mullet

Red mullet has a beautiful pink skin, which is enhanced in this dish by being cooked in red wine and orange juice.

Serves 4

INGREDIENTS

1 3/4 oz golden raisins
2/3 cup red wine
2 tbsp olive oil
2 medium onions, sliced
1 zucchini cut into 2 inch sticks
2 oranges
2 tsp coriander seeds, lightly ground
4 red mullet, boned and filleted
1 x 1 3/4 oz can anchovy fillets, drained
2 tbsp chopped, fresh oregano

1 Place the golden raisins in a bowl. Pour over the red wine and leave to soak for 10 minutes.

2 Heat the oil in a large skillet. Add the onions and sauté for 2 minutes.

3 Add the zucchini and fry for 3 minutes or until tender.

4 Using a zester, pare long, thin strips from one of the oranges. Using a sharp knife, remove the skin from both of the oranges, segment the oranges by slicing between the lines of pith.

5 Add the orange zest to the skillet. Add the red wine, golden raisins, red mullet, and anchovies to the pan and leave to simmer for 10–15 minutes or until the fish is cooked through.

6 Stir in the oregano, set aside and leave to cool. Place the mixture in a large bowl and leave to chill, covered, in the refrigerator for at least 2 hours to allow the flavors to mingle. Transfer to serving plates and serve.

COOK'S TIP

Red mullet is usually available all year round – frozen, if not fresh – from your fishmonger or supermarket. If you cannot get hold of it try using telapia. This dish can also be served warm, if you prefer.

3

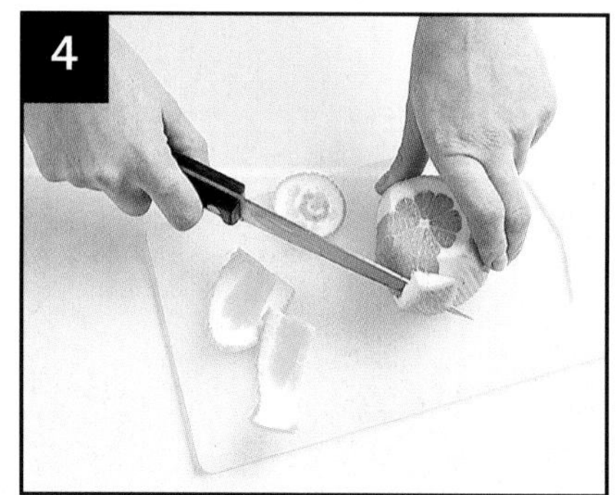
4

5

Broiled Stuffed Sole

A delicious stuffing of sun-dried tomatoes and fresh lemon thyme are used to stuff whole sole.

Serves 4

INGREDIENTS

- 1 tbsp olive oil
- 2 tbsp butter
- 1 small onion, finely chopped
- 1 garlic clove, chopped
- 3 sun-dried tomatoes, chopped
- 2 tbsp lemon thyme
- 1 3/4 oz bread crumbs
- 1 tbsp lemon juice
- 4 small whole sole, gutted and cleaned
- salt and pepper
- lemon wedges, to garnish
- fresh green salad leaves, to serve

1 Heat the oil and butter in a skillet until it just begins to froth.

2 Add the onion and garlic to the skillet and cook, stirring, for 5 minutes until just softened.

3 To make the stuffing, mix the tomatoes, thyme, bread crumbs, and lemon juice in a bowl, and season to taste.

4 Add the stuffing mixture to the pan, and stir to mix.

5 Using a sharp knife, pare the skin from the bone inside the gut hole of the fish to make a pocket. Spoon the tomato and herb stuffing into the pocket.

6 Cook the fish, under a preheated broiler, for 6 minutes on each side or until golden brown.

7 Transfer the stuffed fish to serving plates and garnish with lemon wedges. Serve with fresh green salad leaves.

COOK'S TIP

*Lemon thyme (*Thymus x citriodorus*) has a delicate lemon scent and flavor. Ordinary thyme can be used instead, but mix it with 1 teaspoon of lemon peel to add extra flavor.*

2

4

5

Celery & Salt Cod Casserole

Salt cod is dried and salted in order to preserve it. It has an unusual flavor, which goes particularly well with celery in this dish.

Serves 4

INGREDIENTS

- 9 oz salt cod, soaked overnight
- 1 tbsp oil
- 4 shallots, finely chopped
- 2 garlic cloves, chopped
- 3 celery sticks, chopped
- 1 x 14 oz can tomatoes, chopped
- $\frac{2}{3}$ cup fish stock
- $1\frac{3}{4}$ oz pine nuts
- 2 tbsp roughly chopped tarragon
- 2 tbsp capers
- crusty bread or mashed potato, to serve

1 Drain the salt cod, rinse it under plenty of running water, and drain again thoroughly. Remove and discard any skin and bones. Pat the fish dry with paper towels and cut it into chunks.

2 Heat the oil in a large skillet. Add the shallots and garlic and cook for 2–3 minutes. Add the celery and cook for a further 2 minutes, then add the tomatoes and stock.

3 Bring the mixture to a boil, reduce the heat, and leave to simmer for 5 minutes.

4 Add the fish and cook for 10 minutes or until tender.

5 Meanwhile, place the pine nuts on a cookie sheet. Place under a preheated broiler and toast for 2–3 minutes or until golden.

6 Stir the tarragon, capers, and pine nuts into the fish casserole and heat gently to warm through.

7 Transfer to serving plates and serve with fresh crusty bread or mashed potato.

COOK'S TIP

Salt cod is a useful ingredient to keep in the storecupboard and, once soaked, can be used in the same way as any other fish. It does, however, have a stronger flavor than normal, and it is slightly salty. It can be found in fishmongers, larger supermarkets, and delicatessens.

Herrings with Hot Pesto Sauce

By making a simple pesto sauce, but omitting the cheese, it is possible to heat the paste without it becoming stringy, so it can be used as a hot sauce.

Serves 4

INGREDIENTS

4 whole herrings or small mackerel, cleaned and gutted
2 tbsp olive oil
8 oz tomatoes, peeled, seeded, and chopped
8 canned anchovy fillets, chopped
about 30 fresh basil leaves
$1^3/_4$ oz pine nuts
2 garlic cloves, minced

1 Cook the herrings under a preheated broiler for about 8–10 minutes on each side, or until the skin is slightly charred on both sides.

2 Meanwhile, heat 1 tablespoon of the olive oil in a saucepan.

3 Add the tomatoes and anchovies to the saucepan and cook over a medium heat for 5 minutes.

4 Meanwhile, place the basil, pine nuts, garlic, and remaining oil into a food processor and blend to form a smooth paste. Alternatively, pound the ingredients by hand in a mortar and pestle.

5 Add the pesto mixture to the saucepan containing the tomato and anchovy mixture, and stir to heat through.

6 Spoon some of the pesto sauce on to warm individual serving plates. Place the fish on top and pour the rest of the pesto sauce over the fish. Serve immediately.

COOK'S TIP

Try grilling the fish for an extra char-grilled flavor, if you prefer.

Fresh Baked Sardines

Here, fresh sardines are baked with eggs, herbs, and vegetables to form a dish similar to an omelet.

Serves 4

INGREDIENTS

2 tbsp olive oil
2 large onions, sliced into rings
3 garlic cloves, chopped
2 large zucchini, cut into sticks
3 tbsp fresh thyme, stalks removed
8 sardine fillets or about 2 lb 4 oz whole sardines, filleted
2 3/4 oz Parmesan cheese, grated
4 eggs, beaten
2/3 pint milk
salt and pepper

1. Heat 1 tablespoon of the oil in a skillet. Add the onions and garlic and sauté for 2–3 minutes.

2. Add the zucchini to the skillet and cook for about 5 minutes or until golden.

3. Stir 2 tablespoons of the thyme into the mixture.

4. Place half of the onions and zucchini in the base of a large ovenproof dish. Top with the sardine fillets and half of the Parmesan cheese.

5. Place the remaining onions and zucchini on top and sprinkle with the remaining thyme.

6. Mix the eggs and milk together in a bowl and season to taste with salt and pepper. Pour the mixture over the vegetables and sardines in the dish. Sprinkle the remaining Parmesan cheese over the top.

7. Bake in a preheated oven at 350°F for 20–25 minutes or until golden and set. Serve hot, straight from the oven.

VARIATION

If you cannot find sardines that are large enough to fillet, use small mackerel instead.

2

4

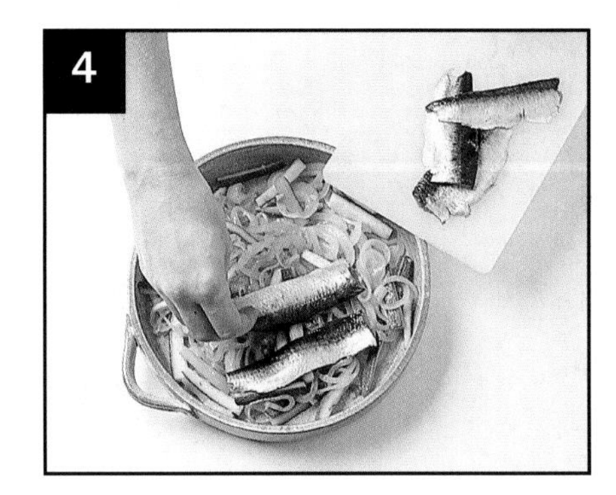
4

Mussel Casserole

Mussels are not difficult to cook, just a little messy to eat. The flavors are worth it, however, and serving this dish with a finger bowl helps to keep things clean!

Serves 4

INGREDIENTS

2 lb 4 oz mussels
$\frac{2}{3}$ cup white wine
1 tbsp oil
1 onion, finely chopped
3 garlic cloves, chopped
1 red chili, finely chopped
$3\frac{1}{2}$ oz tomato paste
1 tbsp chopped marjoram
toast or crusty bread, to serve

1 Scrub the mussels to remove any mud or sand.

2 Remove the beards from the mussels by pulling away the hairy bit between the two shells. Rinse the mussels in a bowl of clean water. Discard any mussels that do not close when they are tapped – they are dead and should not be eaten.

3 Place the mussels in a large saucepan. Pour in the wine and cook for 5 minutes, shaking the pan occasionally until the shells open. Remove and discard any mussels that do not open.

4 Remove the mussels from the saucepan with a perforated spoon. Strain the cooking liquid through a fine sieve set over a bowl, reserving the liquid.

5 Heat the oil in a large skillet. Add the onion, garlic, and chili and cook for 4–5 minutes or until softened.

6 Add the reserved cooking liquid to the pan and cook for 5 minutes or until reduced.

7 Stir in the tomato paste, marjoram, and mussels and cook until hot.

8 Transfer to serving bowls and serve with toast or plenty of crusty bread to mop up the juices.

COOK'S TIP

Finger bowls are individual bowls of warm water with a slice of lemon floating in them. They are used to clean your fingers at the end of a meal.

2

Sole Fillets in Marsala & Cream

A rich wine and cream sauce makes this an excellent dinner party dish. You can make the stock the day before so it takes only minutes to cook and serve the fish.

Serves 4

INGREDIENTS

STOCK:
- 2 1/2 cups water
- bones and skin from the sole fillets
- 1 onion, peeled and halved
- 1 carrot, peeled and halved
- 3 fresh bay leaves

SAUCE;
- 1 tbsp olive oil
- 1 tbsp butter
- 4 shallots, finely chopped
- 3 1/2 oz baby button mushrooms, wiped and halved
- 1 tbsp peppercorns, lightly crushed
- 8 sole fillets
- 1/3 cup Marsala wine
- 2/3 pint heavy cream

1 To make the stock, place the water, fish bones, and skin, onion, carrot, and bay leaves in a saucepan and bring to a boil.

2 Reduce the heat and leave the mixture to simmer for 1 hour or until the stock has reduced to about 2/3 cup. Drain the stock through a fine sieve, discarding the bones and vegetables, and set aside.

3 To make the sauce, heat the oil and butter in a skillet. Add the shallots and cook, stirring, for 2–3 minutes or until just softened.

4 Add the mushrooms to the skillet and cook, stirring, for a further 2–3 minutes or until they are just beginning to brown.

5 Add the peppercorns and sole fillets to the skillet. Fry the sole fillets for 3–4 minutes on each side or until golden brown.

6 Pour the wine and stock over the fish and leave to simmer for 3 minutes. Remove the fish with a slice or a draining spoon, set aside, and keep warm.

7 Increase the heat and boil the mixture in the pan for about 5 minutes or until the sauce has reduced and thickened.

8 Pour in the cream, return the fish to the pan, and heat through. Serve with the cooked vegetables of your choice.

1

4

5

Red Mullet Fillets with Orecchiette, Amaretto, & Orange Sauce

This succulent fish and pasta dish is ideal for serving on a warm, summer's evening – preferably al fresco.

Serves 4

INGREDIENTS

- $3\frac{3}{4}$ cup plain all purpose flour
- 8 red mullet fillets
- 2 tbsp butter
- $\frac{5}{8}$ cup fish stock
- 1 tbsp crushed almonds
- 1 tsp pink peppercorns
- 1 orange, peeled and cut into segments
- 1 tbsp orange liqueur
- grated peel of 1 orange
- 1 lb dried orecchiette
- 1 tbsp olive oil
- $\frac{5}{8}$ cup heavy cream
- 4 tbsp amaretto
- salt and pepper

TO GARNISH:

- 2 tbsp snipped fresh chives
- 1 tbsp toasted almonds

1 Season the flour with salt and pepper and sprinkle into a shallow bowl. Press the fish fillets into the flour to coat. Melt the butter in a skillet. Add the fish and fry over a low heat for 3 minutes, until browned.

2 Add the fish stock to the pan and cook for 4 minutes. Carefully remove the fish, cover with foil, and keep warm.

3 Add the almonds, pink peppercorns, half the orange, the orange liqueur, and orange peel to the pan. Simmer until the liquid has reduced by half.

4 Meanwhile, bring a large saucepan of lightly salted water to a boil. Add the orecchiette and olive oil and cook for 15 minutes until tender but still firm to the bite.

5 Meanwhile, season the sauce with salt and pepper and stir in the cream and amaretto. Cook for 2 minutes. Return the fish to the pan to coat with the sauce.

6 Drain the pasta and transfer to a serving dish. Top with the fish fillets and their sauce. Garnish with the remaining orange segments, the chives, and toasted almonds. Serve immediately.

1

2

3

Casserole of Fusilli & Smoked Haddock with Egg Sauce

This quick, easy, and inexpensive dish would be ideal for a mid-week family supper.

Serves 4

INGREDIENTS

- 2 tbsp butter, plus extra for oiling
- 1 lb smoked haddock fillets, cut into 4 slices
- $2^1/_2$ cups milk
- $^1/_4$ cup all purpose flour
- pinch of freshly grated nutmeg
- 3 tbsp heavy cream
- 1 tbsp chopped fresh parsley
- 2 eggs, hard cooked and mashed to a pulp
- 4 cups dried fusilli
- 1 tbsp lemon juice
- salt and pepper
- boiled new potatoes and beet, to serve

1 Thoroughly grease a casserole with butter. Put the haddock in the casserole and pour over the milk. Bake in a preheated oven at 400°F for about 15 minutes. Carefully pour the cooking liquid into a pitcher without breaking up the fish.

2 Melt the butter in a pan and stir in the flour. Gradually whisk in the reserved cooking liquid. Season to taste with salt, pepper, and nutmeg. Stir in the cream, parsley, and mashed egg and cook, stirring constantly, for 2 minutes.

3 Meanwhile, bring a large saucepan of lightly salted water to a boil. Add the fusilli and lemon juice and cook until tender, but still firm to the bite.

4 Drain the pasta and spoon or tip it over the fish. Top with the sauce and return the casserole to the oven for 10 minutes.

5 Serve the casserole with boiled new potatoes and beet.

VARIATION

You can use any type of dried pasta for this casserole. Try penne, conchiglie, or rigatoni.

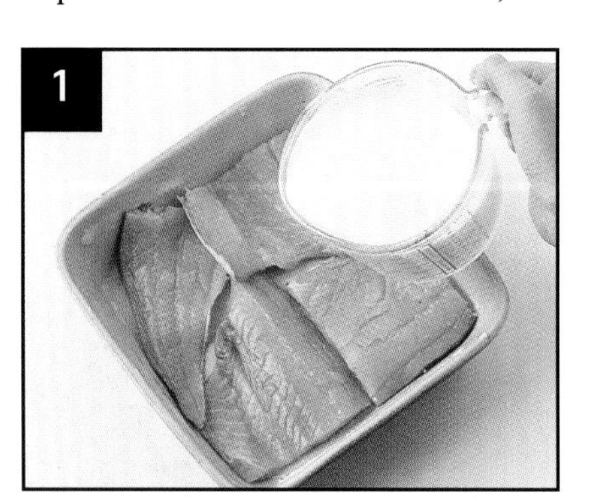

Poached Salmon Steaks with Penne

Fresh salmon and pasta in a mouth-watering lemon and watercress sauce – a wonderful summer evening treat.

Serves 4

INGREDIENTS

4 x 10 oz fresh salmon steaks
4 tbsp butter
3/4 cup dry white wine
sea salt
8 peppercorns
fresh dill sprig
fresh tarragon sprig
1 lemon, sliced
1 lb dried penne
2 tbsp olive oil
lemon slices and fresh watercress, to garnish

LEMON & WATERCRESS SAUCE:
2 tbsp butter
1/4 cup all purpose flour
5/8 cup warm milk
juice and finely grated peel of 2 lemons
2 oz watercress, chopped
salt and pepper

1 Put the salmon in a large, non-stick pan. Add the butter, wine, a pinch of sea salt, the peppercorns, dill, tarragon, and lemon. Cover, bring to a boil, and simmer for 10 minutes.

2 Using a slice, carefully remove the salmon. Strain and reserve the cooking liquid. Remove and discard the salmon skin and center bones. Place on a warm dish, cover, and keep warm.

3 Meanwhile, bring a saucepan of salted water to a boil. Add the penne and 1 tbsp of the oil and cook for 12 minutes until tender but still firm to the bite. Drain and sprinkle over the remaining olive oil. Place on a warm serving dish, top with the salmon steaks, and keep warm.

4 To make the sauce, melt the butter and stir in the flour for 2 minutes. Stir in the milk and about 7 tbsp of the reserved cooking liquid. Add the lemon juice and peel and cook, stirring, for a further 10 minutes.

5 Add the watercress to the sauce, stir gently, and season to taste with salt and pepper.

6 Pour the sauce over the salmon and penne, garnish with slices of lemon and fresh watercress, and serve immediately.

1

4

5

Trout with Pasta colle Acciughe & Smoked Bacon

Most trout available nowadays is farmed rainbow trout, however, if you can, buy wild brown trout for this recipe.

Serves 4

INGREDIENTS

butter, for greasing
4 x $9^1/_2$ oz trout, gutted and cleaned
12 anchovies in oil, drained and chopped
2 apples, peeled, cored, and sliced
4 fresh mint sprigs
juice of 1 lemon
12 slices rindless smoked fatty bacon
1 lb dried tagliatelle
1 tbsp olive oil
salt and pepper

TO GARNISH:
2 apples, cored and sliced
4 fresh mint sprigs

1 Grease a deep cookie sheet with butter.

2 Open up the cavities of each trout and wash thoroughly with warm salt water.

3 Season each cavity with salt and black pepper. Divide the anchovies, sliced apples, and mint sprigs between each of the cavities. Sprinkle the lemon juice into each cavity.

4 Carefully cover the whole of each trout, except the head and tail, with three slices of smoked bacon in a spiral.

5 Arrange the trout on the cookie sheet with the loose ends of bacon tucked underneath. Season with black pepper and bake in a preheated oven at 400°F for 20 minutes, turning the trout over after 10 minutes.

6 Meanwhile, bring a large pan of lightly salted water to a boil. Add the tagliatelle and olive oil and cook for about 12 minutes, until tender but still firm to the bite. Drain the pasta and transfer to a large, warm serving dish.

7 Remove the trout from the oven and arrange on the tagliatelle. Garnish with sliced apples and fresh mint sprigs and serve immediately.

3

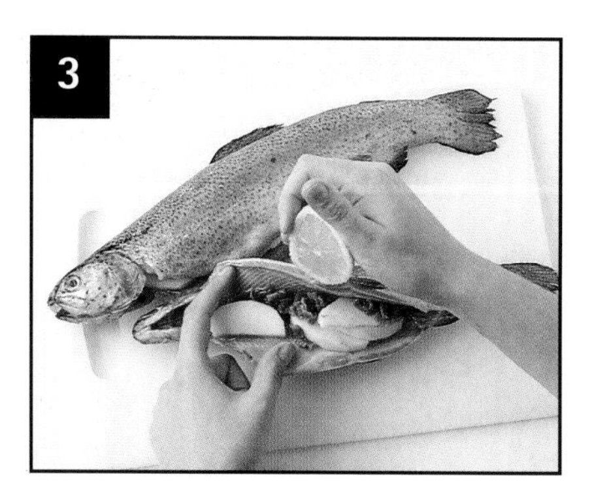
3

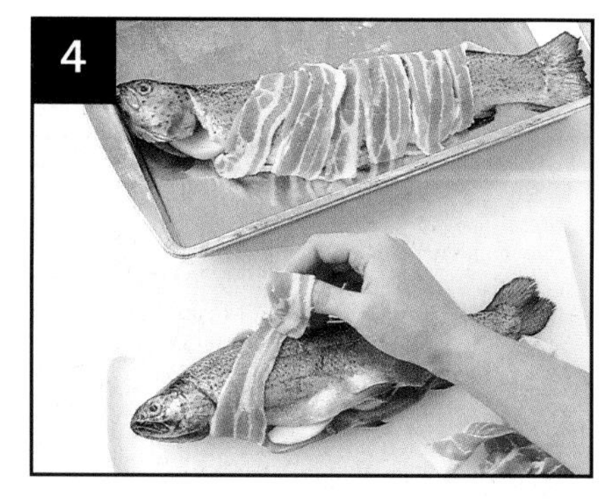
4

Seafood Lasagne

This is one of those recipes where you can use any fish and any sauce you like: from smoked finnan haddock with a little whiskey sauce to cod with cheese sauce.

Serves 4

INGREDIENTS

- 1 lb finnan haddock, filleted, skin removed, and flesh flaked
- 4 oz shrimp
- 4 oz sole fillet, skin removed and flesh sliced
- juice of 1 lemon
- 4 tbsp butter
- 3 leeks, very thinly sliced
- 1/2 cup all purpose flour
- 2 1/3 cups milk
- 2 tbsp honey
- 1 3/4 cups grated mozzarella cheese
- 1 lb pre-cooked lasagne
- 2/3 cup freshly grated Parmesan cheese
- black pepper

1 Put the haddock fillet, shrimp, and sole fillet into a large bowl and season with black pepper and lemon juice. Set aside while you start to make the sauce.

2 Melt the butter in a large saucepan. Add the leeks and cook, stirring occasionally, for 8 minutes. Add the flour and cook, stirring constantly, for 1 minute. Gradually stir in enough milk to make a thick, creamy sauce.

3 Blend in the honey and mozzarella cheese and cook for a further 3 minutes. Remove the pan from the heat and mix in the fish and shrimp.

4 Make alternate layers of fish sauce and lasagne in an ovenproof dish, finishing with a layer of fish sauce on top. Generously sprinkle over the grated Parmesan cheese and bake in a preheated oven at 350°F for 30 minutes. Serve immediately.

VARIATION

For a cider sauce, substitute 1 finely chopped shallot for the leeks, 1¼ cups cider and 1¼ cups heavy cream for the milk, and 1 tsp mustard for the honey. For a Tuscan sauce, substitute 1 finely chopped fennel bulb for the leeks and omit the honey.

1

3

3

Pasta Shells with Mussels

Serve this aromatic seafood dish to family and friends who admit to a love of garlic.

Serves 4–6

INGREDIENTS

- 2 3/4 lb mussels
- 1 cup dry white wine
- 2 large onions, chopped
- 1/2 cup unsalted butter
- 6 large garlic cloves, finely chopped
- 5 tbsp chopped fresh parsley
- 1 1/4 cups heavy cream
- 14 oz dried pasta shells
- 1 tbsp olive oil
- salt and pepper
- crusty bread, to serve

1 Scrub and debeard the mussels under cold running water. Discard any that do not close immediately when sharply tapped. Put the mussels into a large saucepan, together with the wine and half of the onions. Cover and cook over a medium heat, shaking the pan frequently, for 2–3 minutes, until the shells open.

2 Remove the pan from the heat. Drain the mussels and reserve the cooking liquid. Discard any mussels that have not opened. Strain the cooking liquid through a clean cloth into a glass pitcher or bowl and reserve.

3 Melt the butter in a pan over a medium heat. Add the remaining onion and fry until translucent. Stir in the garlic and cook for 1 minute. Gradually stir in the reserved cooking liquid. Stir in the parsley and cream and season to taste with salt and black pepper. Bring to simmering point over a low heat.

4 Meanwhile, bring a large saucepan of lightly salted water to a boil. Add the pasta and olive oil and cook until just tender, but still firm to the bite. Drain the pasta, return to the pan, cover, and keep warm.

5 Reserve a few mussels for the garnish and remove the remainder from their shells. Stir the shelled mussels into the cream sauce and warm briefly.

6 Transfer the pasta to a large, warm serving dish. Pour over the sauce and toss well to coat. Garnish with the reserved mussels and serve with warm, crusty bread.

COOK'S TIP

Pasta shells are ideal because the sauce collects in the cavities and impregnates the pasta with flavor.

1

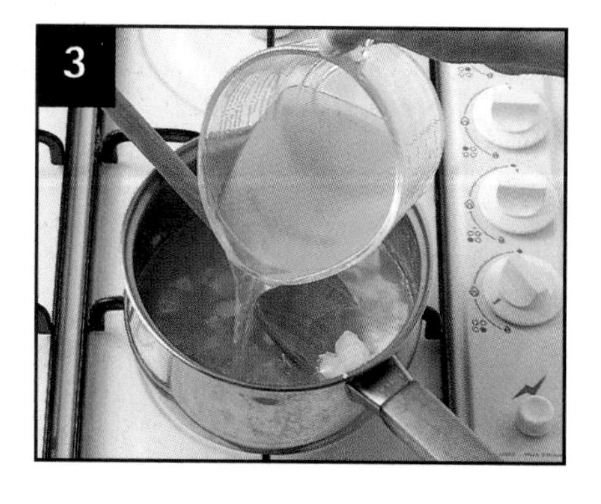

3

3

Vermicelli with Clams

A quickly cooked recipe that transforms store-cupboard ingredients into a dish with style.

Serves 4

INGREDIENTS

14 oz dried vermicelli, spaghetti or other long pasta
2 tbsp olive oil
2 tbsp butter
2 onions, chopped
2 garlic cloves, chopped
2 x 7 oz jars clams in brine
1/2 cup white wine
4 tbsp chopped fresh parsley
1/2 tsp dried oregano
pinch of freshly grated nutmeg
salt and pepper

TO GARNISH:
2 tbsp Parmesan cheese shavings
fresh basil sprigs

1 Bring a large pan of lightly salted water to a boil. Add the pasta and half the olive oil and cook until tender, but still firm to the bite. Drain, return to the pan, and add the butter. Cover the pan, shake well and keep warm.

2 Heat the remaining oil in a pan over a medium heat. Add the onions and fry until they are translucent. Stir in the garlic and cook for 1 minute.

3 Strain the liquid from 1 jar of clams and add the liquid to the pan, with the wine. Stir, bring to simmering point, and simmer for 3 minutes. Drain the second jar of clams and discard the liquid.

4 Add the clams, parsley, and oregano to the pan and season with pepper and nutmeg. Lower the heat and cook until the sauce is heated through.

5 Transfer the pasta to a warm serving dish and pour over the sauce. Sprinkle with the Parmesan cheese, garnish with the basil, and serve immediately.

COOK'S TIP

There are many different types of clams found along almost every coast in the world. Those traditionally used in this dish are the tiny ones – only 1–2 inches across – known in Italy as vongole.

Salt Cod Fritters

These tasty little fried cakes of mashed salt cod mixed with fennel and a little chili make an excellent snack or main course served with vegetables and a chili relish.

Serves 4

INGREDIENTS

3½ oz self-rising flour
1 egg, beaten
⅔ cup milk
9 oz salt cod, soaked overnight
1 small red onion, finely chopped
1 small fennel bulb, finely chopped
1 red chili, finely chopped
2 tbsp oil

TO SERVE:
crisp salad, chili relish, cooked rice, and fresh vegetables

1 Sift the flour into a large bowl. Make a well in the center of the flour and add the egg.

2 Using a wooden spoon, gradually draw in the flour, slowly adding the milk, and mix to form a smooth batter. Leave to stand for 10 minutes.

3 Drain the salt cod and rinse it under cold running water. Drain again thoroughly.

4 Remove and discard the skin and any bones from the fish, then mash the flesh with a fork.

5 Place the fish in a large bowl and combine with the onion, fennel and chili. Add the mixture to the batter and blend together.

6 Heat the oil in a large skillet and, taking about 1 tablespoon of the mixture at a time, spoon it into the hot oil. Cook the fritters, in batches, for 3–4 minutes on each side until golden and slightly puffed. Keep warm while cooking the remaining mixture.

7 Serve with salad and a chili relish for a light meal or with vegetables and rice.

COOK'S TIP

If you prefer larger fritters, use 2 tablespoons per fritter and cook for slightly longer.

Orange Mackerel

Mackerel can be quite rich, but when it is stuffed with oranges and toasted ground almonds it is tangy and light.

Serves 4

INGREDIENTS

2 tbsp oil
4 scallions, chopped
2 oranges
1 3/4 oz ground almonds
1 tbsp oats
1 3/4 oz mixed green and black olives, pitted, and chopped
8 mackerel fillets
salt and pepper
crisp salad, to serve

1 Heat the oil in a skillet. Add the scallions and cook for 2 minutes.

2 Finely grate the peel of the oranges, then, using a sharp knife, cut away the remaining skin and white pith.

3 Using a sharp knife, segment the oranges by cutting down either side of the lines of pith to loosen each segment. Do this over a plate so that you can reserve any juices. Cut each orange segment in half.

4 Lightly toast the almonds, under a preheated broiler, for 2–3 minutes or until golden; watch them as they brown quickly.

5 Mix the scallions, oranges, ground almonds, oats, and olives together in a bowl and season with salt and pepper.

6 Spoon the orange mixture along the center of each fillet. Roll up each fillet, securing it in place with a toothpick or skewer.

7 Bake in a preheated oven at 375°F for 25 minutes until the fish is tender.

8 Transfer to serving plates and serve warm with a salad.

1

5

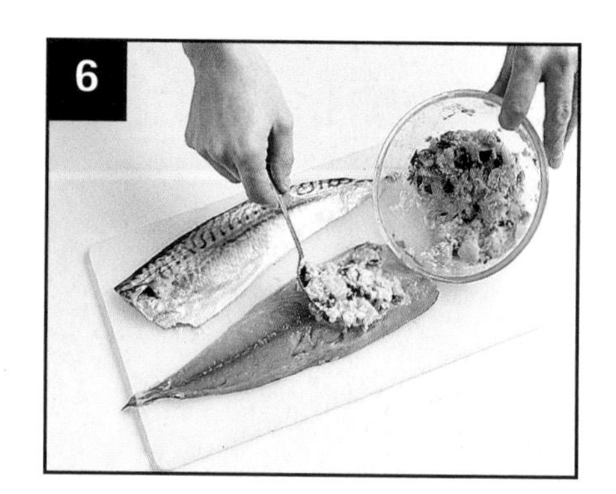
6

Italian Cod

Cod roasted with herbs and topped with a lemon and rosemary crust is a delicious main course.

Serves 4

INGREDIENTS

2 tbsp butter
$1^3/_4$ oz wholemeal bread crumbs
1 oz chopped walnuts
grated peel and juice of 2 lemons
2 sprigs rosemary, stalks removed
2 tbsp chopped parsley
4 cod fillets, each about $5^1/_2$ oz
1 garlic clove, minced
3 tbsp walnut oil
1 small red chili, diced
salad leaves, to serve

1 Melt the butter in a large skillet.

2 Remove the skillet from the heat and add the bread crumbs, walnuts, the peel and juice of 1 lemon, half of the rosemary, and half of the parsley.

3 Press the bread crumb mixture over the top of the cod fillets. Place the cod fillets in a shallow, foil-lined roasting pan.

4 Bake in a preheated oven at 400°F for 25–30 minutes.

5 Mix the garlic, the remaining lemon peel and juice, rosemary, parsley, and chili in a bowl. Beat in the walnut oil and mix to combine. Drizzle the dressing over the cod steaks as soon as they are cooked.

6 Transfer to serving plates and serve immediately.

VARIATION

If preferred, the walnuts may be omitted from the crust. In addition, extra virgin olive oil can be used instead of walnut oil, if you prefer.

COOK'S TIP

The hotness of chilies varies so use them with caution. As a general guide, the smaller the chili, the hotter it will be.

Vegetables, Bakes, & Salads

The pasta and rice recipes in this chapter offer something special for every occasion: filling vegetarian suppers, unusual vegetable side dishes, main course, and side salads. You could even take many of the salads on a picnic and, of course, they are perfect as accompaniments for summer barbecues. There are several innovative new takes on the traditional Italian favorite, the pizza, such as Sun-Dried Tomato and Ricotta Pizza, and delicious salads making good use of local cheeses such as Dolcelatte and Gorgonzola. Some of the dishes included here are classics, while others are imaginative and sometimes surprising new combinations of vegetables and pasta. There are dishes for every occasion from a cosy family supper to superb side dishes and splendid vegetarian spreads.

Green Tagliatelle with Garlic

A rich pasta dish for garlic lovers everywhere.
It is quick and easy to prepare and full of flavor.

Serves 4

INGREDIENTS

- 2 tbsp walnut oil
- 1 bunch scallions, sliced
- 2 garlic cloves, thinly sliced
- 3¼ cups sliced mushrooms
- 1 lb fresh green and white tagliatelle
- 1 tbsp olive oil
- 8 oz frozen spinach, thawed and drained
- ½ cup full-fat soft cheese with garlic and herbs
- 4 tbsp light cream
- ½ cup chopped, unsalted pistachio nuts
- salt and pepper

TO GARNISH:

- 2 tbsp shredded fresh basil
- fresh basil sprigs
- Italian bread, to serve

1 Heat the walnut oil in a large skillet. Add the scallions and garlic and fry for 1 minute, until just softened.

2 Add the mushrooms to the pan, stir well, cover, and cook over a low heat for about 5 minutes, until softened.

3 Meanwhile, bring a large saucepan of lightly salted water to a boil. Add the tagliatelle and olive oil and cook for 3–5 minutes, until tender but still firm to the bite. Drain the tagliatelle thoroughly and return to the saucepan.

4 Add the spinach to the skillet and heat through for 1–2 minutes. Add the cheese to the pan and allow to melt slightly. Stir in the cream and continue to cook, without allowing the mixture to come to a boil, until warmed through.

5 Pour the sauce over the pasta, season to taste with salt and black pepper and mix well. Heat through gently, stirring constantly, for 2–3 minutes.

6 Transfer the pasta to a serving dish and sprinkle with the pistachio nuts and shredded basil. Garnish with the basil sprigs and serve immediately with the Italian bread of your choice.

2

4

5

Spaghetti Olio e Aglio

This easy and satisfying Roman dish originated as a cheap meal for poor people, but has now become a favorite in restaurants and trattorias.

Serves 4

INGREDIENTS

- 1/2 cup olive oil
- 3 garlic cloves, crushed
- 1 lb fresh spaghetti
- 3 tbsp roughly chopped fresh parsley
- salt and pepper

1 Reserve 1 tbsp of the olive oil and heat the remainder in a medium saucepan. Add the garlic and a pinch of salt and cook over a low heat, stirring constantly, until golden brown, then remove the pan from the heat. Do not allow the garlic to burn as it will taint its flavor. (If it does burn, you will have to start all over again!)

2 Meanwhile, bring a large saucepan of lightly salted water to a boil. Add the spaghetti and remaining olive oil and cook for 2–3 minutes, until tender but still firm to the bite. Drain the spaghetti thoroughly and return to the pan.

3 Add the oil and garlic mixture to the spaghetti and toss to coat thoroughly. Season with pepper, add the chopped fresh parsley, and toss to coat again.

4 Transfer the spaghetti to a warm serving dish and serve immediately.

COOK'S TIP

Oils produced by different countries, mainly Italy, Spain and Greece, have their own characteristic flavors. Some produce an oil which has a hot, peppery taste while others have a green flavor.

COOK'S TIP

It is worth buying the best-quality olive oil for dishes such as this one which makes a feature of its flavor, and for salad dressings in addition. Extra virgin oil is produced from the first pressing and has the lowest acidity. It is more expensive than other types of olive oil, but has the finest flavor. Virgin olive oil is slightly more acid, but is also well flavored. Oil simply labeled pure has usually been heat-treated and refined by mechanical means and consequently lacks character and flavor.

1

3

3

Paglia e Fieno

The name of this dish – straw and hay – refers to the colors of the pasta when mixed together.

Serves 4

INGREDIENTS

4 tbsp butter
1 lb fresh peas, shelled
7/8 cup heavy cream
1 lb mixed fresh green and white spaghetti or tagliatelle
1 tbsp olive oil
2/3 cup freshly grated Parmesan cheese, plus extra to serve
pinch of freshly grated nutmeg
salt and pepper

1 Melt the butter in a large saucepan. Add the peas and cook, over a low heat, for 2–3 minutes.

2 Using a measuring pitcher, pour 5/8 cup of the cream into the pan, bring to a boil, and simmer for 1–1½ minutes, until slightly thickened. Remove the pan from the heat.

3 Meanwhile, bring a large pan of lightly salted water to a boil. Add the spaghetti or tagliatelle and olive oil and cook for 2–3 minutes, until just tender but still firm to the bite. Remove the pan from the heat, drain the pasta thoroughly, and return to the pan.

4 Add the peas and cream sauce to the pasta. Return the pan to the heat and add the remaining cream and the Parmesan cheese and season to taste with salt, black pepper, and grated nutmeg.

5 Using 2 forks, gently toss the pasta to coat with the peas and cream sauce, while heating through.

6 Transfer the pasta to a serving dish and serve immediately, with extra Parmesan cheese.

VARIATION

Fry 2 cups sliced button or oyster mushrooms in 4 tbsp butter over a low heat for 4–5 minutes. Stir into the peas and cream sauce just before adding to the pasta in step 4.

1

2

4

Fettuccine with Olive, Garlic, & Walnut Sauce

This mouth-watering dish would make an excellent light, vegetarian lunch for four or a good appetizer for six.

Serves 4–6

INGREDIENTS

- 2 thick slices whole-wheat bread, crusts removed
- $1^1/_4$ cups milk
- $2^1/_2$ cups shelled walnuts
- 2 garlic cloves, minced
- 1 cup pitted black olives
- $^2/_3$ cup freshly grated Parmesan cheese
- 8 tbsp extra virgin olive oil
- $^5/_8$ cup heavy cream
- 1 lb fresh fettuccine
- salt and pepper
- 2-3 tbsp chopped fresh parsley

1 Put the bread in a shallow dish, pour over the milk, and set aside to soak until the liquid has been absorbed.

2 Spread the walnuts out on a cookie sheet and toast in a preheated oven at 375°F for about 5 minutes, until golden. Set aside to cool.

3 Put the soaked bread, walnuts, garlic, olives, Parmesan cheese, and 6 tbsp of the olive oil in a food processor and work to make a paste. Season to taste with salt and black pepper and stir in the cream.

4 Bring a large pan of lightly salted water to a boil. Add the fettuccine and 1 tbsp of the remaining oil and cook for 2–3 minutes, until tender but still firm to the bite. Drain the fettuccine thoroughly and toss with the remaining olive oil.

5 Divide the fettuccine between individual serving plates and spoon the olive, garlic, and walnut sauce on top. Sprinkle over the fresh parsley and serve.

COOK'S TIP

Parmesan quickly loses its pungency and bite. It is better to buy small quantities and grate it yourself. Wrapped in foil, it will keep in the refrigerator for several months.

1

3

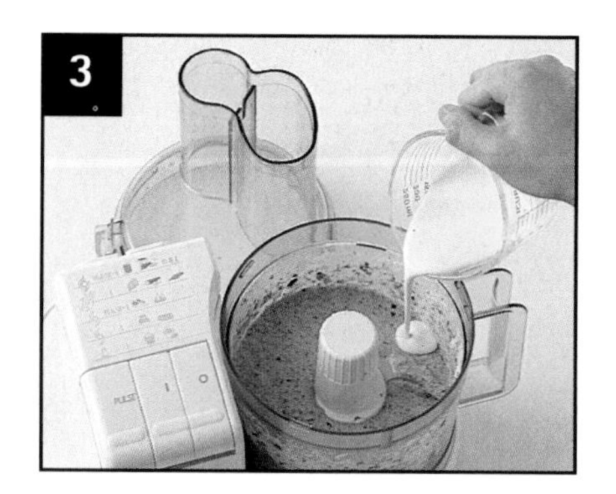

3

Creamy Pasta & Broccoli

This colorful dish provides a mouth-watering contrast in the crisp al dente texture of the broccoli and the creamy cheese sauce.

Serves 4

INGREDIENTS

4 tbsp butter
1 large onion, finely chopped
1 lb dried ribbon pasta
1 lb broccoli, broken into flowerets
5/8 cup boiling vegetable stock
1 tbsp all purpose flour
5/8 cup light cream
1/2 cup grated mozzarella cheese
freshly grated nutmeg
salt and white pepper
fresh apple slices, to garnish

1 Melt half of the butter in a large saucepan over a medium heat. Add the onion and fry for 4 minutes.

2 Add the broccoli and pasta to the pan and cook, stirring constantly, for 2 minutes. Add the vegetable stock, bring back to a boil, and simmer for a further 12 minutes. Season well with salt and white pepper.

3 Meanwhile, melt the remaining butter in a saucepan over a medium heat. Sprinkle over the flour and cook, stirring constantly, for 2 minutes. Gradually stir in the cream and bring to simmering point, but do not boil. Add the grated cheese and season with salt and a little freshly grated nutmeg.

4 Drain the pasta and broccoli mixture and pour over the cheese sauce. Cook, stirring occasionally, for about 2 minutes. Transfer the pasta and broccoli mixture to a warm, large, deep serving dish and serve garnished with slices of fresh apple.

VARIATION

This dish would also be delicious and look just as colorful made with Cape broccoli, which is actually a purple variety of cauliflower and not broccoli at all.

2

2

4

Tagliatelle with Pumpkin

This unusual dish comes from the Emilia Romagna region. Why not serve it with Lambrusco, the local wine?

Serves 4

INGREDIENTS

- 1 lb 2 oz pumpkin or butternut squash, peeled and seeded
- 3 tbsp olive oil
- 1 onion, finely chopped
- 2 garlic cloves, minced
- 4–6 tbsp chopped fresh parsley
- pinch of freshly grated nutmeg
- 1 1/4 cups chicken or vegetable stock
- 4 oz prosciutto
- 9 oz dried tagliatelle
- 5/8 cup heavy cream
- salt and pepper
- freshly grated Parmesan cheese, to serve

1 Cut the pumpkin or butternut squash in half and scoop out the seeds with a spoon. Cut the pumpkin or squash into ½ inch dice.

2 Heat 2 tbsp of the olive oil in a large saucepan. Add the onion and garlic and fry over a low heat for about 3 minutes, until soft. Add half the parsley and fry for 1 minute.

3 Add the pumpkin or squash pieces and cook for 2–3 minutes. Season to taste with salt, pepper and nutmeg.

4 Add half the stock to the pan, bring to a boil, cover, and simmer for about 10 minutes, or until the pumpkin or squash is tender. Add more stock if the pumpkin or squash is becoming dry and looks as if it might burn.

5 Add the prosciutto to the pan and cook, stirring frequently, for a further 2 minutes.

6 Meanwhile, bring a large saucepan of lightly salted water to a boil. Add the tagliatelle and the remaining oil and cook for 12 minutes, until tender, but still firm to the bite. Drain the pasta and transfer to a warm serving dish.

7 Stir the cream into the pumpkin and ham mixture and heat through. Spoon over the pasta, sprinkle over the remaining parsley, and serve. Hand the grated Parmesan separately.

1

5

7

Eggplant Cake

Layers of toasty-brown eggplant, meat sauce, and cheese-flavored pasta make this a popular family supper dish.

Serves 4

INGREDIENTS

1 eggplant, thinly sliced
5 tbsp olive oil
2 cups dried fusilli
2 1/2 cups Béchamel sauce
3/4 cup grated Cheddar cheese
butter, for greasing
1/3 cup freshly grated Parmesan cheese
salt and pepper

LAMB SAUCE:
2 tbsp olive oil
1 large onion, sliced
2 celery stalks, thinly sliced
1 lb ground lamb
3 tbsp tomato paste
5 1/2 oz bottled sun-dried tomatoes, drained and chopped
1 tsp dried oregano
1 tbsp red wine vinegar
5/8 cup chicken stock
salt and pepper

1 Put the eggplant slices in a colander, sprinkle with salt, and set aside for 45 minutes.

2 To make the lamb sauce, heat the oil in a pan. Fry the onion and celery for 3–4 minutes. Add the lamb and fry, stirring frequently, until browned. Stir in the remaining sauce ingredients, bring to a boil, and cook for 20 minutes.

3 Rinse the eggplant slices, drain and pat dry. Heat 4 tbsp of the oil in a skillet. Fry the eggplant slices for about 4 minutes on each side. Remove from the pan and drain well.

4 Bring a large pan of lightly salted water to a boil. Add the fusilli and the remaining oil and cook until almost tender, but still firm to the bite. Drain well.

5 Gently heat the Béchamel sauce, stirring constantly. Stir in the Cheddar cheese. Stir half of the cheese sauce into the fusilli.

6 Make layers of fusilli, lamb sauce, and eggplant slices in a greased dish. Spread the remaining cheese sauce over the top. Sprinkle over the Parmesan and bake in a preheated oven at 375°F for 25 minutes. Serve hot or cold.

3

5

6

Macaroni & Corn Pancakes

This vegetable pancake can be filled with your favorite vegetables, as long as they are cooked beforehand. A favorite alternative is shredded parsnips with 1 tbsp mustard.

Serves 4

INGREDIENTS

- 2 corn-on-the-cobs
- 4 tbsp butter
- 4 oz red bell peppers, cored, seeded and finely diced
- $2^1/_2$ cups dried short-cut macaroni
- $^5/_8$ cup heavy cream
- $^1/_4$ cup all purpose flour
- 4 egg yolks
- 4 tbsp olive oil
- salt and pepper

TO SERVE:
- oyster mushrooms
- fried leeks

1 Bring a saucepan of water to a boil, add the corn, and cook for about 8 minutes. Drain thoroughly and refresh under cold running water for 3 minutes. Carefully cut away the kernels and set aside to dry.

2 Melt 2 tbsp of the butter in a skillet. Add the bell peppers and cook over a low heat for 4 minutes. Drain and pat dry with paper towels.

3 Bring a large saucepan of lightly salted water to a boil. Add the macaroni and cook for about 12 minutes, until tender but still firm to the bite. Drain the macaroni thoroughly and leave to cool in cold water until required.

4 Beat together the cream, flour, a pinch of salt, and the egg yolks in a bowl until smooth. Add the corn and bell peppers to the cream and egg mixture. Drain the macaroni and then toss into the corn and cream mixture. Season well with black pepper to taste.

5 Heat the remaining butter with the oil in a large skillet. Drop spoonfuls of the mixture into the pan and press down until the mixture forms a flat pancake. Fry until golden on both sides and all the mixture is used up. Serve immediately with oyster mushrooms and fried leeks.

1

4

5

Zucchini & Eggplant Lasagne

This rich, baked pasta dish is packed full of vegetables, tomatoes, and Italian mozzarella cheese.

Serves 6

INGREDIENTS

2 1/4 lb eggplant
8 tbsp olive oil
2 tbsp garlic and herb butter
1 lb zucchini, sliced
2 cups grated mozzarella cheese
2 1/2 cups sieved tomatoes
6 sheets pre-cooked green lasagne
2 1/2 cups Béchamel Sauce
2/3 cup freshly grated Parmesan cheese
1 tsp dried oregano
salt and black pepper

1 Thinly slice the eggplant and place in a colander. Sprinkle with salt and set aside for 20 minutes. Rinse and pat dry with paper towels.

2 Heat 4 tbsp of the oil in a large skillet. Fry half the eggplant slices over a low heat for 6–7 minutes, until golden. Drain on paper towels. Repeat with the remaining oil and eggplant slices.

3 Melt the garlic and herb butter in the skillet. Add the zucchini and fry for 5–6 minutes, until golden brown all over. Drain on paper towels.

4 Place half the eggplant and zucchini slices in a large ovenproof dish. Season with pepper and sprinkle over half the mozzarella cheese. Spoon over half the sieved tomatoes and top with 3 sheets of lasagne. Repeat the process, ending with a layer of lasagne.

5 Spoon over the Béchamel sauce and sprinkle over the Parmesan cheese and oregano. Put the dish on a cookie sheet and bake in a preheated oven at 425°F for 30–35 minutes, until golden brown. Serve immediately.

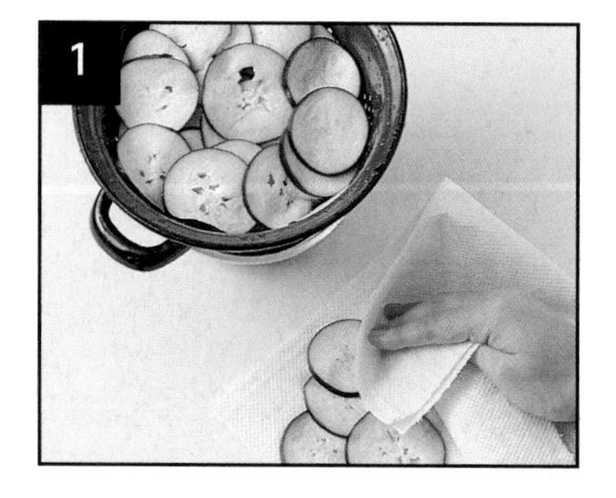

1

4

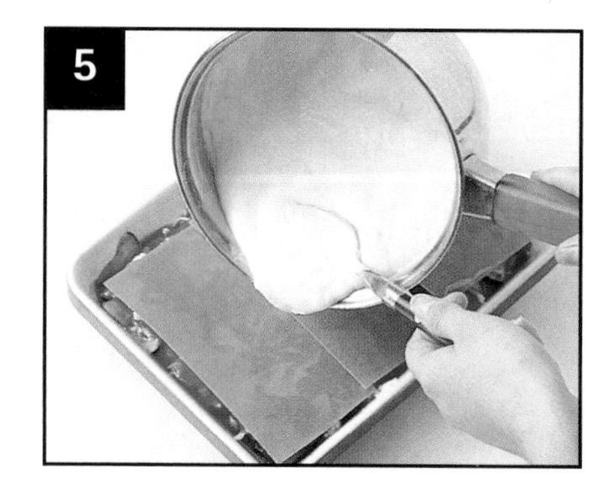

5

Spinach & Wild Mushroom Lasagne

This is one of the tastiest vegetarian dishes. Always check the seasoning of vegetables, as it is most important. You can always add a little more seasoning to a recipe, but you cannot take it out once it has been added.

Serves 4

INGREDIENTS

8 tbsp butter, plus extra for greasing
2 garlic cloves, finely chopped
4 oz shallots
8 oz wild mushrooms, such as chanterelles
1 lb spinach, cooked, drained, and finely chopped
2 cups grated hard cheese
1/4 tsp freshly grated nutmeg
1 tsp chopped fresh basil
2 oz all purpose flour
2 1/2 cups hot milk
2/3 cup grated Cheshire cheese
salt and pepper
8 sheets pre-cooked lasagne

1 Lightly grease an ovenproof dish with a little butter.

2 Melt 4 tbsp of the butter in a saucepan. Add the garlic, shallots, and wild mushrooms and fry over a low heat for 3 minutes. Stir in the spinach, hard cheese, nutmeg, and basil. Season well with salt and black pepper and set aside.

3 Melt the remaining butter in another saucepan over a low heat. Add the flour and cook, stirring constantly, for 1 minute. Gradually stir in the hot milk, whisking constantly until smooth. Stir in 1/4 cup of the Cheshire cheese and season to taste with salt and black pepper.

4 Spread half of the mushroom and spinach mixture over the base of the prepared dish. Cover with a layer of lasagne and then with half of the cheese sauce. Repeat the process and sprinkle over the remaining Cheshire cheese. Bake in a preheated oven at 400°F 30 minutes, until golden brown.

VARIATION

You could substitute 4 bell peppers for the spinach. Roast in a preheated oven at 400°F for 20 minutes. Rub off the skins in cold water, seed, and chop before use.

Ravioli with Vegetable Stuffing

It is important not to overcook the vegetable filling or it will become sloppy and unexciting, instead of firm to the bite and delicious.

Serves 4

INGREDIENTS

1 lb Basic Pasta Dough (see page 6)
1 tbsp olive oil
6 tbsp butter
5/8 cup light cream
1 cup freshly grated Parmesan cheese

STUFFING:
2 large eggplant
3 large zucchini
6 large tomatoes
1 large green bell pepper
1 large red bell pepper
3 garlic cloves
1 large onion
1/2 cup olive oil
2 oz tomato paste
1/2 tsp chopped fresh basil
salt and pepper

1 To make the stuffing, cut the eggplant and zucchini into 1 inch chunks. Put the eggplant pieces in a colander, sprinkle with salt, and set aside for 20 minutes. Rinse and drain.

2 Blanch the tomatoes in boiling water for 2 minutes. Drain, skin, and chop the flesh. Core and seed the bell peppers and cut into 1 inch dice. Chop the garlic and onion.

3 Heat the oil in a saucepan. Add the garlic and onion and fry for 3 minutes. Stir in the eggplant, zucchini, tomatoes, bell peppers, tomato paste, and basil. Season with salt and pepper, cover, and simmer for 20 minutes, stirring frequently.

4 Roll out the pasta dough and cut out 3 inch rounds with a plain cutter. Put a spoonful of the vegetable stuffing on each round. Dampen the edges slightly and fold the pasta rounds over, pressing together to seal.

5 Bring a saucepan of salted water to a boil. Add the ravioli and the oil and cook for 3–4 minutes. Drain and transfer to a greased ovenproof dish, dotting each layer with butter. Pour over the cream and sprinkle over the Parmesan cheese. Bake in a preheated oven at 400°F for 20 minutes. Serve hot.

1

2

3

Pasta & Bean Casserole

A satisfying winter dish, this pasta and bean casserole with a crunchy topping is a slow-cooked, one-pot meal.

Serves 6

INGREDIENTS

- 1 1/4 cups dried navy beans, soaked overnight and drained
- 8 oz dried penne
- 6 tbsp olive oil
- 3 1/2 cups vegetable stock
- 2 large onions, sliced
- 2 garlic cloves, chopped
- 2 bay leaves
- 1 tsp dried oregano
- 1 tsp dried thyme
- 5 tbsp red wine
- 2 tbsp tomato paste
- 2 celery stalks, sliced
- 1 fennel bulb, sliced
- 1 5/8 cups sliced mushrooms
- 8 oz tomatoes, sliced
- 1 tsp dark muscovado sugar
- 4 tbsp dry white bread crumbs
- salt and pepper
- salad greens and crusty bread, to serve

1 Put the navy beans in a large saucepan and add sufficient cold water to cover. Bring to a boil and continue to boil vigorously for 20 minutes. Drain, set aside, and keep warm.

2 Bring a large saucepan of lightly salted water to a boil. Add the penne and 1 tbsp of the olive oil and cook for about 3 minutes. Drain the pasta, set aside, and keep warm.

3 Put the beans in a large, flameproof casserole. Add the vegetable stock and stir in the remaining olive oil, the onions, garlic, bay leaves, oregano, thyme, wine, and tomato paste. Bring to a boil, cover, and cook in a heated oven at 350°F for 2 hours.

4 Add the penne, celery, fennel, mushrooms, and tomatoes to the casserole and season to taste with salt and pepper. Stir in the muscovado sugar and sprinkle over the bread crumbs. Cover the dish and cook in the oven for 1 further hour.

5 Serve hot with salad greens and crusty bread.

3

Linguine with Braised Fennel

This aniseed-flavored vegetable gives that extra punch to this delicious creamy pasta dish.

Serves 4

INGREDIENTS

6 fennel bulbs
5/8 cup vegetable stock
2 tbsp butter
6 slices rindless smoked bacon, diced
6 shallots, quartered
1/4 cup all purpose flour
7 tbsp heavy cream
1 tbsp Madeira wine
1 lb dried linguine
1 tbsp olive oil
salt and pepper

1 Trim the fennel bulbs, then gently peel off and reserve the first layer of the bulbs. Cut the bulbs into quarters and put them in a large saucepan, together with the vegetable stock and the reserved outer layers. Bring to a boil, lower the heat, and simmer for 5 minutes.

2 Using a draining spoon, transfer the fennel to a large dish. Discard the outer layers of the fennel bulb. Bring the vegetable stock to a boil and allow to reduce by half. Set aside.

3 Melt the butter in a skillet. Add the bacon and shallots and fry for 4 minutes. Add the flour, reduced stock, cream, and Madeira and cook, stirring constantly, for 3 minutes, until the sauce is smooth. Season to taste with salt and black pepper and pour over the fennel.

4 Bring a large saucepan of lightly salted water to a boil. Add the linguine and olive oil and cook for 10 minutes, until tender but still firm to the bite. Drain and transfer to a deep ovenproof dish.

5 Add the fennel and sauce and braise in a preheated oven at 350°F for 20 minutes. Serve immediately.

COOK'S TIP

Fennel will keep in the salad drawer of the refrigerator for 2–3 days, but it is best eaten as fresh as possible. Cut surfaces turn brown quickly, so do not prepare it too much in advance of cooking.

1

3

3

Basil & Pine Nut Pesto

Delicious stirred into pasta, soups, and salad dressings, pesto is available in most supermarkets, but making your own gives a much fresher, fuller flavor.

Serves 4

INGREDIENTS

about 40 fresh basil leaves, washed and dried
3 garlic cloves, minced
1 oz pine nuts
$1\,^3/_4$ oz Parmesan cheese, finely grated
2–3 tbsp extra virgin olive oil
salt and pepper
$1\,^1/_2$ lb fresh pasta or 12 oz dried pasta

1 Rinse the basil leaves and pat them dry with paper towels.

2 Put the basil leaves, garlic, pine nuts, and grated Parmesan into a food processor and blend for about 30 seconds or until smooth. Alternatively, pound the ingredients by hand, using a mortar and pestle.

3 If you are using a food processor, keep the motor running and slowly add the olive oil. Alternatively, add the oil drop by drop while stirring briskly. Season with salt and pepper.

4 Meanwhile, cook the pasta in a saucepan of boiling water according to the instructions on the packet or until it is cooked through, but still has bite. Drain.

5 Transfer the pasta to a serving plate and serve with the pesto. Toss to mix well and serve hot.

VARIATION

Try making a walnut version of this pesto. Substitute 1 oz walnuts for the pine nuts and add 1 tablespoon walnut oil in step 2.

COOK'S TIP

You can store pesto in the refrigerator for about 4 weeks. Cover the surface of the pesto with olive oil before sealing the container or bottle, to prevent the basil from oxidizing and turning black.

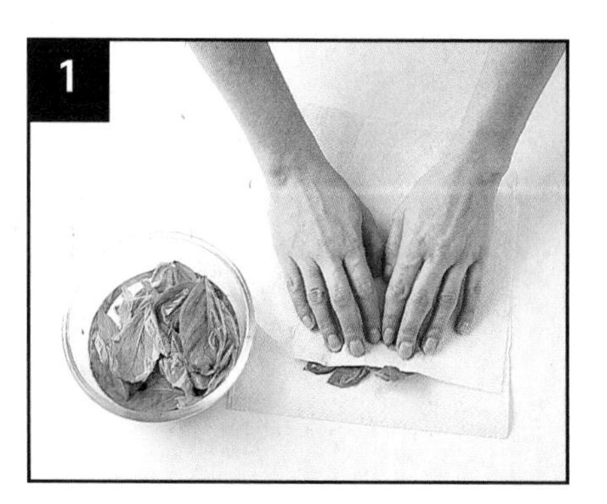
1

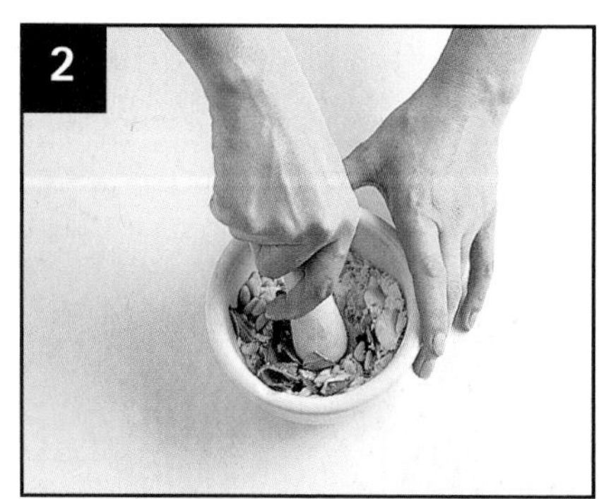
2

3

Basil & Tomato Pasta

Roasting the tomatoes gives a sweeter and smoother flavor to this sauce. Try to buy Italian tomatoes, such as plum or flavia, as these have a better flavor and color.

Serves 4

INGREDIENTS

1 tbsp olive oil
2 sprigs rosemary
2 cloves garlic, unpeeled
1 lb tomatoes, halved
1 tbsp sun-dried tomato paste
12 fresh basil leaves, plus extra to garnish
salt and pepper
$1^1/_2$ lb fresh farfalle or 12 oz dried farfalle

1 Place the oil, rosemary, garlic, and tomatoes, skin side up, in a shallow roasting pan.

2 Drizzle with a little oil and cook under a preheated broiler for 20 minutes or until the tomato skins are slightly charred.

3 Peel the skin from the tomatoes. Roughly chop the tomato flesh and place in a pan.

4 Squeeze the pulp from the garlic cloves and mix with the tomato flesh and sun-dried tomato paste.

5 Roughly tear the fresh basil leaves into smaller pieces and then stir them into the sauce. Season with a little salt and pepper to taste.

6 Cook the farfalle in a saucepan of boiling water according to the instructions on the packet or until it is cooked through, but still has bite. Drain.

7 Gently heat the tomato and basil sauce.

8 Transfer the farfalle to serving plates and serve with the basil and tomato sauce.

COOK'S TIP

This sauce tastes just as good when served cold in a pasta salad.

Tortelloni

These tasty little squares of pasta stuffed with mushrooms and cheese are surprisingly filling. Serve about 3 pieces for a starter and up to 9 for a main course.

Makes 36 pieces

INGREDIENTS

- 10½ oz fresh pasta thin sheets
- 5 tbsp butter
- 1¾ oz shallots, finely chopped
- 3 garlic clove, minced
- 1¾ oz mushrooms, wiped and finely chopped
- ½ stalk celery, finely chopped
- 1 oz pecorino cheese, finely grated, plus extra to garnish
- 1 tbsp oil
- salt and pepper

1 Using a serrated pasta cutter, cut 2 inch squares from the sheets of fresh pasta. To make 36 tortelloni, you will need 72 squares. Once the pasta is cut, cover the squares with plastic wrap to stop them drying out.

2 Heat 3 tbsp of the butter in a skillet. Add the shallots, 1 minced garlic clove, mushrooms, and celery, and cook for 4–5 minutes.

3 Remove the pan from the heat, stir in the cheese and season with salt and pepper.

4 Spoon ½ teaspoon of the mixture on to the middle of 36 pasta squares. Brush the edges of the squares with water and top with the remaining 36 squares. Press the edges together to seal. Leave to rest for 5 minutes.

5 Bring a large pan of water to a boil, add the oil, and cook the tortelloni, in batches, for 2–3 minutes. The tortelloni will rise to the surface when cooked and the pasta should be tender with a slight bite. Remove from the pan with a draining spoon and drain thoroughly.

6 Meanwhile, melt the remaining butter in a pan. Add the remaining garlic and plenty of pepper and cook for 1–2 minutes.

7 Transfer the tortelloni to serving plates and pour over the garlic butter. Garnish with grated pecorino cheese and serve immediately.

1

4

4

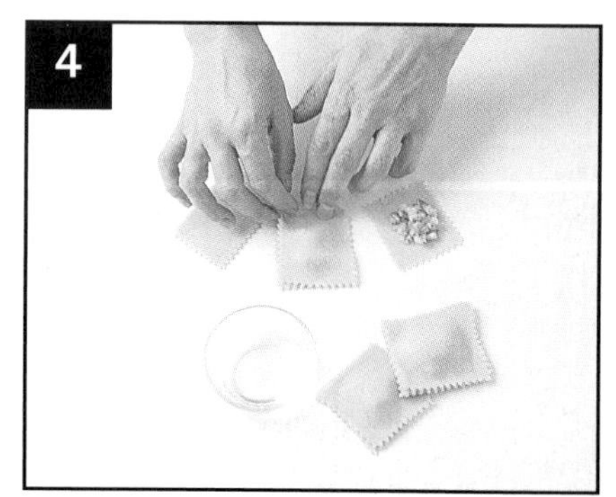

Spicy Tomato Tagliatelle

A deliciously fresh and slightly spicy tomato sauce which is excellent for lunch or a light supper.

Serves 4

INGREDIENTS

3 tbsp butter
1 onion, finely chopped
1 garlic clove, minced
2 small red chilies, seeded and diced
1 lb fresh tomatoes, skinned, seeded, and diced
$^3/_4$ cup vegetable stock
2 tbsp tomato paste
1 tsp sugar
salt and pepper
$1^1/_2$ lb fresh green and white tagliatelle, or 12 oz dried

1 Melt the butter in a large saucepan. Add the onion and garlic and cook for 3–4 minutes or until softened.

2 Add the chilies to the pan and continue cooking for about 2 minutes.

3 Add the tomatoes and stock, reduce the heat and leave to simmer for 10 minutes, stirring.

4 Pour the sauce into a food processor and blend for 1 minute until smooth. Alternatively, push the sauce through a sieve.

5 Return the sauce to the pan and add the tomato paste, sugar, and salt and pepper to taste. Gently reheat over a low heat, until piping hot.

6 Cook the tagliatelle in a pan of boiling water according to the instructions on the packet or until it is cooked, but still has bite. Drain the tagliatelle, transfer to serving plates, and serve with the tomato sauce.

VARIATION

Try topping your pasta dish with $1^3/_4$ oz pancetta or unsmoked bacon, diced and dry-fried for 5 minutes until crispy.

1

2

3

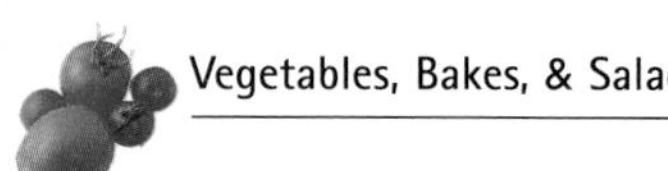

Chicken Risotto alla Milanese

This famous dish is known throughout the world, and it is perhaps the best known of all Italian risottos, although there are many variations.

Serves 4

INGREDIENTS

- 1/2 cup butter
- 2 lb chicken meat, sliced thinly
- 1 large onion, chopped
- 2 1/2 cups risotto rice
- 2 1/2 cups chicken stock
- 2/3 cup white wine
- 1 tsp crumbled saffron
- salt and pepper
- 1/2 cup grated Parmesan cheese, to serve

1 Heat 4 tbsp of butter in a deep skillet, and fry the chicken and onion until golden brown.

2 Add the rice, stir well, and cook for 15 minutes.

3 Heat the stock until boiling and gradually add to the rice. Add the white wine, saffron, salt, and pepper to taste and mix well. Simmer gently for 20 minutes, stirring occasionally, and adding more stock if the risotto becomes too dry.

4 Leave to stand for a few minutes and just before serving add a little more stock and simmer for a further 10 minutes. Serve the risotto, sprinkled with the grated Parmesan cheese and the remaining butter.

COOK'S TIP

A risotto should have moist but separate grains. Stock should be added a little at a time and only when the last addition has been completely absorbed.

VARIATION

The possibilities for risotto are endless – try adding the following just at the end of cooking time: cashew nuts and corn, lightly sautéed zucchini and basil, or artichokes and oyster mushrooms.

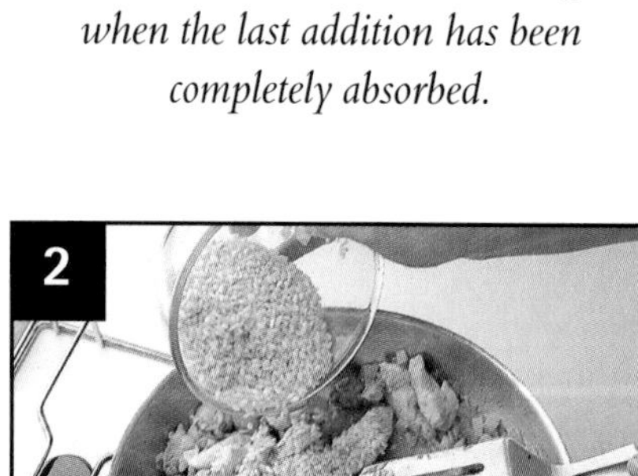

Wild Mushroom Risotto

This creamy risotto is flavored with a mixture of wild and cultivated mushrooms and thyme.

Serves 4

INGREDIENTS

2 tbsp olive oil
1 large onion, finely chopped
1 garlic clove, minced
7 oz mixed wild and cultivated mushrooms, such as ceps, oyster, porcini, and button, wiped and sliced if large
9 oz risotto rice, washed
pinch saffron threads
scant 3 cups hot vegetable stock
$3^1/_2$ oz Parmesan cheese, grated, plus extra for serving
2 tbsp chopped thyme
salt and pepper

1 Heat the oil in a large skillet. Add the onions and garlic and sauté for 3–4 minutes or until softened.

2 Add the mushrooms to the pan and cook for a further 3 minutes or until they are just beginning to brown.

3 Add the rice and saffron to the pan and stir to coat the rice in the oil.

4 Mix together the stock and the wine and add to the pan, a ladleful at a time. Stir the rice mixture and allow the liquid to be fully absorbed before adding more liquid, a ladleful at a time.

5 When all of the wine and stock is incorporated, the rice should be cooked. Test by tasting a grain – if it is still crunchy, add a little more water and continue cooking. It should take at least 15 minutes to cook.

6 Stir in the cheese and thyme, and season with freshly ground black pepper.

7 Transfer the risotto to serving dishes and serve sprinkled with extra Parmesan cheese.

COOK'S TIP

Wild mushrooms each have their own distinctive flavors and make a change from button mushrooms. However, they can be quite expensive, so you can always use a mixture with crimini or button mushrooms instead.

1

2

4

Milanese Sun-Dried Tomato Risotto

A Milanese risotto can be cooked in a variety of ways – but always with saffron. This version with sun-dried tomatoes and wine has a lovely tangy flavor.

Serves 4

INGREDIENTS

- 1 tbsp olive oil
- 2 tbsp butter
- 1 large onion, finely chopped
- 12 oz risotto rice, washed
- about 15 strands saffron
- 2/3 cup white wine
- 3 3/4 cup hot vegetable or chicken stock
- 8 sun-dried tomatoes, cut into strips
- 3 1/2 oz frozen peas, defrosted
- 1 3/4 oz prosciutto, shredded
- 2 3/4 oz Parmesan cheese, grated

1 Heat the oil and butter in a large skillet. Add the onion and cook for 4–5 minutes or until softened.

2 Add the rice and saffron to the skillet, stirring well to coat the rice in the oil, and cook for 1 minute.

3 Add the wine and stock slowly to the rice mixture in the pan, a ladleful at a time, stirring and making sure that all the liquid is absorbed before adding the next ladleful of liquid.

4 About half-way through adding the stock, stir in the tomatoes.

5 When all of the wine and stock is incorporated, the rice should be cooked. Test by tasting a grain – if it is still crunchy, add a little more water and continue cooking. It should take at least 15 minutes to cook.

6 Stir in the peas, prosciutto, and cheese. Cook for 2–3 minutes, stirring, until hot. Serve with extra Parmesan.

COOK'S TIP

Italian rice is a round, short-grained variety with a nutty flavor, which is essential for a good risotto. Arborio is the very best kind to use. The finished dish should have moist but separate grains. This is achieved by adding the hot stock a little at a time, only adding more when the last addition is fully absorbed. Don't leave the risotto to cook by itself: it needs constant watching to see when more liquid is required.

2

4

6

Golden Chicken Risotto

If you prefer, ordinary long grain rice can be used instead of risotto rice, but it won't give you the traditional, deliciously creamy texture that is typical of Italian risottos.

Serves 4

INGREDIENTS

2 tbsp sunflower oil
1 tbsp butter or margarine
1 medium leek, thinly sliced
1 large yellow bell pepper, diced
3 skinless, boneless chicken breasts, diced
12 oz round grain rice
few strands saffron
6 1/4 cups chicken stock
7 oz can corn-on-the-cob
1/2 cup toasted unsalted peanuts
1/2 cup grated Parmesan cheese
salt and pepper

1 Heat the oil and butter or margarine in a large saucepan. Fry the leek and bell pepper for 1 minute, stir in the chicken, and cook, stirring until golden brown.

2 Stir in the rice and cook for 2–3 minutes.

3 Stir in the saffron strands, and salt and pepper to taste. Add the stock, a little at a time, cover, and cook over a low heat, stirring occasionally, for about 20 minutes, until the rice is tender and most of the liquid is absorbed. Do not let the risotto dry out – add more stock if necessary.

4 Stir in the corn-on-the-cob, peanuts, and Parmesan cheese, then adjust the seasoning to taste. Serve hot.

COOK'S TIP

Risottos can be frozen, before adding the Parmesan cheese, for up to 1 month, but remember to reheat this risotto thoroughly as it contains chicken.

1

2

4

Patriotic Pasta

The ingredients of this dish have the same bright colors as the Italian flag – hence its name.

Serves 4

INGREDIENTS

4 cups dried farfalle
4 tbsp olive oil
1 lb cherry tomatoes
3 oz arugula
salt and pepper
Pecorino cheese, to garnish

1 Bring a large saucepan of lightly salted water to a boil. Add the farfalle and 1 tbsp of the olive oil and cook until tender, but still firm to the bite. Drain the farfalle thoroughly and return to the pan.

2 Cut the cherry tomatoes in half and trim the arugula.

3 Heat the remaining olive oil in a large saucepan. Add the tomatoes and cook for 1 minute. Add the farfalle and the arugula and stir gently to mix. Heat through and season to taste with salt and black pepper.

4 Meanwhile, using a vegetable peeler, shave thin slices of Pecorino cheese.

5 Transfer the farfalle and vegetables to a warm serving dish. Garnish with the Pecorino cheese shavings and serve immediately.

COOK'S TIP

Pecorino cheese is a hard sheep's milk cheese which resembles Parmesan and is often used for grating over a variety of dishes. It has a sharp flavor and is only used in small quantities.

COOK'S TIP

Arugula is a small plant with irregular-shaped leaves rather like those of greens. The flavor is distinctively peppery and slightly reminiscent of radish. It has always been popular in Italy, both in salads and for serving with pasta and has recently enjoyed a revival in Britain and the United States, where it has now become very fashionable.

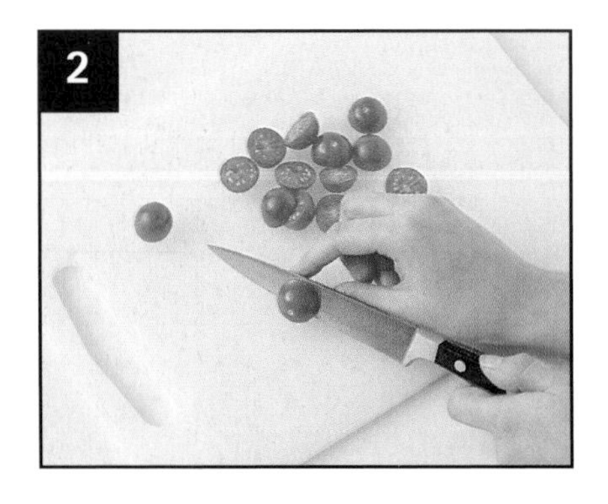
2

3

3

Fettuccine all'Alfredo

This simple, traditional dish can be made with any long pasta, but is especially good with flat noodles, such as fettuccine or tagliatelle.

Serves 4

INGREDIENTS

- 2 tbsp butter
- 7/8 cup heavy cream
- 1 lb fresh fettuccine
- 1 tbsp olive oil
- 1 cup freshly grated Parmesan cheese, plus extra to serve
- pinch of freshly grated nutmeg
- salt and pepper
- fresh parsley sprigs, to garnish

1 Put the butter and 5/8 cup of the cream in a large saucepan and bring the mixture to a boil over a medium heat. Reduce the heat and then simmer gently for about 1½ minutes, or until slightly thickened.

2 Meanwhile, bring a large pan of lightly salted water to a boil. Add the fettuccine and olive oil and cook for 2–3 minutes, until tender but still firm to the bite. Drain the fettuccine thoroughly and then pour over the cream sauce.

3 Toss the fettuccine in the sauce over a low heat until thoroughly coated.

4 Add the remaining cream, the Parmesan cheese, and nutmeg to the fettuccine mixture and season to taste with salt and pepper. Toss thoroughly to coat while gently heating through.

5 Transfer the fettucine mixture to a warm serving plate and garnish with the fresh sprig of parsley. Serve immediately, handing around extra grated Parmesan cheese separately.

VARIATION

This classic Roman dish is often served with the addition of strips of ham and fresh peas. Add 2 cups shelled cooked peas and 6 oz ham strips with the Parmesan cheese in step 4 of the recipe.

1

2

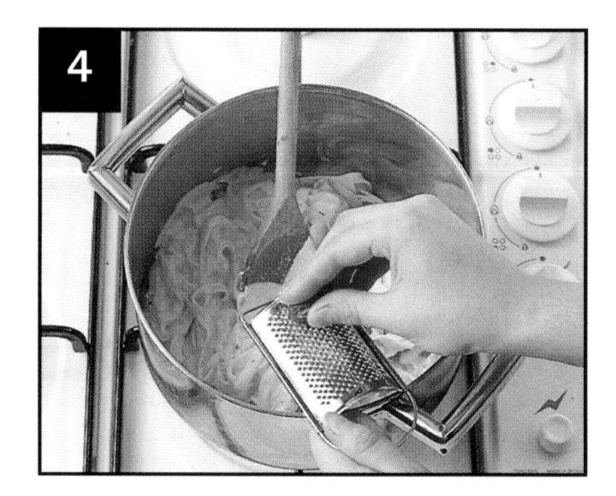

4

Macaroni Bake

This satisfying dish would make an excellent supper for a mid-week family meal.

Serves 4

INGREDIENTS

4 cups dried short-cut macaroni
1 tbsp olive oil
4 tbsp beef dripping
1 lb potatoes, thinly sliced
1 lb onions, sliced
2 cups grated mozzarella cheese
5/8 cup heavy cream
salt and pepper
crusty brown bread and butter, to serve

1 Bring a large saucepan of lightly salted water to a boil. Add the macaroni and olive oil and cook for about 12 minutes, until tender but still firm to the bite. Drain the macaroni thoroughly and set aside.

2 Melt the dripping in a large flameproof casserole, then remove from the heat.

3 Make alternate layers of potatoes, onions, macaroni, and grated cheese in the dish, seasoning well with salt and pepper between each layer and finishing with a layer of cheese on top. Finally, pour the cream over the top layer of cheese.

4 Bake in a preheated oven at 400°F for 25 minutes. Remove the dish from the oven and carefully brown the top of the bake under a hot broiler.

5 Serve the bake straight from the dish with crusty brown bread and butter as a main course. Alternatively, serve as a vegetable accompaniment with your favorite main course.

VARIATION

For a stronger flavor, use mozzarella affumicata, *a smoked version of this cheese, or Swiss cheese instead of the mozzarella.*

Mediterranean Spaghetti

Delicious Mediterranean vegetables, cooked in rich tomato sauce, make an ideal topping for nutty whole-wheat pasta.

Serves 4

INGREDIENTS

2 tbsp olive oil
1 large, red onion, chopped
2 garlic cloves, minced
1 tbsp lemon juice
4 baby eggplant, quartered
$2^1/_2$ cups sieved tomatoes
2 tsp superfine sugar
2 tbsp tomato paste
14 oz can artichoke hearts, drained and halved
1 cup pitted black olives
12 oz dried spaghetti
2 tbsp butter
salt and pepper
fresh basil sprigs, to garnish
olive bread, to serve

1 Heat 1 tbsp of the olive oil in a large skillet. Add the onion, garlic, lemon juice, and eggplant and cook over a low heat for 4–5 minutes, until the onion and eggplant are lightly golden brown.

2 Pour in the sieved tomatoes, season to taste with salt and black pepper and stir in the superfine sugar and tomato paste. Bring to a boil, lower the heat, and then simmer, stirring occasionally, for 20 minutes.

3 Gently stir in the artichoke hearts and black olives and cook for 5 minutes.

4 Meanwhile, bring a large saucepan of lightly salted water to a boil. Add the spaghetti and the remaining oil and cook for 7–8 minutes, until tender but still firm to the bite.

5 Drain the spaghetti and toss with the butter. Transfer the spaghetti to a large serving dish.

6 Pour the vegetable sauce over the spaghetti, garnish with the sprigs of fresh basil, and serve immediately with olive bread.

2

3

5

Creamed Spaghetti & Mushrooms

This easy vegetarian dish is ideal for busy people with little time, but good taste!

Serves 4

INGREDIENTS

4 tbsp butter
2 tbsp olive oil
6 shallots, sliced
6 cups sliced button mushrooms
1 tsp all purpose flour
$^5/_8$ cup heavy cream
2 tbsp port
4 oz sun-dried tomatoes, chopped
freshly grated nutmeg
1 lb dried spaghetti
1 tbsp freshly chopped parsley
salt and pepper
6 triangles of fried white bread, to serve

1 Heat the butter and 1 tbsp of the oil in a large saucepan. Add the shallots and cook over a medium heat for 3 minutes. Add the mushrooms and cook over a low heat for 2 minutes. Season with salt and black pepper, sprinkle over the flour, and cook, stirring constantly, for 1 minute.

2 Gradually stir in the cream and port, add the sun-dried tomatoes and a pinch of grated nutmeg, and cook over a low heat for 8 minutes.

3 Meanwhile bring a large saucepan of lightly salted water to a boil. Add the spaghetti and remaining olive oil and cook for 12–14 minutes, until tender but still firm to the bite.

4 Drain the spaghetti and return to the pan. Pour over the mushroom sauce and cook for 3 minutes. Transfer the spaghetti and mushroom sauce to a large serving plate and sprinkle over the chopped parsley. Serve with crispy triangles of fried bread.

VARIATION

Non-vegetarians could add 4 oz prosciutto, cut into thin strips, and heated gently in 2 tbsp butter, to the pasta with the mushroom sauce.

1

2

4

Vegetable Pasta Stir-Fry

Prepare all the vegetables and cook the pasta in advance, then the dish can be cooked in a few minutes.

Serves 4

INGREDIENTS

- 14 oz dried whole-wheat pasta shells or other short pasta shapes
- 1 tbsp olive oil
- 2 carrots, thinly sliced
- 4 oz baby corn-on-the-cobs
- 3 tbsp corn oil
- 1 inch piece fresh gingerroot, thinly sliced
- 1 large onion, thinly sliced
- 1 garlic clove, thinly sliced
- 3 celery stalks, thinly sliced
- 1 small red bell pepper, cored, seeded, and cut into matchstick strips
- 1 small green bell pepper, cored, seeded, and cut into matchstick strips
- 1 tsp cornstarch
- 2 tbsp water
- 3 tbsp soy sauce
- 3 tbsp dry sherry
- 1 tsp honey
- a dash of hot pepper sauce (optional)
- salt

1 Bring a large saucepan of lightly salted water to a boil. Add the pasta and olive oil and cook until tender, but still firm to the bite. Drain, return to the pan, and keep warm.

2 Bring a saucepan of lightly salted water to a boil. Add the carrots and corn and cook for 2 minutes. Drain, refresh in cold water, and drain again.

3 Heat the corn oil in a preheated wok or large skillet. Add the ginger and stir-fry over a medium heat for 1 minute to flavor the oil. Remove the ginger with a draining spoon and discard.

4 Add the onion, garlic, celery, and bell peppers to the pan and stir-fry for 2 minutes. Add the carrots and baby corn and stir-fry for 2 minutes. Stir in the pasta.

5 Mix together the cornstarch and water to make a smooth paste. Stir in the soy sauce, sherry, and honey. Pour the cornstarch mixture into the pasta and cook, stirring occasionally, for 2 minutes. Stir in a dash of pepper sauce, if liked. Transfer to a serving dish and serve immediately.

Vermicelli Flan

Lightly cooked vermicelli is pressed into a flan ring and baked with a creamy mushroom filling.

Serves 4

INGREDIENTS

- 6 tbsp butter, plus extra, for greasing
- 8 oz dried vermicelli or spaghetti
- 1 tbsp olive oil
- 1 onion, chopped
- 5 oz button mushrooms
- 1 green bell pepper, cored, seeded, and sliced into thin rings
- 5/8 cup milk
- 3 eggs, lightly beaten
- 2 tbsp heavy cream
- 1 tsp dried oregano
- freshly grated nutmeg
- 1 tbsp freshly grated Parmesan cheese
- salt and pepper
- tomato and basil salad, to serve

1 Generously grease a 8 inch loose-based flan pan with butter.

2 Bring a large pan of lightly salted water to a boil. Add the vermicelli and olive oil and cook until tender, but still firm to the bite. Drain, return to the pan, add 2 tbsp of the butter, and shake the pan to coat the pasta.

3 Press the pasta on to the base and around the sides of the flan pan to make a flan case.

4 Melt the remaining butter in a skillet over a medium heat. Add the onion and fry until it is translucent.

5 Add the mushrooms and bell pepper rings to the skillet and cook, stirring, for 2–3 minutes. Spoon the onion, mushroom, and bell pepper mixture into the flan case and press it into the base.

6 Beat together the milk, eggs, and cream, stir in the oregano, and season to taste with nutmeg and black pepper. Carefully pour the mixture over the vegetables and sprinkle over the cheese.

7 Bake the flan in a preheated oven at 350°F for 40–45 minutes, until the filling has set.

8 Slide the flan out of the pan and serve warm with a tomato and basil salad.

3

5

5

Baked Eggplant with Pasta

Combined with tomatoes and mozzarella cheese, pasta makes a tasty filling for baked eggplant shells.

Serves 4

INGREDIENTS

8 oz dried penne or other short pasta shapes
4 tbsp olive oil, plus extra for brushing
2 eggplant
1 large onion, chopped
2 garlic cloves, minced
14 oz can chopped tomatoes
2 tsp dried oregano
2 oz mozzarella cheese, thinly sliced
1/3 cup freshly grated Parmesan cheese
2 tbsp dry bread crumbs
salt and pepper
salad greens, to serve

1 Bring a saucepan of lightly salted water to a boil. Add the pasta and 1 tbsp of the olive oil and cook until tender, but still firm to the bite. Drain, return to the pan, cover, and keep warm.

2 Cut the eggplant in half lengthways and score around the inside with a sharp knife, being careful not to pierce the shells. Scoop out the flesh with a spoon. Brush the insides of the shells with olive oil. Chop the flesh and set aside.

3 Heat the remaining oil in a skillet. Fry the onion until translucent. Add the garlic and fry for 1 minute. Add the chopped eggplant and fry, stirring frequently, for 5 minutes. Add the tomatoes and oregano and season to taste with salt and pepper. Bring to a boil and simmer for 10 minutes, or until thickened. Remove from the heat and stir in the pasta.

4 Brush a cookie sheet with oil and arrange the eggplant shells in a single layer. Divide half the tomato and pasta mixture between them. Sprinkle over the mozzarella, then pile the remaining tomato and pasta mixture on top. Mix the Parmesan cheese and bread crumbs and sprinkle over the top, patting it lightly into the mixture.

5 Bake in a preheated oven at 400°C for 25 minutes, until the topping is golden brown. Serve hot with salad greens.

2

3

4

Pasta with Green Vegetable Sauce

The different shapes and textures of the vegetables make a mouth-watering presentation in this light and summery dish.

Serves 4

INGREDIENTS

- 2 cups dried gemelli or other pasta shapes
- 1 tbsp olive oil
- 1 head green broccoli, cut into flowerets
- 2 zucchini, sliced
- 8 oz asparagus spears
- 4 oz snow peas
- 4 oz frozen peas
- 2 tbsp butter
- 3 tbsp vegetable stock
- 4 tbsp heavy cream
- freshly grated nutmeg
- 2 tbsp chopped fresh parsley
- 2 tbsp freshly grated Parmesan cheese
- salt and pepper

1 Bring a large saucepan of lightly salted water to a boil. Add the pasta and olive oil and cook until tender, but still firm to the bite. Drain, return to the pan, cover and keep warm.

2 Steam the broccoli, zucchini, asparagus spears, and snow peas over a pan of boiling salted water until they are just beginning to soften. Remove from the heat and refresh in cold water. Drain and set aside.

3 Bring a small pan of lightly salted water to a boil. Add the frozen peas and cook for 3 minutes. Drain the peas, refresh in cold water, and then drain again. Set aside with the other vegetables.

4 Put the butter and vegetable stock in a pan over a medium heat. Add all of the vegetables, reserving a few of the asparagus spears, and toss carefully with a wooden spoon until they have heated through, taking care not to break them up.

5 Stir in the cream and heat through without bringing to a boil. Season to taste with salt, pepper, and nutmeg.

6 Transfer the pasta to a warmed serving dish and stir in the chopped parsley. Spoon over the vegetable sauce and sprinkle over the Parmesan cheese. Arrange the reserved asparagus spears in a pattern on top and serve.

2

4

5

Pasta & Sicilian Sauce

This Sicilian recipe of anchovies mixed with pine nuts and golden raisins in a tomato sauce is delicious with all types of pasta.

Serves 4

INGREDIENTS

1lb tomatoes, halved
1 oz pine nuts
$1^3/_4$ oz golden raisins
1 x $1^3/_4$ oz can anchovies, drained and halved lengthways
2 tbsp concentrated tomato paste
$1^1/_2$ lb fresh or 12 oz dried penne

1 Cook the tomatoes under a preheated broiler for about 10 minutes. Leave to cool, then once cool enough to handle, peel off the skin, and dice the flesh.

2 Place the pine nuts on a cookie sheet and lightly toast under the broiler for 2–3 minutes or until golden.

3 Soak the golden raisins in a bowl of warm water for about 20 minutes. Drain the golden raisins thoroughly.

4 Place the tomatoes, pine nuts, and golden raisins in a small pan and gently heat.

5 Add the anchovies and tomato paste, heating the sauce for a further 2–3 minutes or until hot.

6 Cook the pasta in a saucepan of boiling water according to the instructions on the packet or until it is cooked through, but still has bite. Drain thoroughly.

7 Transfer the pasta to a serving plate and serve with the hot Sicilian sauce.

VARIATION

Add $3^1/_2$ oz bacon, grilled for 5 minutes until crispy, then chopped, instead of the anchovies, if you prefer.

COOK'S TIP

If you are making fresh pasta, remember that pasta dough prefers warm conditions and responds well to handling. Do not leave to chill and do not use a marble surface for kneading.

1

3

5

Spinach & Ricotta Pie

This puff pastry pie looks impressive and is actually very easy to make. Serve it hot or cold.

Serves 4

INGREDIENTS

8 oz spinach
1 oz pine nuts
3 1/2 oz ricotta cheese
2 large eggs, beaten
1 3/4 oz ground almonds
1 1/2 oz Parmesan cheese, grated
9 oz puff pastry, defrosted if frozen
1 small egg, beaten

1 Rinse the spinach, place in a large saucepan, and cook for 4–5 minutes until wilted. Drain thoroughly. When the spinach is cool enough to handle, squeeze out the excess liquid.

2 Place the pine nuts on a cookie sheet and lightly toast under a preheated broiler for 2–3 minutes or until golden.

3 Place the ricotta, spinach, and eggs in a bowl and mix together. Add the pine nuts, beat well, then stir in the ground almonds and Parmesan cheese.

4 Roll out the puff pastry and make 2 x 8 inch squares. Trim the edges, reserving the pastry trimmings.

5 Place 1 pastry square on a cookie sheet. Spoon over the spinach mixture, keeping within ½ inch of the edge of the pastry. Brush the edges with beaten egg and place the second square over the top.

6 Using a round-bladed knife, press the pastry edges together by tapping along the sealed edge. Use the pastry trimmings to make leaves to decorate the pie.

7 Brush the pie with the beaten egg and bake in a preheated oven, at 425°F, for 10 minutes. Reduce the oven temperature to 375°F and bake for a further 25–30 minutes. Serve hot.

COOK'S TIP

Spinach is very nutritious as it is full of iron – this is particularly important for women and elderly people who may lack this in their diet.

3

4

6

Olive Oil Bread with Cheese

This flat cheese bread is sometimes called foccacia. *It is delicious served with* antipasto *or simply on its own.*

Makes 1 loaf

INGREDIENTS

1/2 oz dried yeast
1 tsp sugar
9 fl oz hand-hot water
12 oz strong flour
1 tsp salt
3 tbsp olive oil
7 oz pecorino cheese, cubed
1/2 tbsp fennel seeds, lightly minced

1 Mix the yeast with the sugar and 8 tbsp of the water. Leave to ferment in a warm place for about 15 minutes.

2 Mix the flour with the salt. Add 1 tbsp of the oil, the yeast mixture, and the remaining water to form a smooth dough. Knead the dough for 4 minutes.

3 Divide the dough into 2 equal portions. Roll out each portion to a form a round 1/4 inch thick. Place 1 round on a cookie sheet. Scatter the cheese and half of the fennel seeds evenly over the round.

4 Place the second round on top and squeeze the edges together to seal so that the filling does not leak during cooking.

5 Using a sharp knife, make a few slashes in the top of the dough and brush with the remaining olive oil.

6 Sprinkle with the remaining fennel seeds and leave to rise for 20–30 minutes.

7 Bake in a preheated oven at 400°F for 30 minutes or until golden. Serve immediately.

COOK'S TIP

Pecorino is a hard, quite salty cheese, which is sold in most large supermarkets and Italian delicatessens. If you cannot obtain pecorino, use strong Cheddar or Parmesan cheese instead.

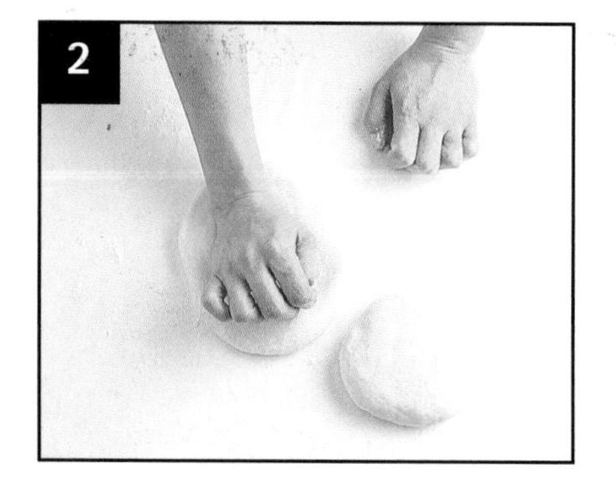
2

3

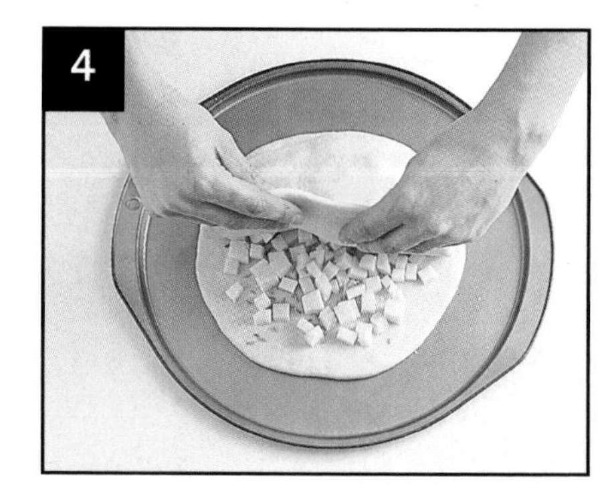
4

Roman Focaccia

Roman focaccia *makes a delicious snack on its own or serve it with cured meats and salad for a quick supper.*

Makes 16 squares

INGREDIENTS

$^{1}/_{4}$ oz dried yeast
1 tsp sugar
$1^{1}/_{4}$ cups hand-hot water

1 lb strong white flour
2 tsp salt
3 tbsp rosemary, chopped
2 tbsp olive oil

1 lb mixed red and white onions, sliced into rings
4 garlic cloves, sliced

1 Place the yeast and the sugar in a small bowl and mix with 8 tablespoons of the water. Leave to ferment in a warm place for 15 minutes.

2 Mix the flour with the salt in a large bowl. Add the yeast mixture, half of the rosemary, and the remaining water and mix to form a smooth dough. Knead the dough for 4 minutes.

3 Cover the dough with oiled plastic wrap and leave to rise for 30 minutes or until doubled in size.

4 Meanwhile, heat the oil in a large pan. Add the onions and garlic and fry for 5 minutes or until softened. Cover the pan and continue to cook for a further 7–8 minutes or until the onions are lightly caramelized.

5 Remove the dough from the bowl and knead it again for 1–2 minutes.

6 Roll the dough out to form a square shape. The dough should be no more than $^{1}/_{4}$ inch thick because it will rise during cooking. Place the dough onto a large cookie sheet, pushing out the edges until even.

7 Spread the onions over the dough and sprinkle with the remaining rosemary.

8 Bake in a preheated oven 400°F for 25–30 minutes or until golden. Cut into 16 squares and serve immediately.

2

Roasted Bell Pepper Bread

Bell peppers become sweet and mild when they are roasted and make this bread delicious.

Serves 4

INGREDIENTS

- 1 red bell pepper, halved and seeded
- 1 yellow bell pepper, halved and seeded
- 2 sprigs rosemary
- 1 tbsp olive oil
- $^1/_4$ oz dried yeast
- 1 tsp sugar
- $1^1/_4$ cups hand-hot water
- 1 lb strong white flour
- 1 tsp salt

1 Grease a 9 inch deep round cake pan.

2 Place the bell peppers and rosemary in a shallow roasting pan. Pour over the oil and roast in a preheated oven, at 400°F, for 20 minutes or until slightly charred. Remove the skin from the bell peppers and cut the flesh into slices.

3 Place the yeast and sugar in a small bowl and mix with 8 tablespoons of hand-hot water. Leave to ferment in a warm place for about 15 minutes.

4 Mix the flour and salt together in a large bowl. Stir in the yeast mixture and the remaining water and mix to form a smooth dough.

5 Knead the dough for about 5 minutes until smooth. Cover with oiled plastic wrap and leave to rise for about 30 minutes or until doubled in size.

6 Cut the dough into 3 equal portions. Roll the portions into rounds slightly larger than the cake pan.

7 Place 1 round in the base of the pan so that it reaches up the sides of the pan by about $^3/_4$ inch. Top with half of the bell pepper mixture.

8 Place the second round of dough on top, followed by the remaining bell pepper mixture. Place the last round of dough on top, pushing the edges of the dough down the sides of the pan.

9 Cover the dough with oiled plastic wrap and leave to rise for 30–40 minutes. Place in the preheated oven and bake for 45 minutes until golden or the base sounds hollow when lightly tapped. Serve warm.

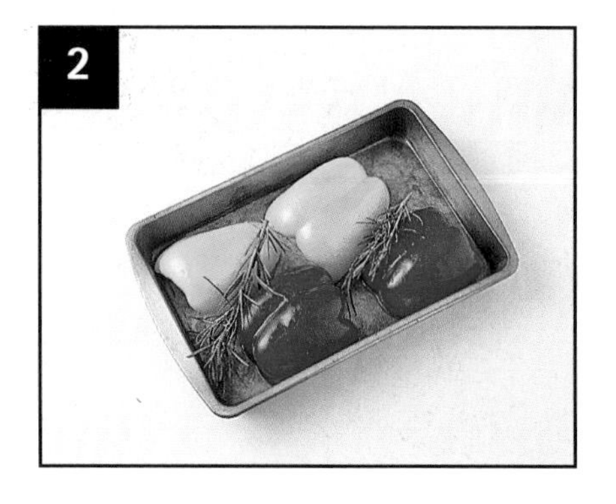

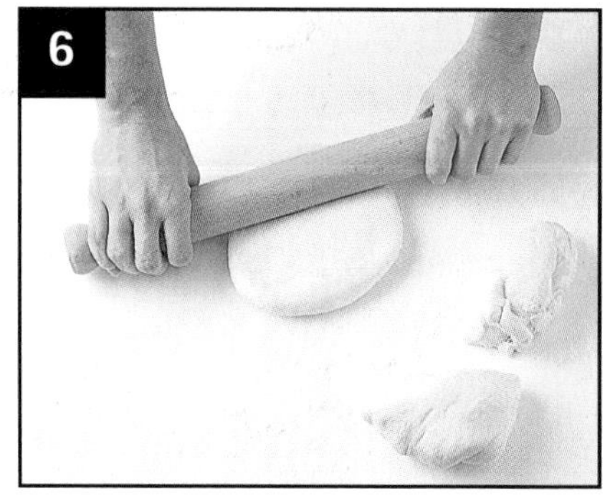

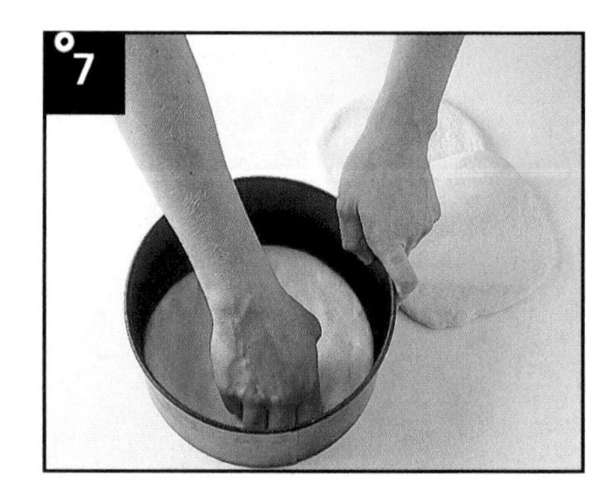

Sun-Dried Tomato Loaf

This delicious tomato bread is great with cheese or soup or to make an unusual sandwich.

Makes 1 loaf

INGREDIENTS

- $^{1}/_{4}$ oz dried yeast
- 1 tsp sugar
- $1^{1}/_{4}$ cups hand-hot water
- 1 tsp salt
- 2 tsp dried basil
- 1 lb strong white flour
- 2 tbsp sun-dried tomato paste or tomato paste
- 12 sun-dried tomatoes, cut into strips

1 Place the yeast and sugar in a bowl and mix with 8 tablespoons of the water. Leave to ferment in a warm place for 15 minutes.

2 Place the flour in a bowl and stir in the salt. Make a well in the dry ingredients and add the basil, the yeast mixture, tomato paste, and half of the remaining water. Using a wooden spoon, draw the flour into the liquid and mix to form a dough, adding the rest of the water gradually.

3 Turn out the dough on to a floured surface and knead for 5 minutes or until smooth. Cover with oiled plastic wrap and leave in a warm place to rise for about 30 minutes or until doubled in size.

4 Lightly grease a 2 lb loaf pan.

5 Remove the dough from the bowl and knead in the sun-dried tomatoes. Knead again for 2–3 minutes.

6 Place the dough in the pan and leave to rise for 30–40 minutes. Once it has doubled in size again, bake in a preheated oven at 375°F for 30–35 minutes or until golden and the base sounds hollow when tapped.

COOK'S TIP

You could make mini sun-dried tomato loaves for children. Divide the dough into 8 equal portions, leave to rise and bake in mini-loaf pans for 20 minutes. Alternatively, make 12 small rounds, leave to rise and bake as rolls for 12–15 minutes.

2

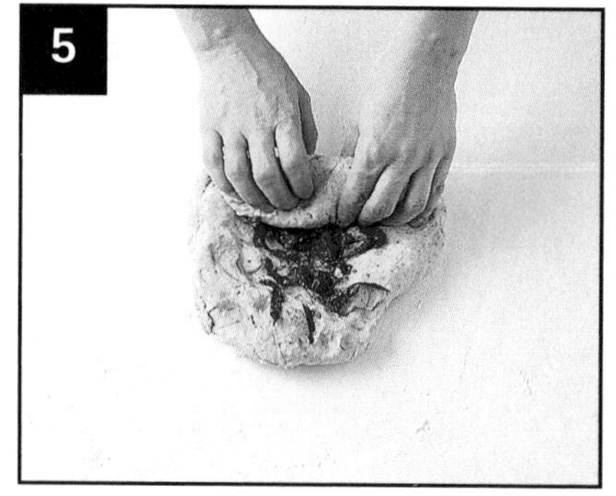
5

6

Pizza Margherita

Pizza means "pie" in Italian. The fresh bread dough is not difficult to make but it does take a little time.

Serves 4

INGREDIENTS

BASIC PIZZA DOUGH:
- 1/4 oz dried yeast
- 1 tsp sugar
- 1 cup hand-hot water
- 12 oz strong flour
- 1 tsp salt
- 1 tbsp olive oil

TOPPING:
- 1 x 14 oz can tomatoes, chopped
- 2 garlic cloves, minced
- 2 tsp dried basil
- 1 tbsp olive oil
- 2 tbsp tomato paste
- 3 1/2 oz Mozzarella cheese, chopped
- 2 tbsp freshly grated Parmesan cheese
- salt and pepper

1 Place the yeast and sugar in a measuring jug and mix with 4 tbsp of the water. Leave the yeast mixture in a warm place for 15 minutes or until frothy.

2 Mix the flour with the salt and make a well in the center. Add the oil, the yeast mixture, and the remaining water. Using a wooden spoon, mix to form a dough.

3 Turn the dough out on to a floured surface and knead for 4–5 minutes or until smooth.

4 Return the dough to the bowl, cover with an oiled sheet of plastic wrap and leave to rise for 30 minutes or until doubled in size.

5 Knead the dough for 2 minutes. Stretch the dough with your hands, then place it on an oiled cookie sheet, pushing out the edges until even and to the shape required. The dough should be no more than 1/4 inch thick because it will rise during cooking.

6 To make the topping, place the tomatoes, garlic, dried basil, olive oil, and salt and pepper to taste in a large skillet and leave to simmer for 20 minutes or until the sauce has thickened. Stir in the tomato paste and leave to cool slightly.

7 Spread the topping evenly over the pizza base. Top with the Mozzarella and Parmesan cheeses and bake in a preheated oven at 400°F for 20–25 minutes. Serve hot.

1

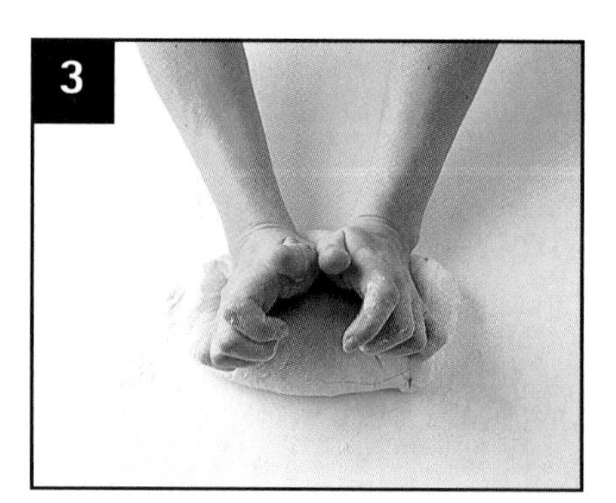

Mushroom Pizza

Juicy mushrooms and stringy Mozzarella top this tomato-based pizza. Use wild mushrooms or a combination of wild and cultivated mushrooms.

Serves 4

INGREDIENTS

1 portion Basic Pizza Dough (see page 302)

TOPPING:
1 x 14 oz can chopped tomatoes
2 garlic cloves, minced
1 tsp dried basil
1 tbsp olive oil
2 tbsp tomato paste
7 oz mushrooms
$5^1/_2$ oz Mozzarella cheese, grated
salt and pepper
basil leaves, to garnish

1 Place the yeast and sugar in a measuring jug and mix with 4 tbsp of the water. Leave the yeast mixture in a warm place for 15 minutes or until frothy.

2 Mix the flour with the salt and make a well in the center. Add the oil, the yeast mixture, and the remaining water. Using a wooden spoon, mix to form a dough.

3 Turn the dough out on to a floured surface and knead for 4–5 minutes or until smooth. Return the dough to the bowl, cover with an oiled sheet of plastic wrap and leave to rise for 30 minutes or until doubled in size.

4 Remove the dough from the bowl. Knead the dough for 2 minutes. Using a rolling pin, roll out the dough to form an oval or a circular shape, place it on an oiled cookie sheet, pushing out the edges until even. The dough should be no more than ¼ inch thick because it rises while cooking.

5 Using a sharp knife, chop the mushrooms into slices.

6 To make the topping, place the tomatoes, garlic, dried basil, olive oil, and salt and pepper in a large pan and simmer for 20 minutes or until the sauce has thickened. Stir in the tomato paste and leave to cool slightly.

7 Spread the sauce over the base of the pizza, top with the sliced mushrooms, and scatter over the Mozzarella.

8 Bake in a preheated oven at 400°F for 25 minutes. Just before serving, garnish with fresh basil leaves.

Sun-Dried Tomatoes & Ricotta Pizza

This is a traditional dish from the Calabrian Mountains in southern Italy, where it is made with naturally sun-dried tomatoes and ricotta cheese.

Serves 4

INGREDIENTS

1 portion Basic Pizza Dough (see page 302)

TOPPING:
4 tbsp sun-dried tomato paste
$5^1/_2$ oz ricotta cheese
10 sun-dried tomatoes
1 tbsp fresh thyme
salt and pepper

1 Place the yeast and sugar in a measuring jug and mix with 4 tbsp of the water. Leave the yeast mixture in a warm place for 15 minutes or until frothy.

2 Mix the flour with the salt and make a well in the center. Add the oil, the yeast mixture, and the remaining water. Using a wooden spoon, mix to form a dough.

3 Turn the dough out on to a floured surface and knead for 4–5 minutes or until smooth.

4 Return the dough to the bowl, cover with an oiled sheet of plastic wrap, and leave to rise for 30 minutes or until doubled in size.

5 Remove the dough from the bowl. Knead the dough for 2 minutes.

6 Using a rolling pin, roll out the dough to form a circle, then place it on an oiled cookie sheet, pushing out the edges until even. The dough should be no more than/4 inch thick because it will rise during cooking.

7 Spread the sun-dried tomato paste over the dough, then add spoonfuls of ricotta.

8 Cut the sun-dried tomatoes into strips and arrange these on top of the pizza.

9 Sprinkle the thyme, and salt and pepper to taste over the top of the pizza. Bake in a preheated oven at 400°F for 30 minutes or until the crust is golden. Serve hot.

COOK'S TIP

The dough for crispy-based pizzas should be rolled out as thinly as possible.

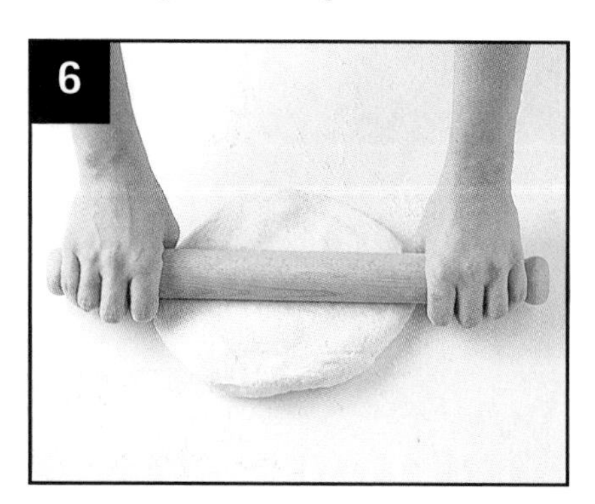

Gorgonzola Pizza

An unusual combination of blue Gorgonzola cheese and pears combine to give a colorful pizza. The wholewheat base adds a nutty flavor and texture.

Serves 4

INGREDIENTS

PIZZA DOUGH:
- 1/4 oz dried yeast
- 1 tsp sugar
- 1 cup hand-hot water
- 6 oz wholewheat flour
- 6 oz strong white flour
- 1 tsp salt
- 1 tbsp olive oil

TOPPING:
- 14 oz pumpkin or squash, peeled and cubed
- 1 tbsp olive oil
- 1 pear, cored, peeled and sliced
- 3 1/2 oz Gorgonzola cheese
- 1 sprig fresh rosemary, to garnish

1 Place the yeast and sugar in a measuring jug and mix with 4 tbsp of the water. Leave the yeast mixture in a warm place for 15 minutes or until frothy.

2 Mix both of the flours with the salt and make a well in the center. Add the oil, the yeast mixture, and the remaining water. Using a wooden spoon, mix to form a dough.

3 Turn the dough out on to a floured surface and knead for 4–5 minutes or until smooth.

4 Return the dough to the bowl, cover with an oiled sheet of plastic wrap and leave to rise for 30 minutes or until doubled in size.

5 Remove the dough from the bowl. Knead the dough for 2 minutes. Using a rolling pin, roll out the dough to form a long oval shape, then place it on an oiled cookie sheet, pushing out the edges until even. The dough should be no more than 1/4 inch thick because it will rise during cooking.

6 To make the topping, place the pumpkin in a shallow roasting pan. Drizzle with the olive oil and cook under a preheated broiler for 20 minutes or until soft and lightly golden.

7 Top the dough with the pear and the pumpkin, brushing with the oil from the pan. Sprinkle over the Gorgonzola. Bake in a preheated oven, at 400°F for 15 minutes or until the base is golden. Garnish with a sprig of rosemary.

5

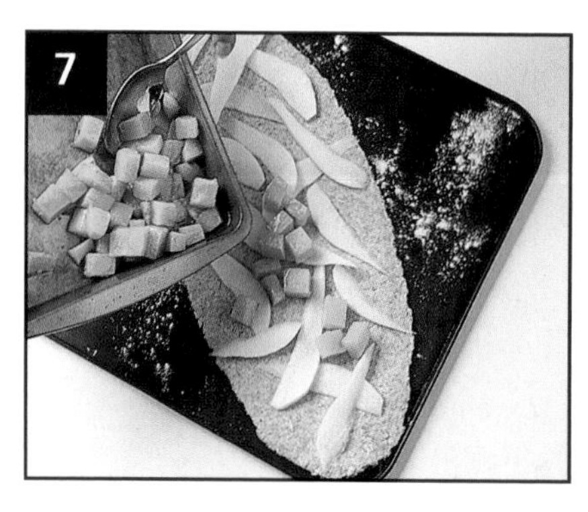
7

7

Folded-Over Pizza

A calzone, *as this pizza is known, can have many different fillings. Here, cured meats mix well with Mozzarella and Parmesan cheese.*

Makes 4 large or 8 small calzone

INGREDIENTS

1 portion of Basic Pizza Dough (see page 302)
freshly grated Parmesan cheese, to serve

TOPPING:
2 3/4 oz mortadella or other Italian pork sausage, chopped
1 3/4 oz Italian sausage, chopped
1 3/4 oz Parmesan cheese, sliced
3 1/2 oz Mozzarella, cut into chunks
2 tomatoes, diced
4 tbsp fresh oregano
salt and pepper

1 Place the yeast and sugar in a measuring jug and mix with 4 tbsp of the water. Leave the yeast mixture in a warm place for 15 minutes or until frothy.

2 Mix the flour with the salt and make a well in the center. Add the oil, the yeast mixture, and the remaining water. Using a wooden spoon, mix to form a dough.

3 Turn the dough out on to a floured surface and knead for 4–5 minutes or until smooth. Return the dough to the bowl, cover with an oiled sheet of plastic wrap and leave to rise for 30 minutes or until doubled in size.

4 Knead the dough for 2 minutes and divide it into 4 pieces. Roll out each portion thinly to form circles. Place them on an oiled cookie sheet. The dough should be no more than 1/4 inch thick because it will rise during cooking.

5 To make the topping, place both Italian sausages, the Parmesan and the Mozzarella on one side of each circle. Top with the tomatoes and oregano. Season.

6 Brush around the edges of the dough with a little water then fold over the circle to form a pasty shape. Squeeze the edges together to seal so that none of the filling leaks out during cooking.

7 Bake in a preheated oven at 400°F for 10–15 minutes or until golden. If you are making the smaller pizzas, reduce the cooking time to 8–10 minutes. Serve with freshly grated Parmesan cheese.

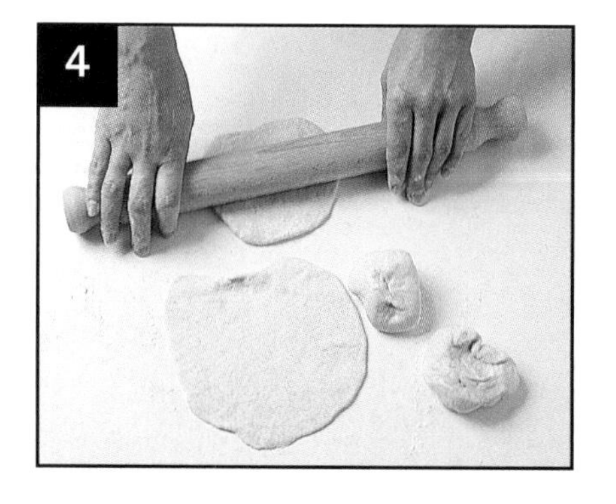

Onion, Ham, & Cheese Pizza

This pizza was a favorite of the Romans. It is slightly unusual because the topping is made without a tomato sauce base.

Serves 4

INGREDIENTS

- 1 portion of Basic Pizza Dough (see page 302)

TOPPING:

- 2 tbsp olive oil
- 9 oz onions, sliced into rings
- 2 garlic cloves, minced
- 1 red bell pepper, diced
- $3^1/_2$ oz prosciutto, cut into strips
- $3^1/_2$ oz Mozzarella cheese, sliced
- 2 tbsp rosemary, stalks removed and roughly chopped

1 Place the yeast and sugar in a measuring jug and mix with 4 tbsp of the water. Leave the yeast mixture in a warm place for 15 minutes or until frothy.

2 Mix the flour with the salt and make a well in the center. Add the oil, the yeast mixture, and the remaining water. Using a wooden spoon, mix to form a dough.

3 Turn the dough out on to a floured surface and knead for 4–5 minutes or until smooth. Return the dough to the bowl, cover with an oiled sheet of plastic wrap and leave to rise for 30 minutes or until doubled in size.

4 Remove the dough from the bowl. Knead the dough for 2 minutes. Using a rolling pin, roll out the dough to form a square shape, then place it on an oiled cookie sheet, pushing out the edges until even. The dough should be no more than $^1/_4$ inch thick because it will rise during cooking.

5 To make the topping, heat the oil in a pan. Add the onions and garlic and cook for 3 minutes. Add the bell pepper and fry for a further 2 minutes.

6 Cover the pan and cook the vegetables over a low heat for 10 minutes, stirring occasionally, until the onions are slightly caramelized. Leave to cool slightly.

7 Spread the topping evenly over the pizza base. Place strips of prosciutto, Mozzarella, and rosemary over the top. Bake in a preheated oven at 400°F for 20–25 minutes. Serve hot.

5

5

7

Mini-Pizzas

Pizette, *as they are known in Italy, are tiny pizzas. This quantity will make 8 individual pizzas or 16 cocktail pizzas to go with drinks.*

Serves 4

INGREDIENTS

- 1 portion Basic Pizza Dough (see page 302)

TOPPING:

- 2 zucchini
- 3½ oz tomato paste
- 2¾ oz pancetta, diced
- 1¾ oz black olives, pitted and chopped
- 1 tbsp mixed dried herbs
- 2 tbsp olive oil

1 Place the yeast and sugar in a measuring jug and mix with 4 tbsp of the water. Leave the yeast mixture in a warm place for 15 minutes or until frothy.

2 Mix the flour with the salt and make a well in the center. Add the oil, the yeast mixture and the remaining water. Using a wooden spoon, mix to form a dough.

3 Turn the dough out on to a floured surface and knead for 4–5 minutes or until smooth. Return the dough to the bowl, cover with an oiled sheet of plastic wrap and leave to rise for 30 minutes or until doubled in size.

4 Knead the dough for 2 minutes and divide it into 8 balls. Roll out each portion thinly to form circles or squares, then place them on an oiled cookie sheet, pushing out the edges until even. The dough should be no more than ¼ inch thick because it will rise during cooking.

5 To make the topping, grate the zucchini finely. Cover with paper towels and leave to stand for 10 minutes to absorb some of the juices.

6 Spread 2–3 teaspoons of the tomato paste over the pizza bases and top each with the grated zucchini, pancetta, and olives. Season with freshly ground black pepper, a sprinkling of mixed dried herbs and drizzle with olive oil.

7 Bake in a preheated oven at 400°F for 15 minutes or until crispy. Season and serve hot.

4

5

6

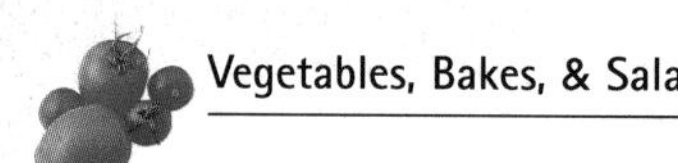

Pizza with Tomato Sauce & Roasted Bell Peppers

This pizza, which is similar to the French Pissaladière, *is made with a pastry base flavored with cheese and topped with a delicious tomato sauce and roasted bell peppers.*

Serves 4

INGREDIENTS

- 8 oz all-purpose flour
- 4½ oz butter, diced
- ½ tsp salt
- 2 tbsp dried Parmesan cheese
- 1 egg, beaten
- 2 tbsp cold water
- 2 tbsp olive oil
- 1 large onion, finely chopped
- 1 garlic clove, chopped
- 1 x 14 oz can chopped tomatoes
- 4 tbsp concentrated tomato paste
- 1 red bell pepper, halved
- 5 sprigs of thyme, stalks removed
- 6 black olives, pitted and halved
- 1 oz Parmesan cheese, grated

1 Sift the flour and rub in the butter to make bread crumbs. Stir in the salt and dried Parmesan. Add the egg and 1 tablespoon of the water and mix with a round-bladed knife. Add more water if necessary to make a soft dough. Cover with plastic wrap and chill for 30 minutes.

2 Meanwhile, heat the oil in a skillet and cook the onions and garlic for about 5 minutes or until golden. Add the tomatoes and cook for 8–10 minutes. Stir in the tomato paste.

3 Place the bell peppers, skin-side up, on a cookie sheet and cook under a preheated broiler for 15 minutes until charred. Place in a plastic bag and leave to sweat for 10 minutes. Peel off the skin and slice the flesh into thin strips.

4 Roll out the dough to fit a 9 inch loose base fluted flan pan. Line with foil and bake in a preheated oven at 400°F for 10 minutes or until just set. Remove the foil and bake for a further 5 minutes until lightly golden. Leave to cool slightly.

5 Spoon the tomato sauce over the pastry base and top with the bell peppers, thyme, olives, and fresh Parmesan. Return to the oven for 15 minutes or until the pastry is crisp. Serve warm or cold.

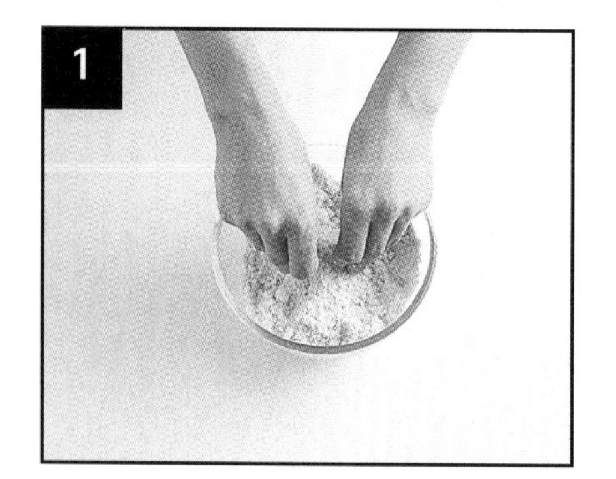

1

1

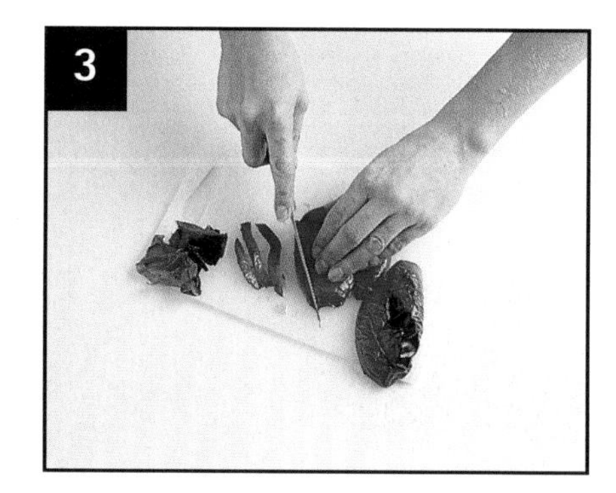

3

Pizza with Creamy Ham & Cheese Sauce

This is a traditional pizza which uses a pastry case and béchamel sauce to make a type of savoury flan. Grating the pastry gives it a lovely nutty texture.

Serves 4

INGREDIENTS

9 oz flaky pastry, well chilled
3 tbsp butter
1 red onion, chopped
1 garlic clove, chopped
1 1/2 oz strong flour
1 1/4 cups milk
1 3/4 oz Parmesan cheese, finely grated, plus extra for sprinkling
2 eggs, hard-cooked, cut into quarters
3 1/2 oz Italian pork sausage, such as salame, cut into strips
salt and pepper
sprigs of fresh thyme, to garnish

1 Fold the sheet of flaky pastry in half and coarsely grate it into 4 individual flan tins, 4 inch across. Using a floured fork, press the pastry flakes down lightly so that they are even, there are no holes, and the pastry comes up the sides of the tin.

2 Line with foil and bake blind in a preheated oven at 425°F for 10 minutes. Reduce the heat to 400°F, remove the foil, and cook for a further 15 minutes or until golden and set.

3 Heat the butter in a pan. Add the onion and garlic and cook for 5–6 minutes or until softened.

4 Add the flour, stirring well to coat the onions. Gradually stir in the milk to make a thick sauce. Season well with salt and pepper and then stir in the Parmesan cheese. Do not reheat once the cheese has been added or the sauce will become stringy.

5 Spread the sauce over the pastry cases. Decorate with the egg and strips of sausage.

6 Sprinkle with a little extra Parmesan cheese, return to the oven and bake for 5 minutes, just to heat through.

7 Serve immediately, garnished with sprigs of fresh thyme.

COOK'S TIP

This pizza is just as good cold, but do not prepare it too far in advance as the pastry will become soggy.

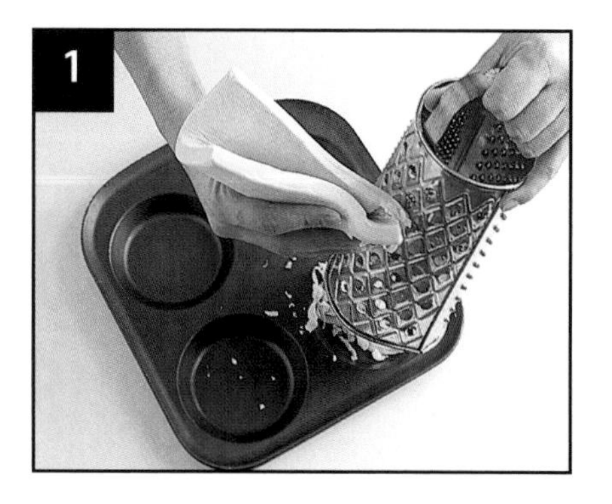
1

1

4

Niçoise with Pasta Shells

This is a more filling variation on the traditional Niçoise salad from southern France.

Serves 4

INGREDIENTS

12 oz dried small pasta shells
1 tbsp olive oil
4 oz French beans
$1^3/_4$ oz can anchovies, drained
$^1/_8$ cup milk
2 small crisp lettuces
1 lb or 3 large beef tomatoes
4 hard-cooked eggs
8 oz can tuna, drained
1 cup pitted black olives
salt and pepper

VINAIGRETTE DRESSING:
2 fl oz extra virgin olive oil
1 fl oz white wine vinegar
1 tsp wholegrain mustard
salt and pepper

1 Bring a large saucepan of lightly salted water to a boil. Add the pasta and the olive oil and cook until tender, but still firm to the bite. Drain and refresh in cold water.

2 Bring a small saucepan of lightly salted water to a boil. Add the beans and cook for 10–12 minutes, until tender but still firm to the bite. Drain, refresh in cold water, drain thoroughly once more, and then set aside.

3 Put the anchovies in a shallow bowl, pour over the milk and set aside for 10 minutes. Meanwhile, tear the lettuces into large pieces. Blanch the tomatoes in boiling water for 1–2 minutes, then drain, skin and roughly chop the flesh. Shell the eggs and cut into quarters. Cut the tuna into large chunks.

4 Drain the anchovies and the pasta. Put all of the salad ingredients, the beans, and the olives into a large bowl and gently mix together.

5 To make the vinaigrette dressing, beat together all the dressing ingredients and keep in the refrigerator until required. Just before serving, pour the vinaigrette dressing over the salad.

COOK'S TIP

It is very convenient to make salad dressings in a screw top jar. Put all the ingredients in the jar, cover securely and shake well to mix and emulsify the oil.

3

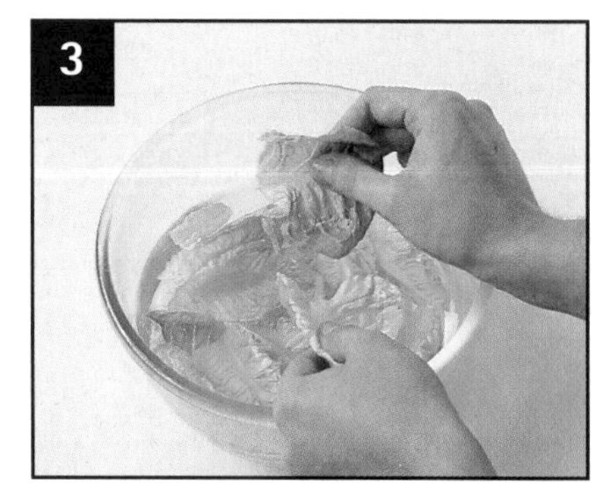

3

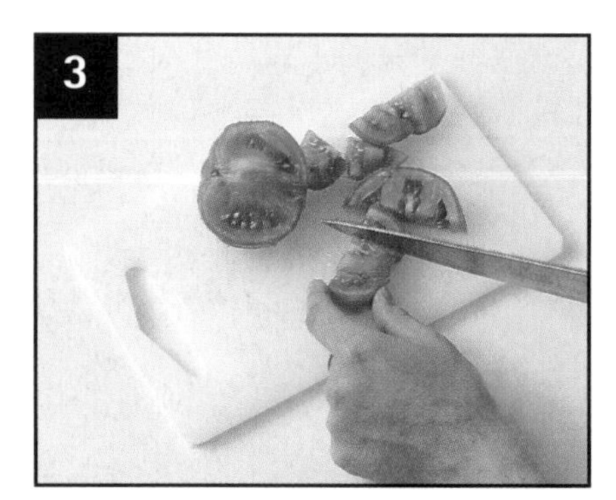

3

Chili & Bell Pepper Pasta Salad

This roasted bell pepper and chili sauce is sweet and spicy.

Serves 4

INGREDIENTS

2 red bell peppers, halved and seeded
1 small red chili
2 garlic cloves
4 tomatoes, halved
$1\,^3/_4$ oz ground almonds
7 tbsp olive oil
$1\,^1/_2$ lb fresh pasta or 12 oz dried pasta
fresh oregano leaves, to garnish

1 Place the bell peppers, skin-side up, on a cookie sheet with the chili and garlic. Cook under a preheated broiler for 15 minutes or until charred. After 10 minutes turn the tomatoes skin-side up.

2 Place the bell peppers and chilies in a plastic bag and leave to sweat for 10 minutes.

3 Remove the skin from the bell peppers and chilies and slice the flesh into strips, using a sharp knife.

4 Peel the garlic and peel and seed the tomatoes.

5 Place the almonds on a cookie sheet and place under the broiler for 2–3 minutes until golden.

6 Using a food processor, blend the bell pepper, chili, garlic, and tomatoes to make a paste. Keep the motor running and slowly add the olive oil to form a thick sauce. Alternatively, mash the mixture with a fork and beat in the olive oil, drop by drop.

7 Stir the toasted ground almonds into the mixture.

8 Warm the sauce in a saucepan until it is heated through.

9 Cook the pasta in a saucepan of boiling water according to the instructions on the packet or until it is cooked through, but still has bite. Drain the pasta and transfer to a serving dish. Pour over the sauce and toss to mix. Garnish with fresh oregano leaves.

VARIATION

Add 2 tablespoons of red wine vinegar to the sauce and use as a dressing for a cold pasta salad, if you wish.

1

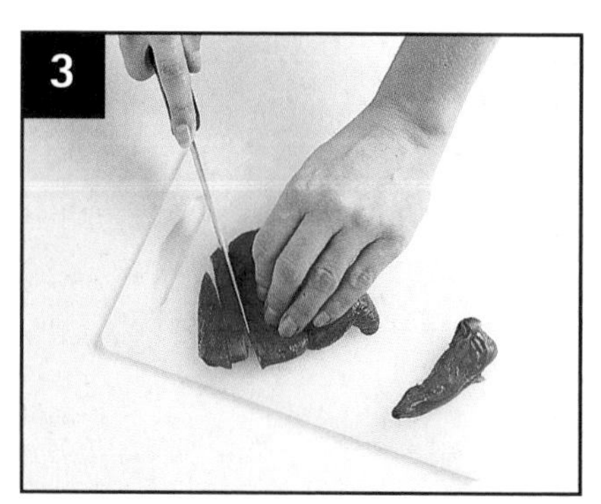
3

5

Pasta Salad with Red & White Cabbage

This crunchy, colorful salad would be a good accompaniment for broiled meat or fish.

Serves 4

INGREDIENTS

2 1/4 cups dried short-cut macaroni
5 tbsp olive oil
1 large red cabbage, shredded
1 large white cabbage, shredded
2 large apples, diced
9 oz cooked smoked bacon or ham, diced
8 tbsp wine vinegar
1 tbsp sugar
salt and pepper

1 Bring a large saucepan of lightly salted water to a boil. Add the macaroni and 1 tbsp of the olive oil and cook until tender, but still firm to the bite. Drain the pasta, then refresh in cold water. Drain the pasta again and set aside.

2 Bring a large saucepan of lightly salted water to a boil. Add the shredded red cabbage and cook for 5 minutes. Drain thoroughly and set aside to cool.

3 Bring a large saucepan of lightly salted water to a boil. Add the white cabbage and cook for 5 minutes. Drain thoroughly and set aside to cool.

4 In a large bowl, mix together the pasta, red cabbage, and apple. In a separate bowl, mix together the white cabbage and bacon or ham.

5 In a small bowl, mix together the remaining oil, the vinegar and sugar and season to taste with salt and pepper. Pour the dressing over each of the 2 cabbage mixtures and, finally, mix them all together. Serve immediately.

VARIATION

Alternative dressings for this salad can be made with 4 tbsp olive oil, 4 tbsp red wine, 4 tbsp red wine vinegar, and 1 tbsp sugar. Or you could substitute 3 tbsp olive oil and 1 tbsp walnut or hazelnut oil for the olive oil.

2

4

5

Goat's Cheese with Penne, Pear, & Walnut Salad

This superb salad was created especially to accompany venison cooked in Chablis, but is equally delicious with other strongly flavored meat dishes.

Serves 4

INGREDIENTS

9 oz dried penne
5 tbsp olive oil
1 head radicchio, torn into pieces
1 Webbs lettuce, torn into pieces
7 tbsp chopped walnuts
2 ripe pears, cored and diced
1 fresh basil sprig
1 bunch of watercress, trimmed
2 tbsp lemon juice
3 tbsp garlic vinegar
4 tomatoes, quartered
1 small onion, sliced
1 large carrot, grated
9 oz goat's cheese, diced
salt and pepper

1 Bring a large saucepan of lightly salted water to a boil. Add the penne and 1 tbsp of the olive oil and cook until tender, but still firm to the bite. Drain the pasta, refresh under cold running water, drain thoroughly again and set aside to cool.

2 Place the radicchio and Webbs lettuce in a large salad bowl and mix together well. Top with the pasta, walnuts, pears, basil, and watercress.

3 Mix together the lemon juice, the remaining olive oil, and the vinegar in a measuring pitcher. Pour the mixture over the salad ingredients and toss to coat the salad leaves well.

4 Add the tomato quarters, onion slices, grated carrot, and diced goat's cheese and toss together, using 2 forks, until well mixed. Leave the salad to chill in the refrigerator for about 1 hour before serving.

COOK'S TIP

Most goat's cheese comes from France and there are many varieties, such as Crottin de Chavignol, Chabi, which is very pungent, and Sainte-Maure, which is available in creamery and farmhouse varieties.

2

2

3

Beet Cannolicchi

Quick and simple, this colorful, warm salad works equally well as a tasty starter or as a main dish.

Serves 4

INGREDIENTS

11 oz dried ditalini rigati
5 tbsp olive oil
2 garlic cloves, chopped
14 oz can chopped tomatoes
14 oz cooked beet, diced
2 tbsp chopped fresh basil leaves
1 tsp mustard seeds
salt and pepper

TO SERVE:
mixed salad greens, tossed in olive oil
4 Italian plum tomatoes, sliced

1 Bring a large saucepan of lightly salted water to a boil. Add the pasta and 1 tbsp of the oil and cook for about 10 minutes, until tender, but still firm to the bite. Drain the pasta thoroughly and set aside.

2 Heat the remaining olive oil in a large saucepan. Add the garlic and fry for 3 minutes. Add the chopped tomatoes and cook for 10 minutes.

3 Remove the pan from the heat and carefully add the beet, basil, mustard seeds, and pasta and season to taste with salt and black pepper.

4 Serve on a bed of mixed salad greens tossed in olive oil, and sliced plum tomatoes.

COOK'S TIP

To cook raw beet, trim off the leaves about 2 inches above the root and ensure that the skin is not broken. Boil in very lightly salted water for 30–40 minutes, until tender. Leave to cool and rub off the skin.

COOK'S TIP

Mustard seeds come from three different plants and may be black, brown, or white. Black and brown mustard seeds have a stronger, more pungent flavor than white mustard.

2

2

3

Fusilli, Avocado, Tomato, & Mozzarella Salad

Tomatoes and mozzarella cheese are a classic Italian combination. Here they are joined with pasta spirals and avocado pear for an extra touch of luxury.

Serves 4

INGREDIENTS

2 tbsp pine kernels
$1^1/_2$ cups dried fusilli
1 tbsp olive oil
6 tomatoes
8 oz mozzarella cheese
1 large avocado pear
2 tbsp lemon juice
3 tbsp chopped fresh basil
salt and pepper
fresh basil sprigs, to garnish

DRESSING:
6 tbsp extra virgin olive oil
2 tbsp white wine vinegar
1 tsp wholegrain mustard
pinch of sugar

1 Spread the pine kernels out on a cookie sheet and toast under a preheated broiler for 1–2 minutes. Remove and set aside to cool.

2 Bring a large saucepan of lightly salted water to a boil. Add the fusilli and olive oil and cook until tender, but still firm to the bite. Drain the pasta and refresh in cold water. Drain again and set aside to cool.

3 Thinly slice the tomatoes and the mozzarella cheese.

4 Cut the avocado pear in half, remove the pit and skin. Cut into thin slices lengthways and sprinkle with lemon juice to prevent discoloration.

5 To make the dressing, whisk together the oil, vinegar, mustard, and sugar in a small bowl, and season to taste with salt and black pepper.

6 Arrange the tomatoes, mozzarella cheese, and avocado pear alternately in overlapping slices on a platter.

7 Toss the pasta with half of the dressing and the chopped basil and season to taste with salt and black pepper. Spoon the pasta into the center of the platter and pour over the remaining dressing. Sprinkle over the pine kernels, garnish with fresh basil sprigs, and serve immediately.

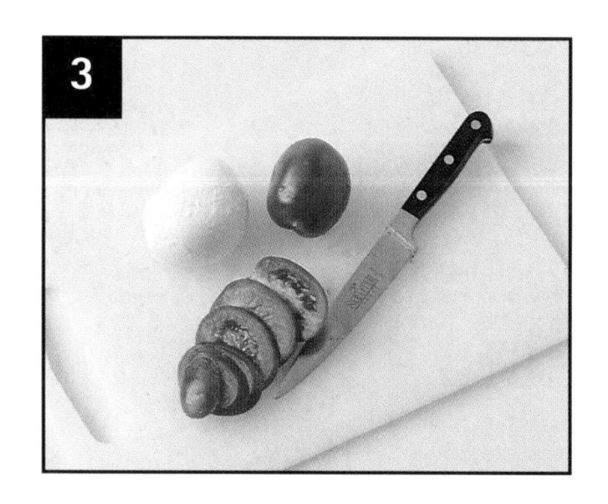
3

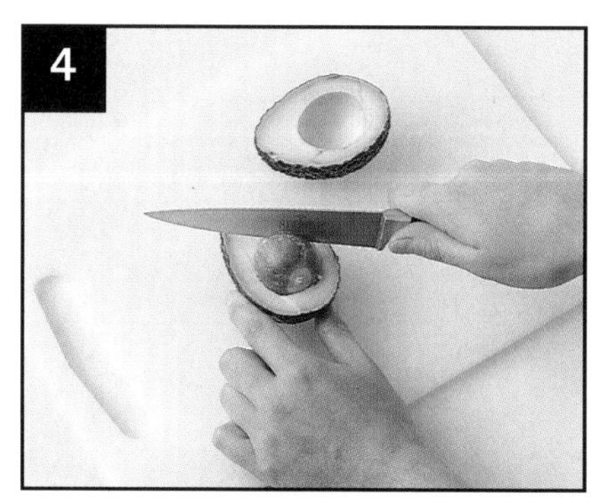
4

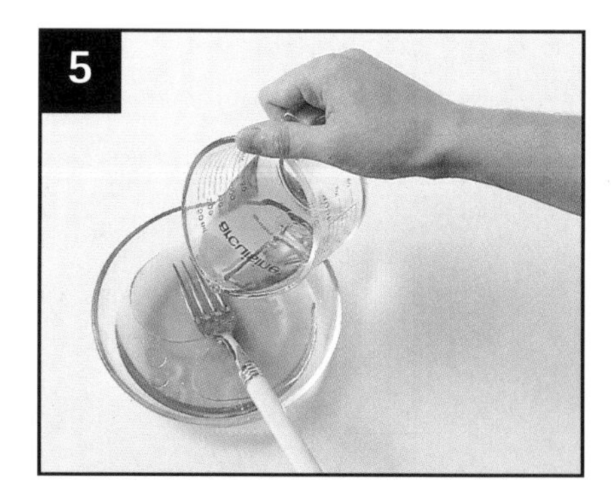
5

Pasta & Garlic Mayo Salad

This crisp salad would make an excellent accompaniment to broiled meat and is ideal for summer barbecues.

Serves 4

INGREDIENTS

2 large lettuces
9 oz dried penne
1 tbsp olive oil
8 red eating apples
juice of 4 lemons
1 head of celery, sliced
3/4 cup shelled, halved walnuts
1 1/8 cups fresh garlic mayonnaise (see Cook's Tip, below right)
salt

1 Wash, drain, and pat dry the lettuce leaves with paper towels. Transfer them to the refrigerator for 1 hour until crisp.

2 Meanwhile, bring a large saucepan of lightly salted water to a boil. Add the pasta and olive oil and cook until tender, but still firm to the bite. Drain the pasta and refresh under cold running water. Drain thoroughly again and set aside.

3 Core and dice the apples, place them in a small bowl and sprinkle with the lemon juice. Mix together the pasta, celery, apples, and walnuts and toss the mixture in the garlic mayonnaise (see Cook's Tip, right). Add more mayonnaise, if liked.

4 Line a salad bowl with the lettuce leaves and spoon the pasta salad into the lined bowl. Serve when required.

COOK'S TIP

Sprinkling the apples with lemon juice will prevent them from turning brown.

COOK'S TIP

To make homemade garlic mayonnaise, beat 2 egg yolks with a pinch of salt and 6 minced garlic cloves. Start beating in 1½ cups olive oil, 1–2 tsp at a time, using a balloon whisk or electric mixer. When about one quarter of the oil has been incorporated, beat in 1–2 tbsp white wine vinegar. Continue beating in the oil, adding it in a thin, continuous stream. Finally, stir in 1 tsp Dijon mustard and season to taste with salt and pepper.

1

3

3

Dolcelatte, Nut, & Pasta Salad

Use colorful salad greens to provide visual contrast to match the contrasts of taste and texture.

Serves 4

INGREDIENTS

2 cups dried pasta shells
1 tbsp olive oil
1 cup shelled and halved walnuts
mixed salad greens, such as radicchio, escarole, arugula, corn salad, and frisée
8 oz dolcelatte cheese, crumbled
salt

DRESSING:
2 tbsp walnut oil
4 tbsp extra virgin olive oil
2 tbsp red wine vinegar
salt and pepper

1 Bring a large saucepan of lightly salted water to a boil. Add the pasta shells and olive oil and cook until just tender, but still firm to the bite. Drain the pasta, refresh under cold running water, drain thoroughly again and set aside.

2 Spread out the shelled walnut halves on to a cookie sheet and toast under a preheated broiler for 2–3 minutes. Set aside to cool while you make the dressing.

3 To make the dressing, whisk together the walnut oil, olive oil, and vinegar in a small bowl, and season to taste with salt and black pepper.

4 Arrange the salad greens in a large serving bowl. Pile the cooled pasta in the middle of the salad greens and sprinkle over the dolcelatte cheese. Pour the dressing over the pasta salad, scatter over the walnut halves, and toss together to mix. Serve immediately.

COOK'S TIP

Dolcelatte is a semi-soft, blue-veined cheese from Italy. Its texture is creamy and smooth and the flavor is delicate, but piquant. You could substitute Roquefort as an alternative. Whichever cheese you choose, it is essential that it is of the best quality and in peak condition.

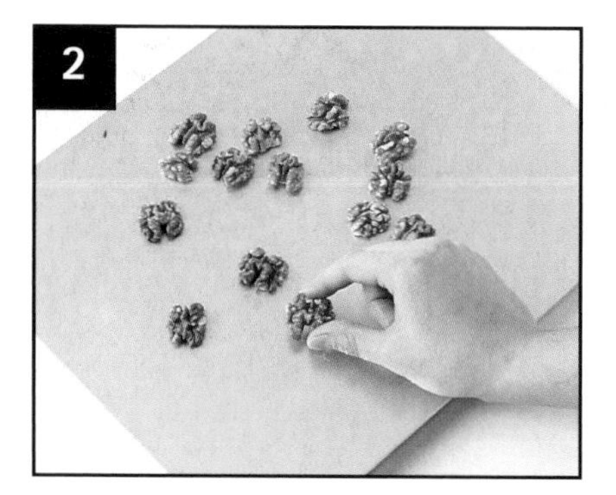

Pasta-Stuffed Tomatoes

This unusual and inexpensive dish would make a good starter for eight people or a delicious lunch for four.

Serves 4

INGREDIENTS

5 tbsp extra virgin olive oil, plus extra for greasing
8 beef tomatoes or large round tomatoes
1 cup dried ditalini or other very small pasta shapes
8 black olives, pitted and finely chopped
2 tbsp finely chopped fresh basil
1 tbsp finely chopped fresh parsley
2/3 cup freshly grated Parmesan cheese
salt and pepper
fresh basil sprigs, to garnish

1 Brush a cookie sheet with olive oil.

2 Slice the tops off the tomatoes and reserve to make lids. If the tomatoes will not stand up, cut a thin slice off the bottom of each tomato.

3 Using a teaspoon, scoop out the tomato pulp into a strainer, but do not pierce the tomato shells. Invert the tomato shells on to paper towels, pat dry, and then set aside to drain.

4 Bring a large saucepan of lightly salted water to a boil. Add the ditalini or other pasta and 1 tbsp of the remaining olive oil and cook until tender, but still firm to the bite. Drain the pasta thoroughly and set aside.

5 Put the olives, chopped basil, parsley, and Parmesan cheese into a large mixing bowl and stir in the drained tomato pulp. Add the pasta to the bowl. Stir in the remaining olive oil, mix together well, and season to taste with salt and pepper.

6 Spoon the pasta mixture into the tomato shells and replace the lids. Arrange the tomatoes on the cookie sheet and bake in a preheated oven at 375°F for 15–20 minutes.

7 Remove the tomatoes from the oven and allow to cool until just warm. Arrange on a serving dish, garnish with the basil sprigs, and serve.

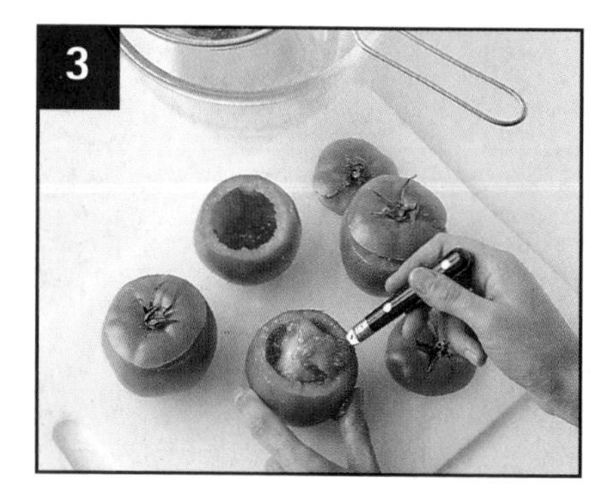
3

5

6

Rare Beef Pasta Salad

This salad is a meal in itself and would be perfect for an al fresco *lunch, perhaps with a bottle of red wine.*

Serves 4

INGREDIENTS

1 lb rump or sirloin steak in one piece
1 lb dried fusilli
5 tbsp olive oil
2 tbsp lime juice
2 tbsp Thai fish sauce (see Cook's Tip, below right)
2 tsp honey
4 scallions, sliced
1 cucumber, peeled and cut into 1 inch chunks
3 tomatoes, cut into wedges
3 tsp finely chopped fresh mint
salt and pepper

1 Season the steak with salt and black pepper. Broil or pan-fry the steak for 4 minutes on each side. Allow to rest for 5 minutes, then slice thinly across the grain.

2 Meanwhile, bring a large saucepan of lightly salted water to a boil. Add the fusilli and 1 tbsp of the olive oil and cook until tender, but still firm to the bite. Drain the fusilli, refresh in cold water and drain again thoroughly. Toss the fusilli in the remaining olive oil.

3 Combine the lime juice, fish sauce, and honey in a small saucepan and cook over a medium heat for 2 minutes.

4 Add the scallions, cucumber, tomatoes, and mint to the pan, then add the steak and mix well. Season to taste with salt.

5 Transfer the fusilli to a large, warm serving dish and top with the steak and salad mixture. Serve just warm or allow to cool completely.

COOK'S TIP

Thai fish sauce, also known as nam pla, *is made from salted anchovies and has quite a strong flavor, so it should be used with discretion. It is available from some supermarkets and from Oriental food stores.*

1

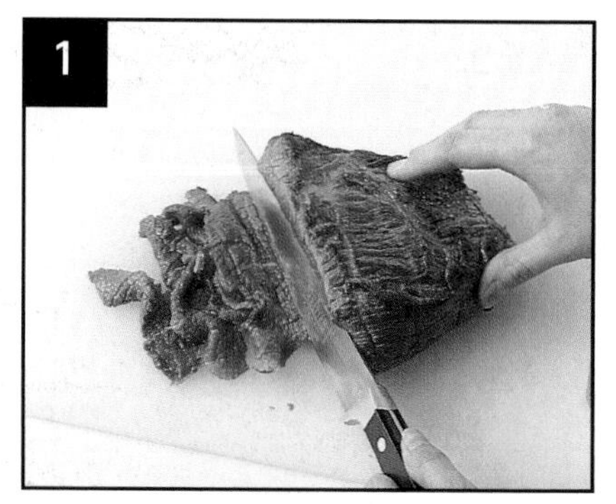
1

3

Neapolitan Seafood Salad with Campanelle

This delicious mix of seafood, salad greens, and ripe tomatoes conjures up all the warmth and sunshine of Naples.

Serves 4

INGREDIENTS

- 1 lb prepared squid, cut into strips
- 1 lb 10 oz cooked mussels
- 1 lb cooked cockles in brine
- 5/8 cup white wine
- 1 1/4 cups olive oil
- 2 cups dried campanelle or other small pasta shapes
- juice of 1 lemon
- 1 bunch chives, snipped
- 1 bunch fresh parsley, finely chopped
- 4 large tomatoes, quartered or sliced
- mixed salad greens
- salt and pepper
- sprig of fresh basil, to garnish

1 Put all of the seafood into a large bowl, pour over the wine and half the olive oil, and set aside for 6 hours.

2 Put the seafood mixture into a saucepan and simmer over a low heat for 10 minutes. Set aside to cool.

3 Bring a large saucepan of lightly salted water to a boil. Add the pasta and 1 tbsp of the remaining olive oil and cook until tender, but still firm to the bite. Drain thoroughly and refresh in cold water.

4 Strain off about half of the cooking liquid from the seafood and discard the rest. Mix in the lemon juice, chives, parsley, and the remaining olive oil. Season to taste with salt and pepper. Drain the pasta and add to the seafood.

5 Cut the tomatoes into quarters. Shred the salad greens and arrange them at the base of a salad bowl. Spoon in the seafood salad and garnish with the quartered or sliced tomatoes and a sprig of basil.

VARIATION

You can substitute cooked scallops for the mussels and clams in brine for the cockles.

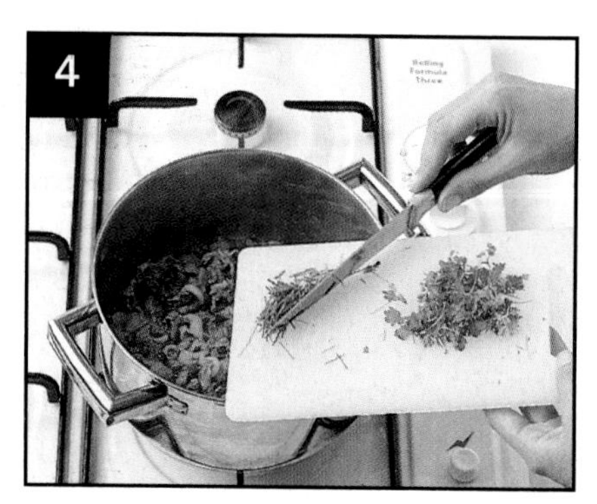

Pasta & Herring Salad

This salad, which so many countries claim as their own, is also considered in Holland to be a typically Dutch dish.

Serves 4

INGREDIENTS

9 oz dried pasta shells
5 tbsp olive oil
14 oz rollmop herrings in brine
6 boiled potatoes
2 large tart apples
2 baby frisée lettuces
2 baby beet
4 hard-cooked eggs
6 pickled onions
6 dill pickles
2 tbsp capers
3 tbsp of tarragon vinegar
salt and pepper

1 Bring a large saucepan of lightly salted water to a boil. Add the pasta and 1 tbsp of the olive oil and cook until tender, but still firm to the bite. Drain the pasta thoroughly and then refresh in cold water.

2 Cut the herrings, potatoes, apples, frisée lettuces, and beet into small pieces. Put all of these ingredients into a large salad bowl.

3 Drain the pasta thoroughly and add to the salad bowl. Toss lightly to mix the pasta and herring mixture together.

4 Carefully shell and slice the eggs. Garnish the salad with the slices of egg, pickled onions, dill pickles, and capers, sprinkle with the remaining olive oil and the tarragon vinegar and serve immediately.

COOK'S TIP

Store this salad, without the dressing, in a container in the refrigerator.

COOK'S TIP

Tarragon vinegar is available from most supermarkets, but you can easily make your own. Add a bunch of fresh tarragon to a bottle of white or red wine vinegar and leave to infuse for 48 hours. It is important to ensure that the tarragon is as fresh as possible and to discard any blemished leaves.

2

2

3

Desserts

If when you think about cooking with pasta, desserts do not usually spring to the forefront of your mind, you will be amazed by the wonderfully self-indulgent sweet pasta treats in this chapter.

The Italians love their desserts, but when there is a special gathering or celebration, then a special effort is made and the delicacies appear. The Sicilians are said to have the sweetest tooth of all, and many Italian desserts are thought to have originated there. You have to go a very long way to beat a Sicilian ice cream – they truly are the best in the world!

Fresh fruit also features in many Italian desserts – oranges are often peeled and served whole, marinated in a fragrant syrup and liqueur. Chocolate, too, is popular in Italy – sample the all-time favorite Tiramisu for a deliciously wicked end to a meal. Whatever your preference, there is sure to be an Italian dessert to tempt and satisfy you – you'll never be disappointed!

Peaches with Creamy Mascarpone Filling

If you prepare these in advance, all you have to do is pop the peaches on the grill when you are ready to serve them.

Serves 4

INGREDIENTS

4 peaches
6 oz mascarpone cheese
$1^1/_2$ oz pecan or walnuts, chopped
1 tsp sunflower oil
4 tbsp maple syrup

1 Cut the peaches in half and remove the pits. If you are preparing this recipe in advance, press the peach halves together again and wrap them in plastic wrap until required.

2 Mix the mascarpone and pecan or walnuts together in a small bowl until well combined. Leave to chill in the refrigerator until required.

3 To serve, brush the peaches with a little oil and place on a rack set over medium hot coals. Grill the peach halves for 5–10 minutes, turning once, until hot.

4 Transfer the peach halves to a serving dish and top with the mascarpone and nut mixture.

5 Drizzle the maple syrup over the peaches and mascarpone filling and serve at once.

VARIATION

You can use nectarines instead of peaches for this recipe, if you prefer. Remember to choose ripe but fairly firm fruit which won't go soft and mushy when it is grilled. Prepare the nectarines in the same way as the peaches and grill for 5–10 minutes.

COOK'S TIP

Mascarpone cheese is high in fat, so if you are following a low-fat diet, use thick natural yogurt instead.

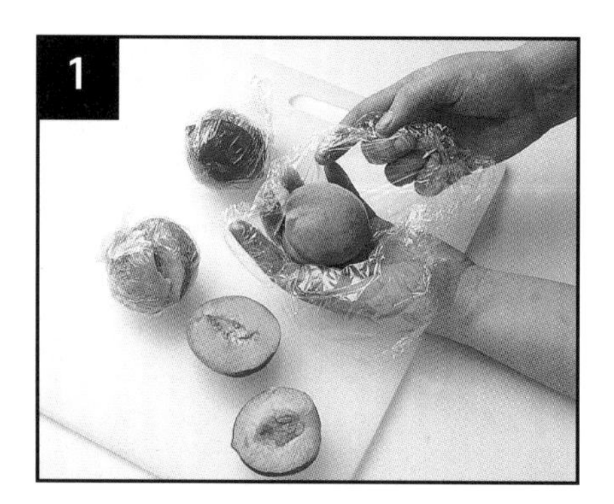

Granita

A delightful end to a meal or a refreshing way to cleanse the palate between courses, granitas are made from slushy ice rather than frozen solid, so they need to be served very quickly.

Serves 4

INGREDIENTS

LEMON GRANITA:
3 lemons
3/4 cup lemon juice
3 1/2 oz superfine sugar
2 1/4 cups cold water

COFFEE GRANITA:
2 tbsp instant coffee
2 tbsp sugar
2 tbsp hot water
2 1/2 cups cold water
2 tbsp rum or brandy

1 To make lemon granita, finely grate the lemon peel. Place the lemon peel, juice, and superfine sugar in a pan. Bring the mixture to the boil and leave to simmer for 5–6 minutes or until thick and syrupy. Leave to cool.

2 Once cooled, stir in the cold water and pour into a shallow freezer container with a lid. Freeze for 4–5 hours, stirring occasionally to break up the ice. Serve as a palate cleanser between dinner courses.

3 To make coffee granita, place the coffee and sugar in a bowl and pour over the hot water, stirring until dissolved.

4 Stir in the cold water and rum or brandy.

5 Pour the mixture into a shallow freezer container with a lid. Freeze the granita for at least 6 hours, stirring every 1–2 hours in order to create a grainy texture. Serve with cream after dinner, if you wish.

COOK'S TIP

If you would prefer a non-alcoholic version of the coffee granita, simply omit the rum or brandy and add extra instant coffee instead.

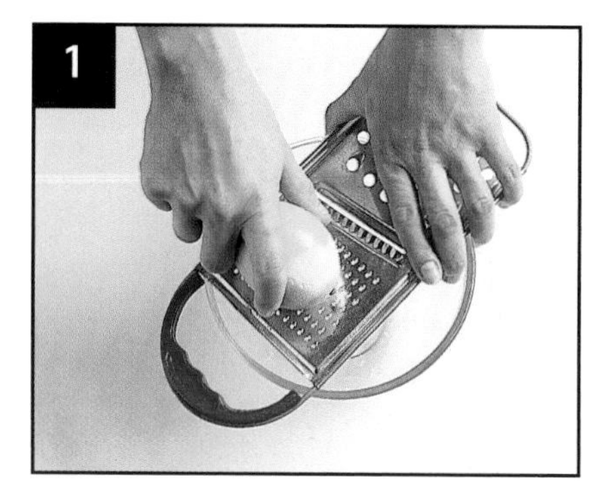

1

1

2

Vanilla Ice Cream

Italy is synonymous with ice cream. This home-made version of real vanilla ice cream is absolutely delicious and so easy to make.

Serves 4–6

INGREDIENTS

$2^1/_2$ cups heavy cream
1 vanilla pod
pared peel of 1 lemon
4 eggs, beaten
2 egg, yolks
6 oz superfine sugar

1 Place the cream in a heavy-based saucepan and heat gently, whisking. Add the vanilla pod, lemon peel, eggs, and egg yolks and heat until the mixture reaches just below boiling point.

2 Reduce the heat and cook for 8–10 minutes, whisking the mixture continuously, until thickened.

3 Stir the sugar into the cream mixture, set aside and leave to cool.

4 Strain the cream mixture through a sieve.

5 Slit open the vanilla pod, scoop out the tiny black seeds and stir them into the cream.

6 Pour the mixture into a shallow freezing container with a lid and freeze overnight until set. Serve when required.

COOK'S TIP

Ice cream is one of the traditional dishes of Italy. Everyone eats it and there are numerous gelato *stalls selling a wide variety of flavors, usually in a cone. It is also serve in scoops, and even sliced!*

COOK'S TIP

To make tutti frutti ice cream, soak $3^1/_2$ oz mixed dried fruit, such as golden raisins, cherries, apricots, candied peel, and pineapple, in 2 tablespoons of Marsala wine or sweet sherry for 20 minutes. Follow the method for vanilla ice cream, omitting the vanilla pod, and stir in the Marsala or sherry-soaked fruit in step 5, just before freezing.

1

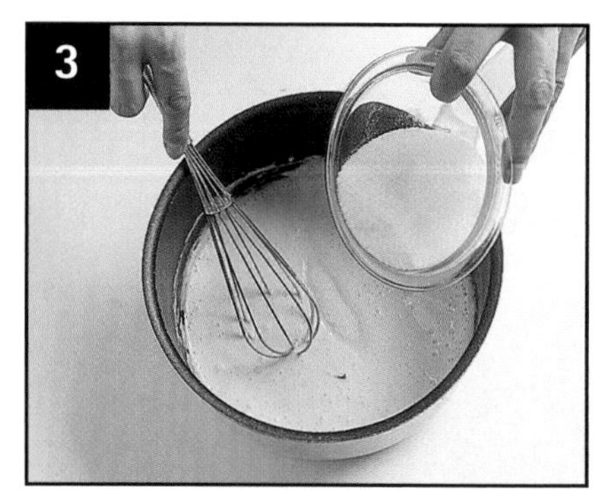
3

5

Peaches in White Wine

A very simple but incredibly pleasing dessert, which is especially good for a dinner party on a hot summer day.

Serves 4

INGREDIENTS

4 large ripe peaches
2 tbsp confectioners' sugar, sifted
pared peel and juice of 1 orange
3/4 cup medium or sweet white wine, chilled

1 Using a sharp knife, halve the peaches, remove the pits, and discard them. Peel the peaches, if you prefer. Slice the peaches into thin wedges.

2 Place the peach wedges in a glass serving bowl and sprinkle over the sugar.

3 Using a sharp knife, pare the peel from the orange. Cut the orange peel into matchsticks, place them in a bowl of cold water and set aside.

4 Squeeze the juice from the orange and pour over the peaches together with the wine.

5 Leave the peaches to marinate and chill in the refrigerator for at least 1 hour.

6 Remove the orange peel from the cold water and pat dry with paper towels.

7 Garnish the peaches with the strips of orange peel and serve immediately.

COOK'S TIP

There is absolutely no need to use expensive wine in this recipe, so it can be quite economical to make.

COOK'S TIP

The best way to pare the peel thinly from citrus fruits is to use a potato peeler.

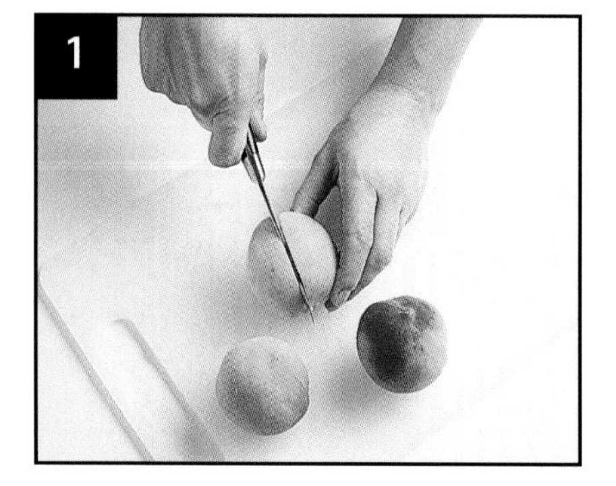

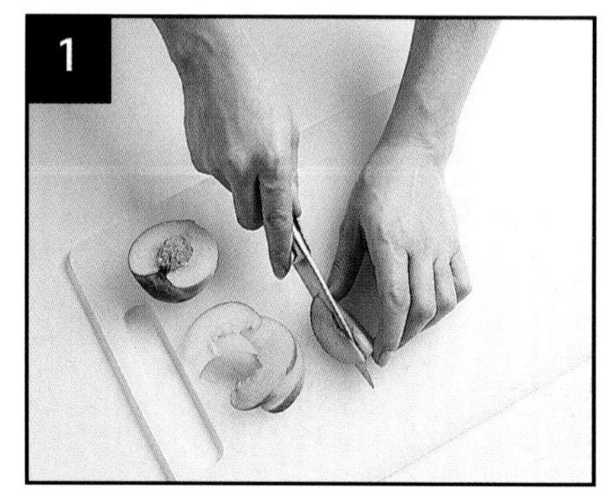

Sicilian Orange & Almond Cake

This is a light and tangy citrus cake better eaten as a dessert than as a cake. It is especially good served after a large meal.

Serves 8

INGREDIENTS

- 4 eggs, separated
- 4½ oz superfine sugar, plus 2 tsp for the cream
- finely grated peel and juice of 2 oranges
- finely grated peel and juice of 1 lemon
- 4½ oz ground almonds
- 1 oz self-rising flour
- ¾ cup light cream
- 1 tsp cinnamon
- 1 oz slivered almonds, toasted
- confectioners' sugar, to dust

1 Grease and line the base of a 7 inch round deep cake pan.

2 Blend the egg yolks with the sugar until the mixture is thick and creamy. Whisk half of the orange peel and all of the lemon peel into the egg yolks.

3 Mix the juice from both oranges and the lemon with the ground almonds and stir into the egg yolks. The mixture will become quite runny at this point. Fold in the flour.

4 Whisk the egg whites until stiff and gently fold into the egg yolk mixture.

5 Pour the mixture into the pan and bake in a preheated oven, at 350°F, for 35–40 minutes, until golden and springy to the touch. Leave to cool in the pan for 10 minutes and then turn out. It is likely to sink slightly at this stage.

6 Whip the cream to form soft peaks. Stir in the remaining orange peel, cinnamon, and sugar.

7 Once the cake is cold, cover with the toasted almonds, dust with confectioners' sugar, and serve with the cream.

VARIATION

You could serve this cake with a syrup. Boil the juice and finely grated peel of 2 oranges, 2¾ oz superfine sugar, and 2 tbsp of water for 5–6 minutes until slightly thickened. Stir in 1 tbsp of orange liqueur just before serving.

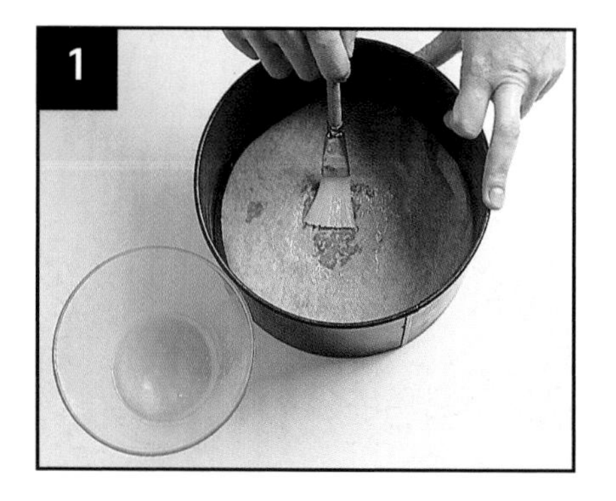

Tuscan Pudding

These baked mini-ricotta puddings are delicious served warm or chilled and will keep in the refrigerator for 3–4 days.

Serves 4

INGREDIENTS

1 tbsp butter
$2^3/_4$ oz mixed dried fruit
9 oz ricotta cheese
3 egg yolks
$1^3/_4$ oz superfine sugar
1 tsp cinnamon
finely grated peel of 1 orange, plus extra to decorate
soured cream, to serve

1 Lightly grease 4 mini pudding basins or ramekin dishes with the butter.

2 Put the dried fruit in a bowl and cover with warm water. Leave to soak for 10 minutes.

3 Beat the ricotta cheese with the egg yolks in a bowl. Stir in the superfine sugar, cinnamon, and orange peel, and mix to combine.

4 Drain the dried fruit in a sieve set over a bowl. Mix the drained fruit with the ricotta cheese mixture.

5 Spoon the mixture into the basins or ramekin dishes.

6 Bake in a preheated oven, at 350°F, for 15 minutes. The tops should be firm to the touch but not brown.

7 Decorate the puddings with grated orange peel. Serve warm or chilled with a dollop of soured cream.

VARIATION

Use the dried fruit of your choice for this delicious recipe.

COOK'S TIP

Soured cream has a slightly sour, nutty taste and is very thick. It is suitable for cooking, but has the same fat content as heavy cream. It can be made by stirring cultured buttermilk into heavy cream and refrigerating overnight.

1

3

4

Tiramisu

This is a traditional chocolate dessert from Italy, although at one time it was known as Zuppa Inglese *because it was a favorite with the English society living in Florence in the 1800s.*

Serves 6

INGREDIENTS

- $10^1/_2$ oz dark chocolate
- 14 oz mascarpone cheese
- $^2/_3$ cup heavy cream, whipped until it just holds its shape
- 14 fl oz black coffee with $1^3/_4$ oz superfine sugar, cooled
- 6 tbsp dark rum or brandy
- 36 lady-fingers, about 14 oz
- cocoa powder, to dust

1 Melt the chocolate in a bowl set over a saucepan of simmering water, stirring occasionally. Leave the chocolate to cool slightly, then stir it into the mascarpone and cream.

2 Mix the coffee and rum together in a bowl. Dip the lady-fingers into the mixture briefly so that they absorb the liquid but do not become soggy.

3 Place 3 lady-fingers on 3 serving plates.

4 Spoon a layer of the mascarpone and chocolate mixture over the lady-fingers.

5 Place 3 more lady-fingers on top of the mascarpone layer. Spread a layer of mascarpone and chocolate mixture and place 3 more lady-fingers on top.

6 Leave the tiramisu to chill in the refrigerator for at least 1 hour. Dust with a little cocoa powder just before serving.

COOK'S TIP

Tiramisu can also be served semi-frozen, like ice-cream. Freeze the tiramisu for 2 hours and serve immediately as it defrosts very quickly.

VARIATION

Try adding $1^3/_4$ oz toasted, chopped hazelnuts to the chocolate cream mixture in step 1, if you prefer.

1

1

2

Lemon Mascarpone Cheesecake

The mascarpone gives this baked cheesecake a wonderfully tangy flavor.

Serves 8

INGREDIENTS

- 1½ tbsp unsalted butter
- 5½ oz ginger cookies, crushed
- 1 oz candied ginger, chopped
- 1 lb 2 oz mascarpone cheese
- finely grated peel and juice of 2 lemons
- 3½ oz superfine sugar
- 2 large eggs, separated
- fruit coulis (see Cook's Tip), to serve

1 Grease and line the base of a 10 inch spring-form cake pan or loose-bottomed pan.

2 Melt the butter in a pan and stir in the crushed cookies and chopped ginger. Use the mixture to line the pan, pressing the mixture about ¼ inch up the sides.

3 Beat together the cheese, lemon peel and juice, sugar, and egg yolks until smooth.

4 Whisk the egg whites until they are stiff and fold into the cheese and lemon mixture.

5 Pour the mixture into the pan and bake in a preheated oven, at 350°F, for 35–45 minutes until just set. Don't worry if it cracks or sinks – this is quite normal.

6 Leave the cheesecake in the pan to cool. Serve with fruit coulis (see Cook's Tip).

VARIATION

Ricotta cheese can be used instead of the mascarpone to make an equally delicious cheesecake. However, it should be strained before use to remove any lumps.

COOK'S TIP

Fruit coulis can be made by cooking 14 oz fruit, such as blueberries, for 5 minutes with 2 tablespoons of water. Sift the mixture, then stir in 1 tablespoon (or more to taste) of sifted confectioners' sugar. Leave to cool before serving.

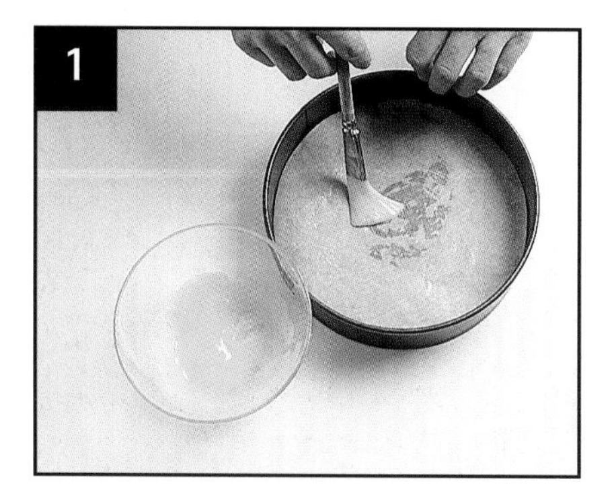
1

2

2

Sweet Mascarpone Mousse

A sweet cream cheese dessert that complements the tartness of fresh summer fruits rather well.

Serves 4

INGREDIENTS

1 lb mascarpone cheese
3½ oz superfine sugar
4 egg yolks
14 oz frozen summer fruits, such as raspberries and redcurrants
redcurrants, to garnish
amaretti cookies, to serve

1 Place the mascarpone cheese in a large mixing bowl. Using a wooden spoon, beat the mascarpone cheese until smooth.

2 Stir the egg yolks and sugar into the mascarpone cheese, mixing well. Leave the mixture to chill in the refrigerator for about 1 hour.

3 Spoon a layer of the mascarpone mixture into the bottom of 4 individual serving dishes. Spoon a layer of the summer fruits on top. Repeat the layers in the same order, reserving some of the mascarpone mixture for the top.

4 Leave the mousses to chill in the refrigerator for about 20 minutes. The fruits should still be slightly frozen.

5 Serve the mascarpone mousses with amaretti cookies.

COOK'S TIP

Mascarpone (sometimes spelled mascherpone*) is a soft, creamy cheese from Italy. It is becoming increasingly more available, and you should have no difficulty finding cartons in your local supermarket, or Italian delicatessen.*

VARIATION

Try adding 3 tablespoons of your favorite liqueur to the mascarpone cheese mixture in step 1, if you prefer.

1

2

2

Zabaglione

This well-known dish is really a light but rich egg mousse flavored with Marsala.

Serves 4

INGREDIENTS

5 egg yolks
3½ oz superfine sugar
⅔ cup Marsala wine or sweet sherry
amaretti cookies, to serve (optional)

1 Place the egg yolks in a large mixing bowl.

2 Add the superfine sugar to the egg yolks and whisk until the mixture is thick and very pale and has doubled in volume.

3 Place the bowl containing the egg yolk and sugar mixture over a saucepan of simmering water.

4 Add the Marsala wine or sherry to the egg yolk and sugar mixture and continue whisking until the foam mixture becomes warm. This process may take as long as 10 minutes.

5 Pour the mixture, which should be frothy and light, into 4 wine glasses.

6 Serve the zabaglione warm with fresh fruit or amaretti cookies, if you wish.

VARIATION

Iced or Semifreddo Zabaglione *can be made by following the method here, then continuing to whisk the foam while standing the bowl in cold water. Beat ⅔ cup light cream until it just holds its shape. Fold into the foam and freeze for about 2 hours, until just frozen.*

VARIATION

Any other type of liqueur may be used instead of the Marsala wine or sweet sherry, if you prefer. Serve soft fruits, such as strawberries or raspberries, with the zabaglione – it's a delicious combination!

Italian Bread Pudding

This deliciously rich pudding is cooked with cream and apples and is delicately flavored with orange.

Serves 4

INGREDIENTS

1 tbsp butter
2 small eating apples, peeled, cored and sliced into rings
$2^3/_4$ oz granulated sugar
2 tbsp white wine
$3^1/_2$ oz bread, sliced with crusts removed (slightly stale French baguette is ideal)
$1^1/_4$ cups light cream
2 eggs, beaten
pared peel of 1 orange, cut into matchsticks

1 Lightly grease a 2 pint deep ovenproof dish with the butter.

2 Arrange the apple rings in the base of the dish. Sprinkle half of the sugar over the apples.

3 Pour the wine over the apple slices. Add the slices of bread, pushing them down with your hands to flatten them slightly.

4 Mix the cream with the eggs, the remaining sugar, and the orange peel and pour the mixture over the bread. Leave to soak for 30 minutes.

5 Bake the pudding in a preheated oven, at 350°F, for 25 minutes until golden and set. Serve warm.

COOK'S TIP

Light cream is the type of cream most commonly used for cooking. However, this type of cream should not be boiled as it will curdle. Also, always add hot liquids to the cream rather than the cream to the liquids, in order to avoid curdling. Light cream has an 18 percent fat content.

VARIATION

For a variation, try adding dried fruit, such as apricots, cherries, or dates, to the pudding, if you prefer.

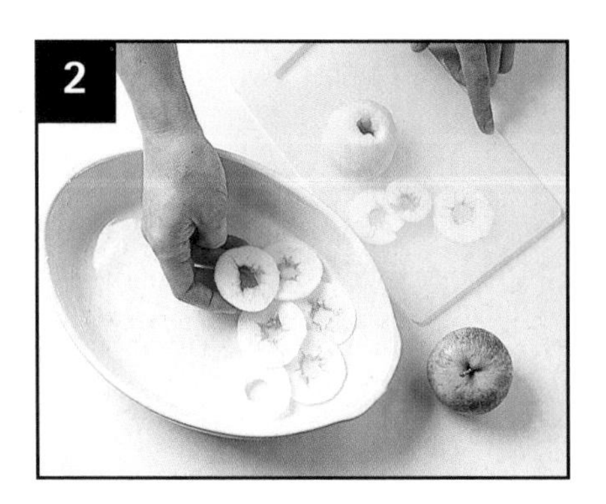
2

3

3

Raspberry Fusilli

This is the ultimate in self-indulgence - a truly delicious dessert that tastes every bit as good as it looks.

Serves 4

INGREDIENTS

$^{1}/_{2}$ cup fusilli
4 cups raspberries
2 tbsp superfine sugar
1 tbsp lemon juice
4 tbsp slivered almonds
3 tbsp raspberry liqueur

1 Bring a large pan of lightly salted water to the boil. Add the fusilli and cook until tender, but still firm to the bite. Drain the fusilli thoroughly, return to the pan and set aside to cool.

2 Using a spoon, firmly press $1^{1}/_{3}$ cups of the raspberries through a strainer set over a large mixing bowl to form a smooth paste.

3 Put the raspberry paste and sugar in a small saucepan and simmer over a low heat, stirring occasionally, for 5 minutes. Stir in the lemon juice and set the sauce aside until required.

4 Add the remaining raspberries to the fusilli in the pan and mix together well. Transfer the raspberry and fusilli mixture to a serving dish.

5 Spread the almonds out on a cookie sheet and toast under the broiler until golden brown. Remove and set aside to cool slightly.

6 Stir the raspberry liqueur into the reserved raspberry sauce and mix together well until very smooth. Pour the raspberry sauce over the fusilli, generously sprinkle over the toasted almonds and serve.

VARIATION

You could use almost any sweet, really ripe berry for making this dessert. Strawberries and blackberries are especially suitable, combined with the correspondingly flavored liqueur. Alternatively, you could use a different berry mixed with the fusilli, but still pour over raspberry sauce.

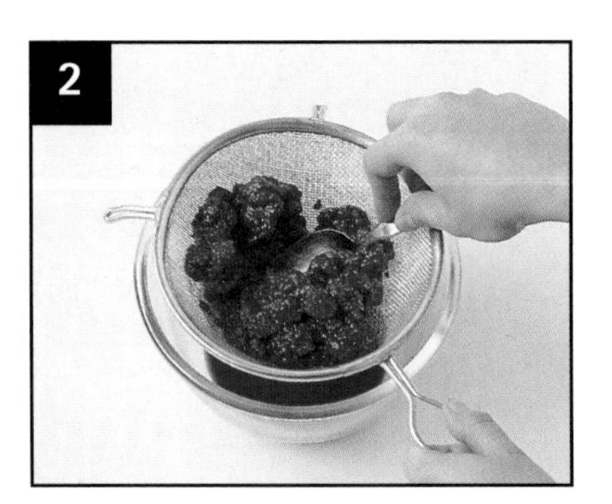

Honey & Walnut Nests

Pistachio nuts and honey are combined with crisp cooked angel hair pasta in this unusual Greek dessert.

Serves 4

INGREDIENTS

8 oz angel hair pasta
8 tbsp butter
1 1/2 cups shelled pistachio nuts, chopped
1/2 cup sugar
1/3 cup honey
5/8 cup water
2 tsp lemon juice
salt
Greek-style yogurt, to serve

1 Bring a large saucepan of lightly salted water to a boil. Add the angel hair pasta and cook until tender, but still firm to the bite. Drain the pasta and return to the pan. Add the butter and toss to coat the pasta thoroughly. Set aside to cool.

2 Arrange 4 small flan or poaching rings on a cookie sheet. Divide the angel hair pasta into 8 equal quantities and spoon 4 of them into the rings. Press down lightly. Top the pasta with half of the nuts, then add the remaining pasta.

3 Bake in a preheated oven at 350°F for 45 minutes, until golden brown.

4 Meanwhile, put the sugar, honey and water in a saucepan and bring to the boil over a low heat, stirring constantly until the sugar has dissolved completely. Simmer for 10 minutes, add the lemon juice and simmer for a further 5 minutes.

5 Using a spatula, carefully transfer the angel hair nests to a serving dish. Pour over the honey syrup, sprinkle over the remaining nuts and set aside to cool completely before serving. Hand the Greek-style yogurt separately.

COOK'S TIP

Angel hair pasta is also known as capelli d'Angelo. *Long and very fine, it is usually sold in small bunches that already resemble nests.*

2

2

2

Baked Sweet Ravioli

These scrumptious little packets are the perfect dessert for anyone with a really sweet tooth.

Serves 4

INGREDIENTS

PASTA:

- $3^{3}/_{4}$ cups all purpose flour
- 10 tbsp butter, plus extra for greasing
- $^{3}/_{4}$ cup superfine sugar
- 4 eggs
- 1 oz yeast
- 4 fl oz warm milk

FILLING:

- $^{2}/_{3}$ cup chestnut paste
- $^{1}/_{2}$ cup cocoa powder
- $^{1}/_{4}$ cup superfine sugar
- $^{1}/_{2}$ cup chopped almonds
- 1 cup crushed amaretti cookies
- $^{5}/_{8}$ cup orange marmalade

1 To make the sweet pasta dough, sift the flour into a mixing bowl, then mix in the butter, sugar, and 3 eggs.

2 Mix together the yeast and warm milk in a small bowl and when thoroughly combined, mix into the dough.

3 Knead the dough for 20 minutes, cover with a clean cloth, and set aside in a warm place for 1 hour to rise.

4 Mix together the chestnut paste, cocoa powder, sugar, almonds, crushed amaretti cookies, and orange marmalade in a separate bowl.

5 Grease a cookie sheet with butter.

6 Lightly flour the work counter. Roll out the pasta dough into a thin sheet and cut into 2 inch rounds with a plain pastry cutter.

7 Put a spoonful of filling on to each round and then fold in half, pressing the edges to seal. Arrange on the prepared cookie sheet, spacing the ravioli out well.

8 Beat the remaining egg and brush all over the ravioli to glaze. Bake in a preheated oven at 350°F for 20 minutes. Serve hot.

3

4

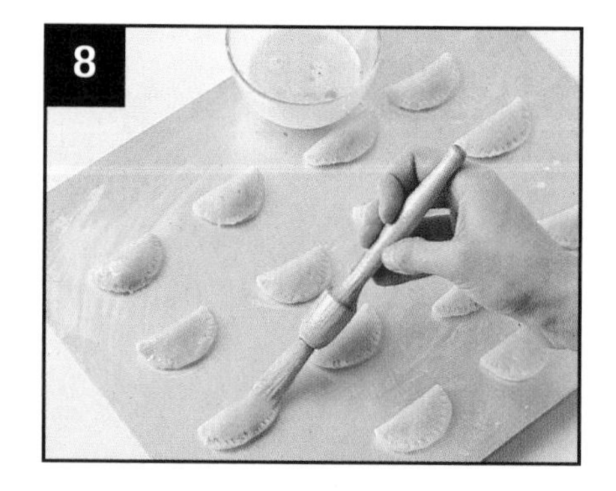

German Noodle Pudding

This rich and satisfying pudding is a traditional Jewish recipe.

Serves 4

INGREDIENTS

- 4 tbsp butter, plus extra for greasing
- 6 oz ribbon egg noodles
- 1/2 cup cream cheese
- 1 cup cottage cheese
- 1/2 cup superfine sugar
- 2 eggs, lightly beaten
- 1/2 cup soured cream
- 1 tsp vanilla extract
- a pinch of ground cinnamon
- 1 tsp grated lemon peel
- 1/4 cup slivered almonds
- 3/8 cup dry white bread crumbs
- confectioner's sugar, for dusting

1 Grease an ovenproof dish with butter.

2 Bring a large pan of water to the boil. Add the noodles and cook until almost tender. Drain and set aside.

3 Beat together the cream cheese, cottage cheese, and superfine sugar in a mixing bowl. Beat in the eggs, a little at a time. Stir in the soured cream, vanilla extract, cinnamon, and lemon peel, and fold in the noodles. Transfer the mixture to the prepared dish and smooth the surface.

4 Melt the butter in a skillet. Add the almonds and fry, stirring constantly, for about 1–1½ minutes, until lightly colored. Remove the skillet from the heat and stir the bread crumbs into the almonds.

5 Sprinkle the almond and bread crumb mixture over the pudding and bake in a preheated oven at 350°F for 35–40 minutes, until just set. Dust with a little confectioner's sugar and serve immediately.

VARIATION

Although not authentic, you could add 3 tbsp raisins with the lemon peel in step 3, if liked.

3

3

5

Cream Custards

Individual pan-cooked cream custards are flavored with nutmeg and topped with caramelized orange sticks.

Serves 4

INGREDIENTS

2 cups light cream
$3\frac{3}{4}$ oz superfine sugar
1 orange
2 tsp grated nutmeg
3 large eggs, beaten
1 tbsp honey
1 tsp cinnamon

1 Place the cream and sugar in a large non-stick saucepan and heat gently, stirring, until the sugar caramelizes.

2 Finely grate half of the orange peel and add it to the pan along with the nutmeg.

3 Add the eggs to the mixture in the pan and cook over a low heat for 10–15 minutes, stirring constantly. The custard will eventually thicken.

4 Strain the custard through a fine sifter, into 4 shallow serving dishes. Leave to chill in the refrigerator for 2 hours.

5 Meanwhile, pare the remaining orange peel and cut it into matchsticks.

6 Place the honey and cinnamon in a pan with 2 tablespoons of water and heat gently. Add the orange peel to the pan and cook for 2–3 minutes, stirring, until the mixture has caramelized.

7 Pour the mixture into a bowl and separate out the orange sticks. Leave to cool until set.

8 Once the custards have set, decorate them with the caramelized orange peel and serve.

COOK'S TIP

The cream custards will keep for 1–2 days in the refrigerator. Decorate with the caramelized orange peel just before serving.

Orange & Grapefruit Salad

Sliced citrus fruits with a delicious almond and honey dressing make an unusual and refreshing dessert.

Serves 4

INGREDIENTS

2 grapefruit, ruby or plain
4 oranges
pared peel and juice of 1 lime
4 tbsp runny honey
2 tbsp warm water
1 sprig of mint, roughly chopped
$1^3/_4$ oz chopped walnuts

1. Using a sharp knife, slice the top and bottom from the grapefruits, then slice away the rest of the skin and pith.

2. Cut between each segment of the grapefruit to remove the fleshy part only.

3. Using a sharp knife, slice the top and bottom from the oranges, then slice away the rest of the skin and pith.

4. Cut between each segment of the oranges to remove the fleshy part. Add to the grapefruit.

5. Place the lime peel, 2 tablespoons of lime juice, the honey and the warm water in a small bowl. Whisk with a fork to mix the dressing.

6. Pour the dressing over the segmented fruit, add the chopped mint and mix well. Leave to chill in the refrigerator for 2 hours for the flavors to mingle.

7. Place the chopped walnuts on a cookie sheet. Lightly toast the walnuts under a preheated medium broiler for 2–3 minutes until browned.

8. Sprinkle the toasted walnuts over the fruit and serve.

VARIATION

Instead of the walnuts, you could sprinkle toasted almonds, cashew nuts, hazelnuts, or pecans over the fruit, if you prefer.

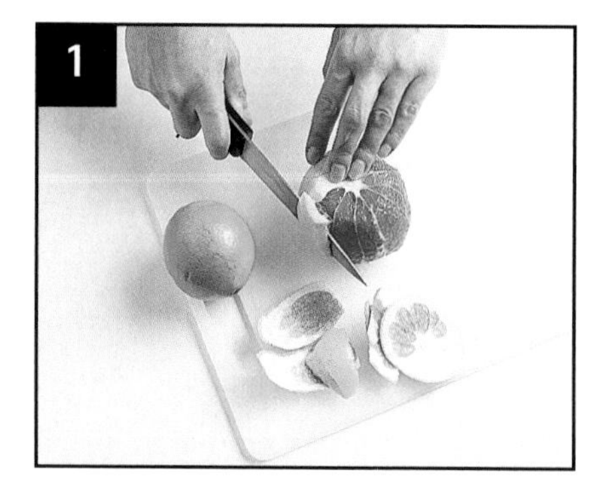
1

2

5

Brown Sugar Pavlovas

This simple combination of fudgey meringue topped with yogurt and raspberries is the perfect finale to any meal.

Serves 4

INGREDIENTS

- 2 large egg whites
- 1 tsp cornstarch
- 1 tsp raspberry vinegar
- $3^1/2$ oz light muscovado sugar, crushed free of lumps
- $^3/4$ cup low-fat unsweetened yogurt
- 6 oz raspberries, thawed if frozen
- 2 tbsp redcurrant jelly
- 2 tbsp unsweetened orange juice
- rose-scented geranium leaves, to decorate

1 Preheat the oven to 300°F. Line a large baking sheet with baking parchment. In a large, grease-free bowl, whisk the egg whites until very stiff and dry. Fold in the cornstarch and vinegar.

2 Gradually whisk in the sugar, a spoonful at a time, until the mixture is thick and glossy.

3 Divide the mixture into 4 and spoon on to the baking sheet, spaced well apart. Smooth each into a round, about 4 inch across, and bake in the oven for 40–45 minutes until lightly browned and crisp. Leave to cool on the tray.

4 Place the redcurrant jelly and orange juice in a small pan and heat, stirring, until melted. Leave to cool for 10 minutes.

5 Meanwhile, using a spatula, carefully remove each pavlova from the baking parchment and transfer to a serving plate. Top with unsweetened yogurt and raspberries.

6 Spoon over the redcurrant jelly mixture to glaze. Decorate and serve.

VARIATION

Make a large pavlova by forming the meringue into a round, measuring 7 inches across, on a lined baking sheet and bake for 1 hour.

Pan-Cooked Apples in Red Wine

This simple combination of apples and raspberries cooked in red wine is a colorful and tempting dessert.

Serves 4

INGREDIENTS

- 4 dessert apples
- 2 tbsp lemon juice
- $1\frac{1}{2}$ oz low-fat spread
- 2 oz light muscovado sugar
- 1 small orange
- 1 cinnamon stick, broken
- $\frac{2}{3}$ cup red wine
- 8 oz raspberries, hulled and thawed if frozen
- sprigs of fresh mint, to decorate

1 Peel and core the apples, then cut them into thick wedges. Place the apples in a bowl and toss in the lemon juice to prevent the fruit from discoloring.

2 In a skillet, gently melt the low-fat spread over a low heat, add the sugar, and stir to form a paste.

3 Stir the apple wedges into the pan and cook, stirring, for 2 minutes until well coated in the sugar paste.

4 Using a vegetable peeler, pare off a few strips of orange peel. Add the orange peel to the pan along with the cinnamon pieces. Extract the juice from the orange and pour into the pan with the red wine. Bring to a boil, then simmer for 10 minutes, stirring.

5 Add the raspberries to the pan and cook for 5 minutes until the apples are tender.

6 Discard the orange peel and cinnamon pieces. Transfer the apple and raspberry mixture to a serving plate together with the wine sauce. Decorate with a sprig of fresh mint and serve hot.

VARIATION

For other fruity combinations, cook the apples with blackberries, blackcurrants, or redcurrants. You may need to add more sugar if you use currants as they are not as sweet as raspberries.

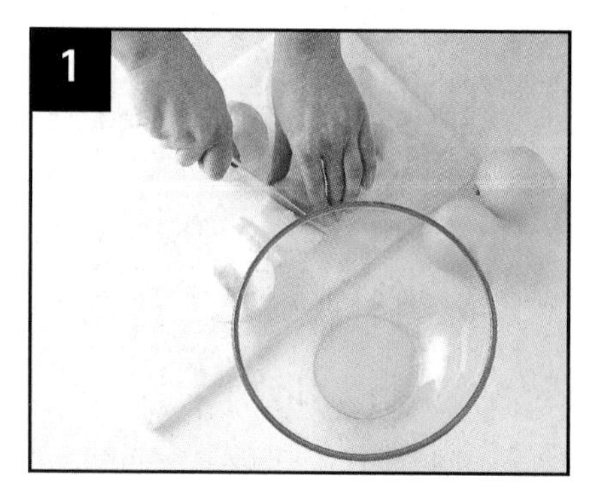

Index